A RAFT ON THE RIVER

The True Story of a Young Girl's Struggle to
Survive in the Shadow of the Holocaust

Miriam Feuer Sorger

~~~~~~~~~~~~~~~~

as written by

Stuart W. Mirsky
~~~~~~~~~~~~~~~~

A RAFT ON THE RIVER
by Miriam Feuer Sorger and Stuart W. Mirsky

First Published 2007
By Paul Mould Publishing UK

ISBN: 978-1-904959-68-7

Cover art (original oil: "Sunrise on the Dniester") and design by Elissa Rosoff.

Dedication

MY NAME is Miriam Sorger but I was born Miriam Feuer in the town of Kolomyia in Galicia more than eighty years ago. In those days Galicia was part of Poland though it was soon conquered by the Russians, the Germans, and then, finally, the Russians again, all within the space of six brutal years. After the break-up of the Soviet Union in the early 1990's, when the Ukraine became an independent state, Galicia was included within its borders. The Polish city where I was born is Ukrainian now – the world I knew is long gone.

Like many of my generation I lived in the shadow of the Holocaust in those years. But I was more fortunate than many. Too frightened to remain where the German occupiers had sent us, the Kolomyia ghetto, I found a way to get past the barbed wire barricades where my family had been confined and went into hiding in what was then southeastern Poland, pretending to be someone I wasn't for close to three years. Nearly everyone I loved and left behind was lost.

In 1949, I came to America with my husband Milek Sorger, himself a Holocaust survivor and together we raised four children here. Joseph, my oldest, was born while we were still in Poland after the war years but Adele, David and Neil were all born in the United States. Over the years I've told and retold the story of my escape and survival, despite the presence of the Nazis and their relentless campaign to find and kill Jews in the lands they occupied. Who can imagine such things in today's world when we live so comfortably, safe from the fears and concerns that haunted us in Eastern Europe in the mid-twentieth century?

My children, and especially my son David, have often begged me to "write it all down" so my memories wouldn't be lost. You're not getting any younger, Mama, David would tell me, afraid to offend me yet anxious to persuade me to write about what I recalled. But the war years took a lot from me, including my chance at a proper education, and the stories I had to tell, reflecting the years I spent in hiding trying to avoid discovery and stay alive, are so many and so involved that I feared I lacked the skills. Thankfully a local author, Stuart Mirsky, came to my rescue. We met and had many discussions about what I remembered and he agreed to set everything down for me in a way that captured the actual flow of events in those years. With his help, I have now managed to tell my story in this book one final time – for my children, my grandchildren and for all those who come after us.

My thanks go to everyone who patiently listened to me all these years and in particular to my son, David, who pushed me to complete this book. I want to dedicate it to all those who didn't have the good fortune I had to survive, and especially to my mother Adela, who did all she could to keep us safe for as long as she could; to my brothers, Samuel and Meir, who stood by us until they were no longer able to; to my sisters, Gusta, Bertha and Feiga, whose beautiful futures were ripped from them in that terrible time; and to my grandmother, Shprintzer Kirschner, who died at the hands of a Gestapo official because she was too old and feeble to follow his instructions.

I want to remember others of our family, as well, who lost their lives in those terrible years including my sister Bertha's husband, Yakuv Eckhouse of Horodenka, and Bertha's newborn daughter whom we never knew, my two little cousins, Aaron and Israel, who my mother struggled fiercely, if futilely, to protect, and my husband's older brother and sister, Solomon and Rachel, both of whom died at the hands of the Nazis before the Kolomyia ghetto had even been built.

Mine is a story of one person's escape and survival but, because of what I saw and remember, it's also the story of what happened to so many others who lost their lives through no fault of their own in that terrible time. I'm grateful to have lived long enough to be able to help keep their names and memories alive.

Miriam Feuer Sorger
June 25th, 2007
Belle Harbor, NY

Introduction

I HAD just finished editing the manuscript of ***Bitter Freedom: Memoirs of a Holocaust Survivor*** by Jafa Wallach (Hermitage, 2006), which recounts the harrowing tale of a handful of Polish Jews who hid from the Nazis for twenty-two months in the 1940's in a small Polish town called Lesko, buried alive barely thirty feet from Gestapo headquarters. I was working on preparing the manuscript for publication when my mother, Ruth Mirsky, came to me with another Holocaust story. I had heard so many by then that I wasn't keen on hearing a new one. Still, she insisted, this one was different.

It was the tale, she said, of her friend Miriam Sorger's survival against all odds during the Nazi occupation of Poland – a tale of one young girl's desperate and lonely flight through the countryside, hiding in plain sight as an ethnic Pole. In fact, Miriam's tale of her lost girlhood, adrift in a world bent on killing her, turned out to be as intriguing and compelling as the story of the people in ***Bitter Freedom*** who made it through the war years by hunkering down in the darkness of a grave-sized hole they had excavated beneath a damp cellar floor.

I agreed to meet with my mother's friend to hear more. For a number of weeks thereafter I sat and listened, over coffee and some of the best homemade rugelach I had ever tasted, transfixed by Miriam Sorger's words. There were times when I couldn't wipe the tears away from my eyes fast enough as she recounted what had happened to her family in those years. It was hard to keep up any semblance of objectivity and dispassion.

When Miriam was finally done, I just sat there with no words of my own to offer her. I realized then and there that her story was one that needed preserving, too, and agreed to undertake the writing of it if she were willing. She was. And so

I began a six month process of collecting the facts, sorting and organizing the material and visualizing the long lost world of war torn Eastern Poland as Miriam knew it. This book reflects that effort. It includes within its pages both a faithful recounting of Miriam's recollections and some dramatization, based on the facts, which I have added to enrich and flesh out the original bones of her story.

Miriam is not a professional writer and did not always have ready to hand the kind of detailed recollections that any good narrative needs to breathe life into it. But as we sat together, week after week, I was surprised to see how much detail came back to her after so many years. Where it didn't, I have taken the liberty of interpolating what I believe things would have looked like to a teenage Jewish girl, on her own in Nazi-occupied Poland, struggling to stay alive. Miriam reviewed the material in draft and together we made the necessary corrections. As such, this story is Miriam's primarily, with a little literary help from me.

Miriam lived through her ordeal by a combination of luck and pluck. Afraid to remain in the ghetto, where people were being killed all around her, she preferred to take her chances on the outside. Finding a way to escape the barbed wire that had been strung around the ghetto to keep the Jews in, she ran unaided into the countryside and spent the next few years as a secret fugitive, living a lie, in constant fear of discovery – even as she discovered unimagined reserves within herself.

Hers is a tale of flight, escape and deception. She endured and witnessed in the shadow of some of the most heinous crimes one human being can commit against another before finally finding her way home again in the wake of the Nazi defeat, only to learn the awful fate of those she had had to leave behind. Although her losses in those years were great, the message of her courage and survival is a powerful one, showing that human beings, even the youngest among us, have reserves within themselves that are quite beyond ordinary comprehension. Miriam came face to face with evil and lived to tell the world what she saw.

Most important of all, of course, she lived.

A Note on the Text:

Because the area in which the story takes place has fallen under so many different jurisdictions over the centuries, and because it's no longer part of Poland today, there is great variety, and a certain instability, in both nomenclature and spellings. Old Polish words, some of which may originally have been of German or other derivation, have variants in modern Polish, as well as in Ukrainian and Russian, many of which overlap across the years because of the continued co-existence of the different national groups in that part of the world. Sometimes, too, there's just an absence of a reliable standard, reflecting variations in local dialects as much as the presence of two competing alphabets. The city of Kolomyia, for instance, where much of the story takes place, has been variously spelled Kolomea, Kolomyya, and Kolomyja, nor do these fully exhaust the possibilities.

The different spellings tend to reflect the language and conventions of whoever was in charge at any given time. Under Austrian and, later, Polish rule, the Latin alphabet was used in the area while the Russians brought their own Cyrillic alphabet when they came, adding additional obstacles to the development of settled rules. More, despite the fact that Polish and English both use the Latin alphabet, Polish spellings and pronunciations remain a challenge for English readers because the Polish language frequently uses Latin letters to represent different sounds than English does.

The area of Polish Galicia, in which Kolomyia is situated, for instance, can also be rendered in Polish as Galicja while the Ukrainian variant is transliterated as Halychyna. In Russian, it's Galitsiya. Unfortunately, this is not any easier for most of the other names either. Indeed, in reviewing maps of the area, we frequently found similar names designating distinctly different locations, while different names often attached to the same places over time. In nineteenth century maps, for instance, Horodenka, Chortkow and Tluste appear much as Miriam remembers them, but the spellings change later on, giving us Gorodenka, Chortkiv (sometimes Czortkow), and Tolstoye. The important town of Podhajce in the story (pronounced Pod-hy-ts-uh) turned out to have numerous iterations, too, including Podhaice, Pidhajci, Pidhaitsi and Podgaytsy.

Some strictly Polish words also proved difficult to render into a reader friendly English. For instance, Kozcaczwka, the name of both a river and a street, leaves those unfamiliar with Polish spellings on uncertain ground. For the record, it's pronounced Ko-zha-chuf-ka, at least as Miriam recalls it.

Other names were also a challenge including Brzezany, Brezhany or Berezhany; Tarnopol, Ternupil or Ternopil; and Lvov, Lviv or Lwow. Sometimes the variant spellings just reflect competing ways of transliterating the relevant pronunciations into English because of a lack of definitive standards. At other times, however, variant pronunciations are also involved.

In telling Miriam's story, we tried to stick with a single standard throughout, of course, and tended to choose either the most familiar looking spelling or the one that enabled the easiest pronunciation for English speakers. Unfortunately, as with Kozcaczwka, this was not always an easy task. For less familiar words, we tried to more closely approximate English spellings but, since the names of particular streets or rivers are often standardized, some variant transliterations were unavoidable. In general, "v" is pronounced somewhere between an English "v" and "w" (as though swallowing the "v"), "czwk" as "chufk," "j" as "y", "cz" as an English "ch," and "zc" as a hard English "sh", approximating "zh".

Miriam's Polish is not as precise as it once was and mine, unfortunately, is non-existent. But together we labored to make the names and places accessible to non-Polish speakers. Any errors that may be found here are strictly my own and I can only apologize for them in advance.

Stuart W. Mirsky
August 30, 2007
Belle Harbor, NY

A RAFT ON THE RIVER

Miriam Feuer Sorger

~~~~~~~~~~~~~~~

as written by

Stuart W. Mirsky
~~~~~~~~~~~~~~~

CONTENTS

". . . Today the Germans came and took eighty young men to work in the fields, supposedly to dig potatoes. Some people were glad, imagining the men would be able to bring a few potatoes home to their relatives. But I knew all too well what the Germans meant by potatoes."

– Anna Semyonovna in a letter to her son from the Berdichev Ghetto, Ukraine, shortly before it was liquidated.*

* From ***Life and Fate*** by Vasily Grossman, translated by Robert Chandler, published by Harvill. *Reprinted by permission of Random House Group Ltd.*

Chapter 1

New Year's Eve

IT WAS DECEMBER 31, 1949, New Year's Eve, and we were 'greenhorns' in New York. We had come to America barely a year earlier after the war in Europe had ended. We came from Poland, through the Russian and British occupied areas of Germany, pretending to be German Jews because the authorities would have sent us back otherwise.

Poland held nothing for us anymore, nor did the city of Kolomyia, where I had grown up and where most of my immediate family had died. So we had set out over the war torn roads and fields of Eastern Europe, trying to reach the west. We traveled by trucks when we could, trains when we had to, and disguised ourselves as best we could, carrying false papers. But we didn't look like much, presenting a very scraggly appearance that did not make a good impression on the people and towns we passed through. But very few people traveling on the roads looked much better than we did in those days.

One night we were jammed onto a train traveling through the British zone. Suddenly the train, which had been moving slowly along the tracks, with no lights so it would not be seen, came to a halt. The man we had paid to take us west came round to all the rail cars, telling us the British were nearby and that we had to burn everything we had with us from Poland, anything that could still give us away, that might tell the British we weren't really the returning German Jews we were pretending to be. Milek, my husband, came to the car in which I was huddled with the other women. He told me to give him everything I had. "We can't take a chance they'll find anything with Polish writing on it," he whispered hurriedly. I didn't want to give him the identity card which I had worked so hard to obtain from the German authorities, the card which said I wasn't a Jew, but he said everything, and I had my baby, he was only six weeks old, my little Joseph, to consider.

They were making a fire nearby in a clearing in the woods and Milek said, please Miriam, give me the papers and so I took out my *kenncarte* and held it out to him but he kept insisting "everything Miriam." I still had the little tin cross I had worn during the war. I didn't want to give that up, too, but Milek repeated in a hushed whisper, "You must Miriam."

These two things were all I had left from what I had lived through and I didn't want to part with them. But the man we had paid to take us west said we mustn't hold anything back, not if we wanted to get safely to America. The cross and my identity card – I didn't want to let them go, but Milek took my hand and gently squeezed it and slowly I opened up my fist and gave him the *kenncarte* and then I took the cross from my neck and handed it to him, too. Then I watched his back as he walked away to burn the card and the cross in the fire they had built nearby.

Milek's mother was with us, and others we were traveling with, and we were all afraid of being taken by the British before we could reach the sea. So I did what I had to and tried to forget what had been, a life so different from what I had dreamed of while still a young girl growing up with my mother and three sisters in the little *korchma* on Kozcaczwka Street, which ran northwards out of Kolomyia to the very edge of the Kozcaczwka River, the sleepy little stream after which it had been named.

My husband was a tall man with a full head of very dark hair when he was young. I had liked him the minute I saw him on that first day in Mieske Park in Kolomyia after the war, after I had come home. He took a shine to me, too, though my friend Hilda had had other ideas. Hilda and her family took me in when I first came back to Kolomyia. I was looking for my mother and sisters, for my brother and his family, for anyone who was still alive – though no one was – and I felt a great sense of gratitude to Hilda and her parents for taking me in because I had no one left. Milek only had eyes for me when we first met and I, a shy little girl until then, took pleasure in the interest he showed in me.

Milek liked to tell jokes and was always very upbeat, despite everything he had seen and been through. He was determined to get us all out of Europe so we could start over in America. But he had weak lungs, my Milek, the result of lying for months in the muddy ground at the bottom of a pit in which he had hidden with his parents toward the end of the war. His father and mother had been well off before the war and had money to pay a Polish couple to take them in and hide them under a horse's feeding trough in their barn. Milek, who had escaped for a time by moving around with false papers, and by staying indoors when he could, had finally been forced to join them when the risks of living openly among the Poles became too high. Milek was the only one of his siblings left by then because the Germans had already killed his brother and sister.

Milek's father, Duvid Yusher Sorger, had been a prosperous businessman before the war. But that didn't save you if you were a Jew. First the Russians came and took everything away if you had any property or wealth. And then the Nazis came. They took the rest.

My husband's father had had a beautiful home in the town of Obertyn, not far from Kolomyia. It was a big brick house but, when the Russians came in 1939, they lost everything. The Russians just took over that house and told my husband's family they had to go. They said to my father-in-law, "if you even look at this house when you pass it in the street afterwards we'll arrest you and throw you into the cellar and you'll never see the light of day again." They turned the house into their headquarters and made a jail in the cellar and after that, Milek told me, his parents always averted their eyes when they walked by their old home, afraid the Communists would do what they had threatened.

But my mother-in-law was a clever woman and she found ways to smuggle some of their things out when they left, along with some money, and because of that they had enough to pay the Polish family to hide them when the Nazis came. My father-in-law had been in the leather business. During the war leather was very dear and my mother-in-law had managed to hide quite a bit of it from the Communists when they came. It paid for a lot afterwards, including their lives.

Milek was not the only one who was affected by the time spent hiding in the underground bunker the Polish farm couple built for them. Though my husband and his parents could come out by night most of the time – the farm was very isolated – they had to spend their days lying quietly in the pit, with only a small hole for a little fresh air. When it rained the water seeped into the ground and they had to lie there all day in the wet mud and the filth. It had a terrible affect on my father-in-law especially and, after the war, he was very ill with pleurisy because his lungs had been so weakened by his ordeal. I never actually met him because of that. He died soon after Milek and I were first introduced in the park in Kolomyia, around the time Milek had promised to take me to meet him.

My own family had not been so well off. My father had died when I was very young and my mother, Adela Feuer, had to raise us by herself. Israel Feuer, my father, was an only son and had inherited a little inn at the edge of Kolomyia from his parents who died before I was born. That was how he made a living until his death and how my mother kept us going afterwards. The inn, or *korchma* as it was called in Polish, was a place where people from nearby villages, like Piadyki which was just over the bridge, came when traveling into or out of Kolomyia on their way to the central marketplace. All the farmers and traders from miles around would meet at the central market to exchange goods and to buy what they needed and many came into Kolomyia on the street where we had our inn so business was good when there was peace and people could come and go freely to trade their goods.

Our street, *Uliza* Kozcaczwka, was on the very edge of Kolomyia, the last road out of town. It led down towards the Kozcaczwka River for which it was named. A small bridge, rising slightly in the middle, carried the road over the river into the adjacent village of Piadyki where mostly local

Ukrainian farmers lived. On our street there were mainly Poles with only a very few Jews. Everyone got on well in those days, except for the Ukrainians who didn't like either the Poles or the Jews very much. But everything was still quiet before the war and no one made a big fuss about such things.

The Ukrainian peasants from the nearby farms and villages always came to our *korchma* when they were on their way to and from the market. It was a place where people could stop for a meal and some beer – or something stronger. One of my jobs was to pump the beer from the barrels we kept in the cellar. When the beer tap would be empty Mama would send me down into the cellar, saying "now you have to fill up the beer again, Mutzka." That's what everyone called me when I was little, though my given name was Miriam. It was hard work, pumping the beer up through the pipes, but I remember having great fun doing it, pulling the lever up and down to force the brew upwards and into the barrel my brother or sisters tapped to fill the mugs for our guests. The strong, sweet smell of the beer filled the old cellar and I loved going down there just to breathe it in.

We had three large rooms in the front of our house which we rented to overnight travelers and a big dining room with six wooden tables where my mother and sisters would bring customers a meal and whatever they wanted to drink. The peasants always liked the dark beer or vodka best but we also sold whiskey and rum. My mother made a delicious treat the Ukrainians especially loved, *studeniecz* it was called, a tasty gel made from cow fat. In Yiddish we call it *pchah*. She also served the customers tea or a dark beverage, made from a combination of chicory and ground brown oats because coffee was so hard to come by. We also sold fresh cheeses, pretzels, honey cakes and bread which Mama took in from the bakery every morning. Mama cooked for our customers, of course, if they wanted a meal after they had come into town from one of the more distant villages or before setting out for home again on their return trip. Her food was well known. It wasn't very fancy but people appreciated it and usually asked for second helpings. Mama always obliged them when she could.

My brother Meir used to bring in meat for the peasants to round out the menu. At first we had only kosher meats because Mama was very observant. But the local Ukrainians had a taste for food we never kept in our home and when things started to become more difficult for us, because a store run by Poles had opened on our street and offered a wider selection of the things the Ukrainians liked, Meir decided to bring unkosher food into the *korchma* to win back the customers we had lost. Without telling Mama he brought in kielbasa and ham, which he bought from the Poles, and started serving these together with cheese to our customers, violating all the rules of *kashruth.* Our customers were happy with this change and started to return but, when she realized what was happening, Mama was furious at Meir and the rest of us for supporting him. She finally left the house in disgust, going to live with our grandmother, Shprintzer Kirschner, in nearby Horodenka which was past Piadyki heading east toward the Dniester River.

We had a terrible rift in the family then because my mother wouldn't come home for nearly a year and we girls were all distraught, crying and arguing with Meir over this constantly. It felt like we had driven Mama away. Finally Meir had to give in and went to Horodenka to see Mama, promising he would fix things if she returned. We spent weeks koshering the kitchen and the eating areas after that and when we were done Meir went off to fetch Mama back.

We girls all lined up when she came home, Meir bringing her up to the front door in a little wagon he had hired for that purpose. Mama got down and looked around at us and at the house and we all trembled, afraid she would turn around and go back to Horodenka in disgust with us again. But she didn't. Meir stood back, looking sheepish, until Mama went into the house to carefully inspect everything, from top to bottom. It seemed like hours before she was done but we were glad when she finally announced she would stay, even if it meant business at the *korchma* would now be worse again.

Meir never went against Mama's wishes concerning the inn after that and was always a dependable rock for the rest of us – until the Russians finally took him away and left us without any men in the house in 1940. They took him into their army, one year after they had annexed our part of Poland – a year before the Nazis came – and we never saw him again.

But I was now in New York, far away from all these things. It was barely a year since we had come to America, and Milek and I were living in a nice apartment in Manhattan at 610 Riverside Drive on West 137th Street, an apartment my mother's sister, my aunt Yetta, had found for us. My mother's siblings had all come to America well before the war and we had been the only ones still left in Poland from my mother's immediate family. Our New York apartment was large and in good repair, but everything seemed to be in good repair in America in those days compared to the world we had left behind. Because we were going to a New Year's Eve party that night, we were all dressed up. It was to be a big event that members of our group, all war refugees like ourselves, were throwing in the Diplomat Hotel downtown from where we were living.

I had never been to the Diplomat before and was very excited. I was wearing a new black dress my aunt had made me for the occasion. We couldn't afford to buy fancy dresses in those days but sewing our own clothes wasn't strange to us. Our friends, Benny and Eva Muntzer, were driving. They owned a car and that impressed us very much. Our apartment was on the second floor so we just walked down the steps to ground level and went out to the street where the Muntzers were already waiting for us. Benny was laughing as Milek, admiring the black fancy car, held the door open for me so I could climb into the back. Then he got in beside me. He was coughing a little. He had a constant cough because of what he had been through during the war years. We sat close together as Benny drove off, downtown, and I could feel Milek tremble against my side every time a cough wracked his body. Benny and Eva were smoking in the front and smoke always irritated his lungs.

Eva turned and looked back at me. She was all dressed up and looking lovely and I felt plain by comparison but Milek took my hand and we laughed and joked all the way to the Diplomat. When we got there, Benny parked his car and we all walked together along the sidewalk to the hotel. There were people everywhere, heading up the wide stone steps into the double doors that formed the entranceway. I still marveled at the buildings in New York, so different from what I had left behind, so big and untouched by war. Inside, the walls were covered with a textured gold paint and there was one huge chandelier hanging over the center of the dance floor. It seemed to be swaying to the waves of music coming from the band playing up on the stage.

We pushed our way into the ballroom between the tightly pressed bodies. Above us was an overhanging balcony with people moving about there, too, some leaning over, looking down at us just as we looked up at them. The music was playing and you could barely hear yourself talk but Milek grabbed my hand and pulled me onto the floor almost at once, leaving Benny and Eva behind. He was coughing harder than before from all the cigarette smoke in that place – it seemed like everyone smoked in those days – and I knew he was anxious to get out where people were moving around and couldn't smoke, where the air would be comparatively clear.

That dance floor was the only place where the air seemed to be free of the bluish clouds from all the cigarettes. Milek took me around at once and we started to move about to the music. He was a wonderful dancer though I was still a little awkward. I had missed quite a bit in my teenage years and one of the things I'd missed was the chance to dance with other girls my age, to learn the steps and how to follow a man's lead on the dance floor like girls did in those days.

But Milek was wonderful and guided me around the other dancing couples who packed the floor. All I had to do was let him take over and it just felt wonderful. We danced like that for a long time – I can't remember how long, but it seemed like we just kept moving through one number after another as the band changed selections – it felt good to be there among friends, so far away from that other world, the one we had left behind. Milek liked to dance and I wasn't going to ask him to stop when he was so happy. Finally, though, we were both pretty tired and I felt him moving us toward the edge of the dance floor again. I knew he was ready to take a break and I was glad because I was, too. We had almost maneuvered our way off the floor when I felt a shoulder bumping me and then a hand against my back. We stopped and I turned to see who was there.

It was another couple. They had been dancing, too, but now they were just standing and staring at us. The man was looking directly at me. He wasn't very tall and I thought his face seemed familiar. He had a full head of black hair and was wearing a pair of dark rimmed glasses. Milek was looking down at him but the man couldn't seem to take his eyes off me. "I know you," he finally said.

"I'm sorry," I offered, "but I don't . . ."

He was laughing and cut me off. "Oh yes, I know you," he went on. "You know me, too. I always knew you were one of us," he whispered conspiratorially. "Where's that cross you used to wear?"

I put my hand to my neck, involuntarily feeling for a cross that wasn't there. If he knew about my cross, I thought, then surely he was someone I knew. Still, I couldn't place his face. He took off his glasses for a moment and continued staring at me. "Don't you recognize me?" he said.

I thought maybe I was beginning to remember his face.

"Dr. Kleiman," he said at last, tapping his hand against his chest, "the dentist. From Podhajce . . ."

I just looked at him. His face seemed to take a different shape for me and suddenly I remembered. The dentist! I had visited him after the war while I was still in Podhajce, the city where I had gone to hide from the Nazis – not that you could hide from them anywhere, but that's where I had ended up. And he had been a dentist in that town.

"Tzvi Kleiman," he was saying, still tapping himself on the chest. "I saw you in the war, at the priest's house. You were the one who used to put the food out. I always knew you were one of us." He was laughing again. "Who else would have done such a thing? Who else would have cared? Why didn't you tell us who you were?" It sounded almost like an accusation.

I looked at him and then at Milek. I didn't know what to say and then Milek started to laugh, too, but it was a forced, uncomfortable laugh. Dr. Kleiman looked up at him with a big grin and then, again, at me. I just didn't know what to say. It all seemed so long ago though only some five years had gone by since the war had ended for us. So much had happened to us in that time.

Today five years seems like such a small amount of time – but then, to us, it was a lifetime.

I remembered him then, of course – the dentist I had gone to after the Russians came and we could all start living again. I hadn't known that he had been one of those in the fields, coming out by night to steal what they could, just to keep themselves alive. Of course, I should have known. Wasn't he there after the Germans had gone? Where else would he have been, after all, while they were hunting and killing all the Jews in Podhajce? Even then, when I had sought him out for my tooth, how could I not have made the connection? Where had he been when the Germans had been there? A Jew couldn't live in those days if they knew who you were. And it was much harder for a man to pretend to be someone he wasn't than for a woman.

I clutched Milek's hand more tightly and answered Dr. Kleiman softly. "I was afraid," was all I could say. I didn't know what else to tell him. He was looking at me so intently.

"Well, yes," he said finally, "I guess you were. We all were, weren't we?"

Milek held me closer to him and said, "It's very nice meeting you, Dr. Kleiman."

"Yes, yes," Kleiman said, rushing to get his words out now. "I treated your wife after the war, you know. She was pretending to be a Catholic girl. I saw her – we saw her – in the priest's house, the Ukrainian priest, during the war. She used to put food out in the night. For whom? The field mice? It was a very fine thing to do so we thought this one must be a Jew. Who else would do such a thing for us, for people who were starving and being hunted down like animals?"

I managed to smile but I was embarrassed and looked down at my own feet. I didn't want praise for what I had done. I just wanted to forget. But Dr. Kleiman brought it all rushing back, a great flood of memories, things I had thought I had left behind with the burning of my *kenncarte* and that little cross in the forest clearing in Germany.

Milek was shaking Tzvi Kleiman's hand and Dr. Kleiman's wife was looking at me, too, smiling as her husband had done.

I don't remember what she said but I think she was thanking me.

Then Milek had hold of me again and I could only lean against him as he began to dance us away, the music starting up once more as we moved off from the dentist and his wife toward the edge of the dance floor where the heavy cigarette smoke still hung like a ghostly bluish curtain in the air. Coughing, Milek pushed our way through it, looking for our table, and I followed him, still holding tightly to his hand.

Chapter 2

The House on Kozcaczwka Street

THE EARLIEST thing I remember was a great quiet in the house we lived in on Kozcaczwka Street, everyone tiptoeing around in stocking feet, no one wearing shoes. I couldn't understand why. Everyone was speaking in very muted tones, if they spoke at all, and people were coming and going. Mama was sitting on a bench or a box or something and her hair was wild and sticking out from the sides of her head. Her face was pale, her eyes red. My oldest brother, Samuel, was talking in a corner of the main room with Meir, my other brother.

Samuel was married already and had a home of his own so it was unusual for him to be staying with us for so long. My sisters were clustered around Mama but were afraid to go too close to her. People were coming in and going to Mama, sitting by her, talking to her, and then abruptly getting up and leaving.

The few mirrors we had in the house were draped with cloth so you couldn't see yourself. I was very confused and wandered about from room to room, looking at the people, trying to hear what my older sisters and my brothers were saying. But everyone seemed to be ignoring me. I didn't know why and was frightened, but later I came to understand. My father had died and we were in mourning.

It was August 1932 and the heat in our house was stifling, even with the windows opened in every room. I was only six years old.

My mother was a strong woman and people came to our house to pay their respects to her as much as to say good-bye to my father. Even many of the Ukrainians came. They always liked my mother because she was kind to them and had a certain skill with home remedies. In fact, in those days there weren't many doctors around and the peasants didn't have money to pay the ones that could be found in the city anyway so they often came to Mama for help. She kept her kitchen well stocked with herbal remedies and poultices and would often rush out, if a peasant came to the house, and go with them to their homes where she would treat whoever was sick in their families. She was very good at it, too, or so the peasants said because they kept coming to her for years. Later her reputation as a local healer would serve us well, at least in the beginning.

But now my father was dead and Mama was alone, except for us, and she had to worry about keeping us together and fed. My father, Israel Feuer, had fought in World War I in the Austrian army, when Austria still controlled Galicia, the part of Poland in which we lived. He hadn't been the same after the war. He was injured in the fighting, I think, but he kept things going and ran the inn for years when he came home until his health started failing. Then Mama had to do more until finally Father was too sick to help at all.

I was born in 1926, the last of my parents' children. The oldest was my brother Samuel who was born in 1905 and was about twenty six when our father died. Samuel was a short, stocky man, built like an ox. He was very strong and clever and had a good head for business. He made a living trading in wheat and, for a while, he owned a dairy business. He lived with his wife Breina just over the bridge in Piadyki. They had two sons, good boys both, Lazar and Israel. Israel must have been born after my father's death because he bore his name.

After Samuel came my oldest sister, Regina. She was born in 1909 and was about twenty two when my father died. She still lived at home with us but I think she was already involved with a young man, a Polish boy, named Rudeck Hudema, a musician. He used to come to our inn and play for the guests there at dinner time but I think he really came to see my sister. Mama was not at all happy about this and did everything she could to discourage the relationship. She did not think Poles and Jews should marry. She didn't dislike Poles anymore than she disliked Ukrainians but she was an observant Jew and thought that people should stick to their own.

Meir, my other brother, was seventeen when my father died. He had been born in 1914 and still lived with us. After my father's death, he became the mainstay of our house, taking care of all the heavy work at the inn although my mother was always in charge, except for that brief period when Meir turned the kitchen *tref* and Mama left us in disgust. Meir looked up to Samuel and was very close with him. Samuel, after my father died, would often come by to see how we were doing and help us out. He would guide Meir when he had difficult decisions to make. My brother Samuel always had money and he used to leave whatever we needed with Mama and Meir after his visits. Even though times were sometimes difficult for us, we never went hungry or lacked clothing to wear thanks to Samuel. We could always depend on him. And, of course, Meir was there in the house to look after us as well.

My sister Gusta was born in 1919 and was only twelve years old at the time our father died. Gusta's was a sad story. Some time after the loss of our father – it was winter – Gusta was coming home from school. Our school was not far away from the inn by the standards of those days but there were no busses so you had to walk, no matter what the weather was like. In bad weather this could be especially hard. Gusta was trying to get home from school in a snow storm on that day and having a bad time of it.

She saw a farmer, one of the Ukrainians from Piadyki, driving his sleigh through the snow. The wind was very bad, blowing the snow all around and making it hard to see where you were going, or even what was right in font of you, but Gusta had sharp eyes and she recognized the farmer's sleigh when she saw it almost immediately. Maybe she knew his horses. She realized that the farmer would be driving right by our house on his way back to Piadyki so she rushed through the drifts and driving wind to catch up with him, thinking he would take her home. But the wind was blowing very fiercely and, when she called to him, he couldn't hear her.

Convinced the farmer, who knew our family and often came by the inn, would give her the ride she needed to make it safely home in the storm, Gusta grabbed onto the sleigh and tried to pull herself up. But the farmer was surprised by the sudden weight on his sleigh. He didn't understand what was going on because he hadn't heard or seen Gusta in the storm. Now, seeing someone trying to climb up to him, someone he didn't recognize because of the poor visibility, he turned and struck at Gusta with the whip he used on his horses, slashing her across the face and she fell off the sleigh, into the snow.

We don't know what happened for certain, if she was caught under the sleigh or if the fall was what did it, but her knee was broken in the fall. The farmer was beside himself when he realized what he had done, of course. He knew Gusta and hadn't meant to hurt her. If he had recognized her in time he would surely have taken her up on the sleigh with him. But he hadn't and because of that Gusta was crippled for the rest of her life, her knee never healing right.

Gusta became housebound after this and we all had to take turns looking after her. She couldn't get around well and Meir sometimes had to carry her from room to room. But as she grew older she became more independent and could move about on her own, supporting herself, if needed, by holding on to pieces of furniture or by using a stick Meir cut for her as a sort of crutch. There was no question of her going to school any longer. After the accident she had to confine herself to studying what she could on her own in the house. In the end, Mama brought in a seamstress from outside and apprenticed Gusta to her so she could learn a trade and be able to care for herself as she grew older. Sadly, she was not to have that need.

My sister Bertha was born in 1921 so she was much closer in age to me. Bertha, who was ten when my father died, was a beautiful girl and a wonderful singer. She used to sing at the inn for our customers and everyone admired her rich, resonant voice. She was very talented in other ways, too. She used to write her own songs and put them to music. I have no talent like that and can't imagine what it must be like to be able to do such things. Bertha was admired for it by everyone.

Even at ten, people thought she was going to grow up to be a lovely woman and everyone believed she had a great future ahead of her. I still remember one of the songs she used to sing because of its haunting melody, a melody she had composed herself. I'm sure I can't do it justice now, nor do I remember it as well as I should but it's all I have left of her – her beautiful song and a few pictures I was able to find of her after the war. This is how it went:

Jak szybko plynie zycie- How swiftly life swims onward

Tak szybkomijia czos - Such speed, time flies away

Zarok, zadzein, zachwile - A year, a day, a minute

Razem nie niebedzie nas - Together, we cannot stay.

I nasze mlode lata uplynie - Our youth swims out beyond us

Shibko udal - So fast, so far away

Aw sercu pozosta nie - Tho' in my heart you linger,

Tesknoto smutek zal - To pine for all my days.

Bertha used to sing this and other songs with Rudeck Hudema, my sister Regina's admirer, accompanying her on his fiddle. All our guests would pause in their conversations, putting down their spoons and forks and the cups they held to listen to her sweet, mellow voice as it filled the dining room. Even my mother would come to the kitchen window and listen in silence as Bertha's blonde head nodded and lifted with each note. Afterwards there would be silence and then the guests would clap and we would, too, Mama and Meir and my other sisters and me. Everyone thought our Bertha had a wonderful future before her.

I had one other sister, Feiga, born about two years before me, in 1924. At the time of my father's death she was seven or eight I think. Like Bertha, Feiga was a lovely girl with blonde hair. She was the smartest of us all I remember, a very good student, and we would become very close as I grew older. But Feiga was headstrong and always did what she wanted, except once – and then it would have been better if she had.

Later, in 1935, we gained two additional members to the family when two little boys, the sons of Mama's cousin Hindi, came to live with us. Hindi and her husband lived in Stanislavov and were both deaf mutes though their sons, Aaron and Srulek, were normal. Mama took them in to give them a better chance in life, hoping they would learn to speak and interact normally. When they were older and had trouble learning Hebrew, she sold off some of our property to raise enough money to send them to a special school.

As they grew older they were sometimes treated badly by the local children who accepted us but never really came to accept them. But to me, having them with us was like having two younger brothers. It also meant I was no longer the youngest in the family. I must have been about nine years old when Mama took them in.

After our father died, everything became much harder though I didn't notice because, for a long time, I remained the baby of the family. Mama had to work from morning to evening every day, except *Shabbos* of course, keeping the inn going. Most of our customers were Ukrainians though many Poles stopped by, too. We were always busy in the kitchen, Mama baking or preparing meals, my older sisters or Meir behind the window that served as our counter and which opened into the dining area. There they would rush about, drawing drafts of beer, selling cakes along with bread, pretzels and cheese to passing travelers. And there, too, they would take the money from the diners after they had eaten. Bertha and Feiga waited on the tables and sometimes Meir helped with this as well. We also had a Polish lady, her name was Kashie, who helped out. Mama kept her on until the Russians came and took the inn away from us. For a time we also had a

Ukrainian boy named Ivanko to do the heavier work. Mama was always very kind to him but one day we found him stealing and Mama could never trust him after that. For most of those years, when we still had the inn, I was too young to do a lot myself, especially to wait on the tables, but I helped clean up and, of course, I was the one they sent down to the cellar to pump the beer.

Our house was a one storey affair. We lived in the rear and the restaurant was in the front where travelers could easily find it when they stopped on the road. We had a wide gravel driveway that led off Kozcaczwka Street up to our front entrance and people would draw up their wagons in front when they stopped in. A well outside let them water their horses and also provided water for us because we had no running water in those days. We didn't have any electricity either and lit the house by night with kerosene lamps. The outside of our house was unpainted clapboard and alongside and behind it were several fields we owned. Mama planted vegetables there for our own use and to stock the larders for the inn. We were not the only Jewish family on the street but we practically were.

The house we lived in, our little inn, 62 Kozcaczwka Street, was almost at the very end of the street, just before the river. Across the road from us was a Polish family at 61 Kozcaczwka. The man who lived there was called Janek Kozhanofski, a railroad clerk. The railroad was very important in Kolomyia because our city was the rail hub for the entire area. Many Poles worked for the railroad in various capacities but the Jews in the town were mostly merchants and businessmen, teachers and lawyers, or shopkeepers like we were. While there were a great many Jews in Kolomyia, maybe a third or even half the entire population in the city, we did not live in the center of town where most of the Jews lived. On our street only a few were Jews.

Next door to Mr. Kozhanofski, just at the river's edge, lived the Bielinskis, also Poles. Mr. Bielinski was a railroad conductor. Across from the Bielinskis, at 64 Kozcaczwka, lived a little girl with whom I soon became very good friends. Her name was Wanda Madeira. I think her family had come from Spain at one time because of their name. Wanda was my age and we went to school together. Her father had died, too, I don't remember when, and she lived there with her mother Ruzia, her older sister Angela, and a younger sister and brother, Janschia and Zbyschek. They had a very large piece of property, much larger than ours, that went very far back along the river. They made sausages for a living. The Polish people had a great love for this kind of food and they did a good business.

Their house and the other buildings which they used for their business were set very far back from Kozcaczwka Street. You had to follow a long private road from the street, along the river, to reach them. I went there quite a bit when I was growing up and Wanda came to visit me at our *korchma* almost as often. We were very good friends and became closer as the years wore on.

On the other side of our inn were the Frieds, a Jewish family, and farther down the road, going toward the center of Kolomyia, lived the only other Jewish family on our street, the Schechters. They had a small grocery where Mama used to shop to keep the inn's kitchen stocked. Haim Schechter, the father, was a very religious man and he and his wife, Sura, had two sons, Yakuv and Naftulu. I don't remember what happened to them.

Because we didn't live in the city itself, where most of the Jews were, we were protected from the worst of the troubles when the Germans first came. But that didn't last very long.

After a while things heated up between my oldest sister Regina and Rudeck Hudema and Mama became very concerned. She would take Regina aside and they would have very loud arguments which scared us terribly. Regina was old enough to do as she liked but Mama was very strong willed and not about to let her oldest daughter go off and marry a Catholic boy. She told Regina she would never be accepted by his family and that by doing this she would hurt her own family. But Rudeck kept coming around and finding ways to see Regina and finally Mama decided she had to take drastic action. She contacted an uncle of hers, her mother's brother, Herman Kirschner, who had a jewelry shop in Vienna, and arranged to send Regina to him. We were all upset to see Regina go but Mama packed her things and got her a ticket and promised it would just be for a while so Regina agreed to do it. She had never been out of Kolomyia so the excitement of seeing Vienna was a great temptation for her. I don't know if she said good-bye to Rudeck or not before going. But he was very dejected for a long time afterwards, when she was gone.

Uncle Herman put Regina up in Vienna and gave her a job in his shop and Regina used to write us about her life in Austria. We waited for weeks sometimes for her letters and when they came, delivered by Mr. Kazhnovski, the postman, we would cluster around and ask Mama to read what Regina had written. Sometimes she would oblige us but other times she just shook her head and took the letter and went alone into her room and read it by herself.

At some point Regina or Uncle Herman wrote Mama about a man, a Mr. Blank, I don't recall his first name, who was from Palestine. He was a Jew who had been visiting Vienna and had been in a motorcycle accident and was now in a wheelchair. It seems that he had taken a liking to Regina, or maybe Uncle Herman had put him up to it, I don't know. But eventually a letter came proposing that Regina marry this Mr. Blank as a means of getting her out of Europe. After that, Uncle Herman had written, they could be divorced since this man was ten years older than Regina and she had no interest in him romantically.

Mama decided this was a good idea because she was afraid that when Regina came home she would pick up where she left off with Rudeck. The only problem was that Mr. Blank said he was short of money. He wanted the equivalent of five hundred American dollars to marry Regina and then divorce her in Palestine so Mama raised the money by selling off one of our fields, about three acres of land. She then sent the cash to Uncle Herman who brokered the arrangement and Regina went off as Mrs. Blank, to Palestine.

Unfortunately this did not turn out as well as everyone hoped because, once in Palestine, Mr. Blank decided he didn't want to divorce Regina after all. Then there was a lot of trouble and I think my sister had a very hard time of it though eventually she was able to get out of the marriage. Later she married another – a younger man – in Palestine, but he was something of a Mama's boy and his mother was very much against that marriage. Regina was soon divorced from him, too, though not before becoming pregnant and having a son. My oldest sister had a very difficult life, I'm afraid, though because of Uncle Herman and that Mr. Blank she ended up in Palestine before the Nazis came and that probably saved her life.

During all those years I was growing up, going to school, helping my family in the *korchma* and just enjoying my childhood. I didn't know a great deal about the wider world around us and those days on Kozcaczwka Street seem idyllic to me now. Certainly they were by comparison with what came later.

As I've said, we didn't have a lot but we never wanted for anything thanks to Mama's hard work and my oldest brother, Samuel, who looked after us from nearby Piadyki. Samuel was always going back and forth, traveling the countryside, buying and selling wheat. He was very good at business and always had plenty of money in his pocket. For a while he owned a dairy but decided to let that go when it became too much of a drain on him. The biggest problem in those days was keeping hold of the money you earned. There was a lot of thievery going on and, if people thought you had money, there was always someone who would try to steal it from you.

My brother was not tall but he was very strong and knew how to take care of himself. Still, he had to be careful traveling the country roads in those days and even the streets in Kolomyia. Once he had a special satchel made, with a false bottom in which he could hide his money. But while he was visiting one of the farmers he did business with, someone in the farmer's house managed to find the secret compartment and take his money anyway. At one point he even tried to use his wife, my sister-in-law Breina, to transport his cash. He would have her carry the money back and forth from the dairy under her coat. But a robber waylaid her one day, too, and got away with everything. After that my brother closed down the dairy business, which had required his constant attention, and just took care of everything himself. He didn't want to put my sister-in-law Breina at any further risk.

I used to admire Samuel greatly when he would come to visit us. In some ways he was like a father to me because he was so much older than I was and, of course, I couldn't remember my father because I had been so young when he died. When Samuel came to the inn I would always try to make it a point of hanging around there, just to see him. But Mama and Meir often had things to talk about with him and there was no room for children. Then I'd go down to the river, especially in the summer months, when school was out and we kids had little to do but play along the banks of the Kozcaczwka. There I used to meet my friends, Wanda Madeira and Janka and Stasia Bielinski and also Cesia Beck whose father worked in the city jail. Others would be there playing with us too. There was Cesiek Zaremba whose family lived in Piadyki, just over the bridge, and whose father was actually the *burmiszht* or mayor of Kolomyia. And there was Franek. I don't recall his last name now. He was a blonde boy, of German extraction, very handsome. There were many Poles in our area who were German in origin like him. They were called Swabians and were particularly proud of their heritage, though they spoke Polish and went to the Polish churches like most of their neighbors.

We children all used to gather in the summers to play in the high grass along the river bank. The Kozcaczwka was a small river, not like the fast running Prut on the other side of Kolomyia which was deep with treacherous currents. Our river was placid and, in the hot days of summer, you could lie there and dangle your feet in the cool water, watching the tiny insects and dragonflies buzz languidly overhead or skim the brown water's surface. Sometimes small boats would come by and pass under the bridge but most of the time the river was devoid of even that activity. The Kozcaczwka was the kind of river you could swim in, not like the Prut, so we did a lot of swimming when the weather was good, too.

Of course, we used to play ball along the river bank or jump rope while the boys skipped their rocks across the surface of the water. Franek, the Swabian, and his friends would tease us unmercifully, especially the older girls like

Wanda and me. I liked Franek quite a bit and enjoyed taunting him to get his attention. I thought he liked me, too, because he used to talk more to me than to the other girls. And he was always quick with his comebacks when I needled him about his rocks falling short of the farther side of the river.

Wanda also liked him, I think.

But we were only eleven years old around this time. What could we possibly know of such things?

Chapter 3

Poland Falls

THE COMMUNISTS came to Kolomyia in 1939, when I was thirteen. I wasn't very aware of events in the wider world when I was growing up and, though we had heard of terrible things going on in Germany, particularly with regard to Jews, such events seemed very far away to the child I still was in Poland.

Kolomyia was in the part of Poland known as Galicia or "Little Poland," near the foothills of the Carpathian Mountains. To our south were Rumania and Hungary and to our east the Ukraine, part of the Soviet Union which had come to control much of old Czarist Russia after the First World War. Because of our nearness to the Russians, we had a long history with them.

Our city was founded around 1240, in the Middle Ages, part of a German drive to colonize the east, and we lived in the midst of a land where ethnic Ukrainians predominated. Our region, which had once been part of the land of Kievan-Rus, the original Russian state and the first homeland of the Ukrainians, had passed from one nation's hands to another over the centuries. Invasions were an ever present part of our history. Having once formed the base from which the Polish nobility ruled the peoples of southern Russia during the era of Polish expansion, Galicia was later annexed by the Austrian Empire in 1772 and, until the end of the First World War in 1918, it remained in Austrian hands. When that war ended with the defeat and break-up of what had come to be known as the Austro-Hungarian Empire and its Hapsburg ruling house, our land briefly passed under Ukrainian sovereignty, becoming part of the short-lived Western Ukrainian People's Republic. But this didn't last and in 1919 we were annexed by Poland once more.

Perhaps this explains the deep hostility of the Ukrainian population who lived all around us. They disliked both Poles, who had been their rulers in the past and who had now taken over their homeland again, and Jews. Jews, especially, were seen by the local peasantry as supporters and servants of their Polish enemies. The Jews had originally come into the region as agents of the medieval German nobility but later served the Polish landed class who ruled the Ukrainians as successors to the German gentry.

Denied the possibility of owning land in those earlier times, Jews had no other way of earning a living except through commerce and so developed skills in business which the medieval aristocrats found useful. Our community prospered over the centuries and we were very much involved in the life of the cities and towns of Galicia, benefiting, over time, from the increasing liberalization of Austrian society as the rights of citizenship were gradually conferred on us. But the peasants did not look kindly on the people in the cities and towns. Our lives were too different from theirs and, because we were engaged in businesses while they were farmers, we seemed to have much more than they had.

They had their land, of course, but land was cheap in those days and they labored from morning to night, often under the control of others, with little to show for all their hard work. They were not well educated either and believed the advantages we had in our cities, both in money and goods, were unfairly gained at their expense. It didn't help that our language and religion were different from theirs, too. The Ukrainians were members of the Greek Orthodox Church, like the Russians, while the Poles were Catholic.

Of course we Jews were neither.

When Russia joined the Germans in the takeover of Poland in 1939, they divided the country between them and Poland ceased to exist as an independent state. In the west, the Polish lands and people were absorbed by Hitler's Third Reich while in the east, where we were, the Soviet Red Army came to stay. Or so it seemed at the time. I don't remember the exact moment when things changed in Kolomyia but I can still see the Soviet troops rolling in past our house. They rumbled down Kozcaczwka Street in long lines of trucks and horse drawn wagons with unkempt men in nondescript, dust-covered uniforms trailing along behind. They were rowdy and grim looking and they stared, awe struck, at everything. They were mostly country boys, simple folk who were genuinely friendly with the people they believed they had come to liberate.

We all stood on the porch scrutinizing them the first day they appeared, not knowing what to think about this momentous change in our lives. Not only were these Russians, the historic enemies of Poland, they were Russians of a new kind: Bolsheviks, the people who had taken over the lands to our east after the end of the First World War and instituted an iron rule under the man called Stalin.

We were frightened, of course, but the news we were getting from the west was much worse. There Hitler's armies had invaded the Polish homeland itself and refugees were already streaming east, fleeing the Nazis and carrying terrible stories about the German invaders. We already knew about Nazi attitudes towards the Jews, of course. My mother's cousin, Adela Byshel, had returned to Kolomyia from Germany in 1937, two years before the war began, after living in Germany for some time with her two sons. When they came back to Galicia, they brought with them the most horrifying tales. Aunt Adela told us that Jews in Germany were being systematically stripped of their rights, that their property was being confiscated everywhere and that they met only humiliation in the streets. She talked of beatings and other cruelties she had witnessed so, in a way, it was a relief that our invaders were only the Communists from Russia and not those others.

At first, things didn't change that much for us under the Soviets though our new rulers were still gripped with revolutionary fervor and wanted to destroy all vestiges of what they considered bourgeois living in our region. So they went after those who had businesses or property because you couldn't hide such things. My brother Samuel quickly lost his business when the Communists shut down the central marketplace and trading in wheat became impossible. He used his knowledge of wheat, though, to build a new business, at least for a time: the production of bootleg whiskey.

The Soviet presence didn't affect our family much at first because we weren't well off. We only owned the little land on which our house was situated, all that was left after Mama had sold off what she needed to raise the cash to send Regina to Palestine. The Communists did not think our small property was worth confiscating so we continued to use it to grow the vegetables on which we survived.

Maybe the biggest impact on us was what happened with the schools. The Soviets had their own ideas about schooling, very different from the Poles, and they quickly reorganized the educational system around the ethnic divisions in the area. Where before everyone, Poles, Ukrainians and Jews, had gone to the same schools, the Soviets now established new schools for each ethnic group. Now Polish children had to go to Polish schools, Ukrainians to Ukrainian, and Jews to Jewish schools where Yiddish was spoken. Polish, of course, was my native tongue and I also knew Ukrainian because there were so many Ukrainians in our area and these people made up the bulk of our customers at the inn. But I didn't know a lot of Yiddish and so Mama had to find a special tutor for me. She found Yaekel the Melamed. He was a little old man who was distantly related to us. He came to the house to teach us children Yiddish and to help us with our assignments.

But it was still difficult trying to learn things in an entirely new language and it was made harder still because the Soviets didn't recognize the grade levels we had achieved under the old Polish educational system. They told us our education had been poor and pushed us back a number of grades while at the same time increasing the demands of the curriculum that was taught. Polish schools were inadequate we were told and our new Communist teachers made us study twice as hard as we had before so that we would become proper citizens of the new state.

Soon I was going daily to a Yiddish speaking school in the heart of Kolomyia and lost track of most of my old playmates on Kozcaczwka Street as they were now sent off to Polish schools just as I and my sisters were enrolled in Jewish schools. But I made new friends, as children will, including a girl about my own age named Celia Bieber and another, Hilda Spiegel. Celia and Hilda and some others replaced my earlier Polish friends including my best friend, Wanda Madeira. But because we lived so close to one another, on the same street, I still saw Wanda quite a bit and managed to keep our friendship going, too.

My sister Feiga, who was two years ahead of me, was sent by the authorities to a special agricultural school established for Jewish children, the Baron Hirsch School in Slobutka, and Mama was very upset about this. She didn't like it when any of her children were taken away but you couldn't argue with the people who were now in charge. They had their own ideas about how to do things and you had to go along – or else.

We struggled to get on despite the growing number of changes. Things were much more difficult because the commerce in the marketplace, that we had depended on for our business, soon dried up. The Soviets did not allow individual commercial transactions in the markets and so the peasants and traders ceased to travel back and forth along *Uliza* Kozcaczwka to the Kolomyia market anymore and pretty soon there weren't many people coming into the inn for food or drink, or to spend the night either. The Ukrainian peasants were forced to sell their products to government agents who gave them quotas to fill, collecting what they grew centrally at harvest time and paying according to whatever prices the government set. No one was happy with this situation but there wasn't anything anyone could do about it.

One day some Ukrainian men who were working for the new Soviet authorities came to our inn and told Mama that our taxes had been raised. Mama was beside herself. Without trade in the city, she told them, there was little traffic on our street and hardly any business left for us. Mama pleaded with them to lower the taxes since we weren't making enough money to even keep the inn going, she said. But the officials were insistent. They said there was a tax on every business and as long as we ran the inn it had to be paid, even if there was no money coming in to pay it, and that if we didn't pay what they said we owed, they would take the inn away from us.

That's when Mama finally decided to close everything down. From then on it would just be a home for us, a roof over our heads and nothing more, she told us. We just listened in silence. What else could she do? Mama let Kashie, the Polish lady she had employed for years, go, and shut up our extra rooms. She sent Ivanko, the Ukrainian boy, away, too. We still had our small piece of land on which to grow food and Samuel was still able to come by periodically and surreptitiously pass money to Mama, money he was making from secretly distilling whiskey and selling it on the black market. Mama never asked him how he came by this money. She was just glad he had it to give us.

We could also still trade with the Ukrainian farmers who were eager to avoid the scrutiny of our new Communist masters and would bring their produce to us for barter, often at night when no one was about. But you had to be careful because the Soviets had their spies everywhere, informing on their neighbors to make sure no one was secretly accumulating any sort of wealth by stealing what they said was due to the people.

That's how we survived from then on, after the Soviets came in 1939. We didn't have as much as we had had before but we still had a place to live and clothes on our backs and enough food to keep ourselves alive. But everyone was downcast and the Ukrainians especially were very grim and didn't seem to think much of the new authorities. Because things were so much harder, Mama thought it was time to look into finding a home for my older sister, Bertha. She was the talented one and very attractive and Mama thought she would have no trouble finding a husband. Bertha had harbored hopes of some day finding her way to a major city and realizing her ambitions to become an acclaimed singer but Mama told her that times had changed and that it would be better for her, better for everyone, if she now married. Bertha protested. She was still too young she said, and she hadn't found anyone to her liking but Mama reminded her that she was now nineteen and that that was old enough. Bertha was very unhappy, especially when Mama sent to Horodenka, the village where she had grown up and where Bubbeh Shprintzer, our grandmother, still lived, for a *shadchin*, a matchmaker. Soon the matchmaker came to the house to say that she had found a suitable young man from a very respectable family in Horodenka. His name was Yakuv Eckhouse.

Mama and the matchmaker went into the kitchen for some tea, and there they sat for a long time, out of the hearing of the rest of us. When they finally came out it was done. Mama was smiling and the matchmaker was positively glowing with pride in her skills. When Bertha saw both their faces she was beside herself and ran off in tears, her sobs so loud we could hear them for hours afterwards coming from her room.

The wedding was held in our house not long afterwards and many family members were there from Horodenka and nearby Piadyki. My brother Samuel came with Breina, his wife, and they brought Bubbeh Shprintzer with them. By now my grandmother was quite blind and could not find her way about by herself unless someone took her by the arm so Samuel took this duty on himself and guided her to her place for the ceremony. Bubbeh Sprintzer, who lived alone in Horodenka, where she could get by despite her blindness because of the familiarity of her surroundings, seemed lost in our home. When my brother walked beside her, his hand on her thick arm, I could see the family resemblance for Bubbeh Shprintzer was short and stocky like Samuel was.

The rabbi who officiated was a large, thickset man in a long black coat and a very thick beard, his long, greasy curls dangling alongside his fleshy ears as if they had sprouted directly from the base of his great fur hat. Yakuv Echkouse, the groom, was a slight boy who seemed even slighter beside this rabbi. Young Eckhouse had a scholarly look but he was not unattractive and I thought my sister lucky to be marrying him. He had been trained as an electrician, a good trade, and Mama had carefully considered this before accepting him as a suitable match for our beautiful Bertha. Still, he looked more like a talmudic student than a tradesman to me. Maybe he was, too.

Mama said she was sure Bertha would be well provided for by such a husband and was pleased with herself for having arranged an auspicious match. By this time Bertha had given up crying and protesting and had resigned herself to the marriage. I thought she was not displeased with Yakuv when she looked at him, too, and that she was even looking forward to her new life with a husband. At least she managed to smile shyly at him from under the veil that Mama had placed on her head before the ceremony began and he looked enormously pleased to have found himself such a lovely young bride.

The wedding was quick and the reception, afterwards, not very elaborate. There wasn't a lot of money to waste on frivolities by this time nor was it wise to do so as it might attract the attention of the authorities. After everyone had helped themselves to the rugelach and other pastries Mama had prepared for them, my brother Samuel took a few of the men outside to unload his wagon and carry in Bubbeh Shprintzer's things. As part of the marriage arrangements, my grandmother had agreed to give up her home and her independence to come live with us, turning the little house she had owned in Horodenka over to the newlyweds as their wedding gift. Henceforth, Bubbeh Shprintzer would be our responsibility and, especially, my mother's.

Not long afterwards we got some terrible news. With Bertha safely settled in Horodenka with her new husband, life went on as before – until one day, one of the Ukrainians who used to frequent our inn in the old days came knocking at the door, asking to see Mama. Meir let the man inside and he took off his cap out of respect while Meir went to get Mama. When she came out, brushing her hands on her apron, the Ukrainian looked pained and took her aside, whispering something in her ear. When she heard him she just got very quiet and sat down heavily on one of the wooden chairs we kept in that area. Samuel, the Ukrainian told her, had been arrested.

We were in shock. The authorities, said the man, had learned of Samuel's bootlegging and taken him into custody. They had destroyed his still. After a few minutes, Mama got up again and thanked the man for coming to her with the news. She gave him something in his hand, I don't know what it was, and he left. After that she grabbed her coat and, with Meir, went at once to the nearest police station. She didn't know where Samuel was being held but she knew that she had to start somewhere.

But no one in that station, or any other she tried afterwards, would agree to see her. She raised a terrible ruckus about it with the authorities but it was no use. Later we heard that Samuel had been shipped east to a prison camp in Siberia and the word was he would not be coming back anytime soon. This was a terrible blow to us because Samuel was our mainstay. Now Breina and their two sons were without a man to look after them and we would have no one to turn to when food and money became scarce.

When she realized that Samuel might be beyond our reach Mama began to think about the future again. One day she went into her bedroom with a determined look and began to collect whatever she could. She was looking for whatever we had that could be sold for cash in case this would be needed. Whatever money Mama could raise in this way, she knew, would have to tide us over until things improved.

But they didn't improve. Maybe it was because Meir had gone with Mama to the police station or maybe it was merely a coincidence but soon an official came round to the house asking for him. The man wore a long gray coat that seemed to touch the ground and a cap with a hammer and sickle on it. He was very official looking. Mama wanted to know what he wanted but he said he had come to speak with Meir. When Meir finally came out, the man very officiously asked him his name and Meir told him. Then the man consulted a piece of paper he had and said that since Meir was of military age, he had now been drafted into the Soviet army. He was to report in two days if he knew what was good for him. If you refuse, said the official, you'll be shot.

Meir was flabbergasted but he knew it would do no good to argue and he quietly agreed to report for duty as directed.

His leave-taking was very sad for all of us and there was much hugging and kissing and sobbing. Meir said not to worry, that he knew how to take care of himself and would be all right. He would be home before we knew it, he said. In the meantime he carefully told Mama all the things he had left undone, things she would have to be responsible for by herself, now that he was going, and then he kissed Gusta and me, his remaining sisters, and Bubbeh Shprintzer last of all. The blind old woman clung tightly to him for a long time and I thought I could see tears welling up in her vacant eyes. Meir kissed her finally on her forehead, just below her kerchief, touching her parchment like skin with his lips and then he went to Mama and took her in his arms, telling her to stay strong and not to worry. He said this over and over and Mama warned him to look out for himself and to watch out for those Russians.

Meir grinned and said he would and then he broke free of her grip and lifted his belongings and turned away, moving toward the door. We all followed him outside and watched as he walked down the road. We watched him for a long time this way, until he disappeared in the distance, and then we just stood there waving at the place where we had last seen him, just as if he were still there and could see our hands moving in the air over our heads. It seemed like the only thing left that we could do.

That was last time we ever saw Meir, my brother. He died defending Russia against the Germans at Leningrad.

Mama never stopped working to find a way to bring my oldest brother, Samuel, home. He was especially needed now that Meir, too, was gone. At first the authorities wouldn't pay any attention but Mama was relentless and managed to pay a few bribes and eventually found a sympathetic ear. There were more bribes to be paid and Mama went to Breina and together they found money that Samuel had hidden away and used some of it to pay the officials who, though they were Communists, were not above taking a little gift here and there. In the end, Samuel was released, sent back to us after some six months in Siberia. But he was very subdued when he came home and wouldn't talk about what had happened to him, not even to us. He was just so glad to be back that he embraced us all and very nearly lifted Breina off the floor, along with each of his sons. Mama was proud of what she had done because she had found a way to break through the bureaucracy but she didn't talk much about it either. Better, she told us, to forget about everything that has happened and just live on as quietly as we could. Better not to call too much attention to ourselves.

Samuel agreed that this was the best advice, under the circumstances, and told us he would now have to see about earning a living again. He wouldn't be bootlegging anymore though, he assured us. "They told me the next time, if they catch me at it, I won't be coming back." We were all very frightened at the tone in his voice. Gusta and I were especially concerned and I think I must have turned very pale.

"Don't worry Mutzka," my brother said, looking straight at me. "They won't catch me at it anymore."

Samuel's return was a blessing for us because we knew we could rely on him, that he would always find a way to make money and take care of us. He had a good head for figures and for making deals and after he came back from Siberia he came by more often than before, perhaps to make up for the loss we had suffered when Meir was drafted. But the news from the rest of Europe was growing ever more ominous each day as word of the war then going on in the west, between Germany and the other European countries, filtered through to us. Even more frightening, though, was the news from the western part of Poland itself, the part Hitler's armies had swallowed up in 1939. Although things were hard for us under the Communists, although they made it difficult to make a living or to survive without always looking over your shoulder, we knew we were still better off than our fellow Jews who had been living in the western part of Poland when the Nazis came. Those who had managed to flee brought tales east with them, tales of terrible Nazi brutality against the Jews and no one knew what to make of this. Things would settle down in the west we thought. They must. The Nazis would tire of tormenting Jews and everything would somehow return to normal. It was the war, we thought, the war that made life so much harder for everyone. Still, no one was fleeing from the

Communists and running to the Nazis from our part of Poland. That should have been a sign for us.

We children continued to go to school and I joined my friends in Kolomyia each day at the Jewish school where we had our girlish concerns to talk about and this made me forget the problems that seemed to be raging across Europe. Such problems seemed very far away. I was only fifteen by this time and it was 1941. I had my whole life ahead of me and was convinced that there was nothing I couldn't do if I put my mind to it. My family was all around me except for my one brother who had entered the Soviet army somewhere in the east, but he would be coming back, I was certain of it. Hadn't he promised us he would?

As for the rest, well Mama and Bubbeh Shprintzer were with Gusta and me in the old inn and Samuel and his family were just across the bridge in Piadyki. Just a little ways beyond that, in my mother's hometown of Horodenka, lived my sister Bertha with her new husband Yakuv Eckhouse. His family was there and many of my mother's relations, too. True, my mother's other sisters and brothers had all emigrated to America years before but they sent money periodically to Bubbeh Shprintzer and that was another source of much needed funds for us.

My oldest sister, Regina, of course, had gone off to Palestine but that was when I was still a little girl and it had been years since, and I didn't remember her that well any longer. Her absence seemed perfectly ordinary to me, just the way things were. Only my sister Feiga seemed to be missing from our close knit little family because she was at the Baron Hirsch Agricultural School in Slobutka, but she would be coming home soon enough, too, when her education was completed and, until then, we could visit her if we had to. She wasn't beyond our reach.

Ours was a small world, a world we knew intimately. What harm could come to us? Even the Communists couldn't destroy us I knew. Hadn't Mama figured out a way to bring Samuel home? Wouldn't she eventually do the same with Meir? There were always ways to fix things if you thought long enough and hard enough about a problem, and my brother Samuel was back, strong and smart and utterly reliable. I was young and confident in my youth, believing as the young will, in all those who were older and wiser than I was.

Chapter 4

The Beginning of the Nightmare

ONE DAY in June 1941 we were awakened in the early morning hours as a convoy of trucks rumbled past the inn on Kozcaczwka Street, raising great plumes of dust. To our surprise, the trucks all came to a halt directly in front of our house and we ran to the window to see what was happening. There were people on the open, flatbed trucks. A girl jumped from the back of one and ran toward us, up to our house, and we realized it was Feiga. She had a very excited look on her face but she seemed concerned, too. Mama ran out to meet her, grabbing hold of her and hugging her close. Then she pushed her an arm's length away.

"Let me see you," she said forcefully. "You haven't been eating right, have you? You're losing weight." She seemed to be shaking Feiga in her strong hands. I thought she was angry but when I looked more closely, I saw Mama was trembling.

Feiga laughed and said no, she was eating okay, that she just wanted to stop and say goodbye to the rest of us. Mama looked at her firmly and then eyed the trucks, still idling on the road in front of the house. She could see other people on the backs of all the trucks, young people like Feigie.

"Come with me," she said firmly, seizing my sister by the arm and drawing her inside.

Feiga tried to resist but Mama was nothing if not strong, in her arms as well as in spirit, and she half dragged, half pushed my sister up onto the porch and into the house. "What's this about?" she demanded when they were inside. "Where are you going?"

"East," said Feiga breathlessly. "We're going east, to Russia. We'll have new lives there," she said. "The school and all the students are to be relocated . . ."

Mama was flustered. "Relocated?" she repeated. "When was this decided? What is going on? What are these Russians up to now?"

Feiga tried to explain herself but was too excited to speak clearly. All that came out was that the Russians had told them to pack up everything they had that morning and to get onto the trucks. Their future, they had been assured, was now in the east. They were leaving Poland.

Mama was dumbfounded. She just stood and looked at her middle daughter. Then she looked around at the rest of us, as if she were counting heads. "You can't leave Poland," she finally said to Feigie. "What will you do in Russia? How will we see you again?"

"I don't know, Mama," Feigie replied, "but it's all right. We're going to make new lives, a better future for everyone."

"No," Mama said firmly. "No, you're not. You're not going. Your place is right here . . . with us. How can you leave everything you have here, your family, your friends?"

"My friends are on the trucks, Mama."

We could hear impatient shouting coming from the trucks now. They were calling my sister to come back and get on the truck she had left. Someone was honking a horn.

"Mama," said Feigie, "I really have to go . . ."

"No," Mama replied. There was finality in her tone and Feigie looked at her. "No," Mama repeated with emphasis. "You don't have to go."

Outside the trucks were all revving their engines and the shouting from the one Feigie had been on was growing more insistent. There was a lot more honking, too.

My sister looked torn and tears glistened in her eyes. "Mama," she said, "I left my things, I left everything on the truck . . ."

"Let them stay there then," said Mama. "You can get new things but I can't get a new Feigie." Mama's eyes, too, were red with tears. We could see that Feigie wanted to go back, to rejoin her friends on the trucks, that she was excited and seduced by the promise of a new life in the east. But Mama stood there, between Feigie and the door, and would not move. Mama was a broad woman but now she looked tired and her shoulders seemed to slump. She looked like she would topple over if Feigie challenged her and went toward the door. I was thinking about what had happened when Meir went off to join the Russian army, how we had watched him disappear and of the emptiness left in the house when he was gone. And now Feiga wanted to do the same.

The trucks outside started to move out and I ran to the window just in time to see them leaving. They hadn't even sent anyone inside to get Feiga back, they were so impatient to be gone. When Feiga realized what was happening she said, "Mama, they only let me off the truck to say goodbye. I'm supposed to go back. They're waiting for me . . ."

"Not anymore," Gusta said. She was standing at the window with me, having limped over just behind me. "They're going."

"Mama," Feiga's voice was desperate.

"Let them go, Feigie," Mama answered her. "Your place is with us."

"I promised them Mama, that's why they let me off the truck. That's why they stopped here."

"They're in an awful hurry," Mama said, looking out the window. "Why such a hurry? Something's not right. Better to stay here with us. You can't trust the Russians." But it was already too late for Feiga to rejoin them in any event. The trucks were rumbling down the road, heading over the bridge to Piadyki on their way east.

Feiga stayed with us then because she had no choice and because she had not had the will to go against our mother. Mama had always been a strong woman and everyone in the family did as she said most of the time, even Samuel. We knew she meant only the best for us and that she understood the world better than any of us, and so, in this way Mama brought our Feiga home to us again. We were all together once more, except for Meir, of course, and Regina who was in Palestine.

Mama couldn't have known then what was coming, nor could any of us, or that it would have been better, by far, to have let Feiga go.

The following day, when we woke, things were strangely quiet outside. There was no traffic on the road and when we went out into the street there were people standing about. Everyone was just looking at one another. Someone shouted that the police were gone and all the other Russian officials, too.

No one knew what to make of it. Where had they gone? Overnight it seemed they had melted away, gone east we surmised, just like the convoy of trucks that had brought Feigie home the day before. After a little while people shook their heads and headed back inside. It was strange though. You could hear nothing but the birds in the trees and the whirr of insects. People seemed afraid to speak to one another and eventually we all just went back to our own houses. It was June 1941.

The first inkling we had that things were really about to change was in the afternoon, I think, when we heard planes overhead. Again we went outside, searching the sky for the source of the droning sounds we were hearing. I don't remember clearly why I was home that day. Maybe because the teachers had all fled, too, and there was no school. But I was home and my sister Feigie and I rushed into the street to look for the planes we could hear but not yet see.

The first blasts were distant and sporadic. But soon, looking up the road toward the city, we could see smoke billowing into the sky as if from a great fire. Then we heard more explosions. The smoke was coming from the brewery in Kolomyia, the place where we got our beer from, before we had had to shut down the inn. I learned later that the brewery was one of the only places the German planes struck in our area, but they totally destroyed it. Maybe they thought it was something else, something more important? Or maybe they just wanted to let us know they were coming, even though the Russians had already fled and no one remained to fight against them. Or maybe they just didn't care what they were dropping their bombs on.

Mama came out and, when she saw the columns of smoke coming from the city, she herded us back into the house and told us to stay there. She was very insistent about it. We must not go out again, she said, just stay put. We didn't have to be told twice. Though we didn't know what war was, not really, we were too afraid to go out now, not with air raids and bombings so close by. We all went into the main living area of the house and Mama told us to settle down. She was puttering around with something, I don't recall what it was, and looking very nervous. She had the radio on, too, but we couldn't hear anything but a lot of static. Someone came to the door, one of our Polish neighbors, I think, and Mama spoke to him. Then she came back into the room and said the Germans were attacking and that the Russians were fleeing everywhere. We didn't know what to say. I hugged my sisters Gusta and Feiga and I think the three of us were crying. Mama's face looked very serious. Her skin was pale. Maybe she was thinking of Meir.

"Everyone just stay inside for now," Mama finally told us.

We weren't thinking of doing anything else.

Even after the explosions ceased and the distant planes overhead were quiet we sat very still, afraid even to look outside. That night Mama put us all to bed early, even my older sisters Gusta and Feiga who were old enough to do as they liked. None of us complained. There wasn't anything else we could do. Where could we go?

The following morning was silent again, as it had been the day before. When we woke we all ran to look outside but nothing seemed to be moving on Kozcaczwka Street. Mama came out and made some breakfast and called us in to eat. Bubbeh Shprintzer was already at the table and we all ate in silence, everyone afraid to ask what was going to happen next.

It was the noise from outside that first caught our attention. It sounded like someone shouting and then there were more voices, more shouting. Suddenly we heard a banging, like something being broken. I ran to the window in the front and looked out at the street. There were people there, everywhere, along *Uliza* Kozcaczwka. They were crowding the streets, moving in a great surge up from the Piadyki bridge toward Kolomyia. It was the Ukrainians, the peasants, and I could see that many of them were carrying sticks and clubs and banging these against the trees by the side of the road or against the street signs near our house. They moved in a wavelike motion up the street, some running ahead of the others and shouting to those behind them to follow. Some were shaking their fists. I thought one man waved his stick in my direction and I quickly pulled back, away from the window.

Suddenly I realized Mama was beside me, staring at the mob, too. I thought I recognized some of the people in the street but I couldn't be certain. There were so many and most were unfamiliar to me, not from Piadyki perhaps, but from other Ukrainian towns beyond Piadyki. Mama put her hand on my shoulder and tried to pull me away from the window. I heard Gusta and Feiga behind us now, too.

"What's happening, Mama?" Gusta said as she struggled to find a place by the window so that she could see out with the rest of us.

Our mother had no answer. She could only continue to stare at the street while absently tugging at me, mechanically drawing me back.

"The Ukrainians," Feiga said now, hurriedly. "They're all running through the streets."

Suddenly I was aware of someone coming toward our house. It was a man and he was carrying a stick or club in his hands. Then he was outside and we heard banging on the door. Mama was afraid to answer it but the banging became more insistent and finally she broke away from us and went hesitantly toward the source of the loud hammering. Without opening the door she asked who was outside.

"Open," a voice said. It was familiar and Mama cracked the door ever so slightly. Through the space we could see the face of one of the Ukrainian men from Piadyki, a man who had been a regular customer at the inn in the days when it was still operating. He took off his cap and said, "Today, stay inside, Panyi Srulova." That's what the Ukrainians called my mother because she had been the wife of Israel Feuer whom they had called Srulov. "It's not safe to come outside," the man was saying breathlessly, "not safe if you are a Jew. We will not touch your house out of respect, Panyi Srulova. But please, stay inside."

I remembered how my mother had tended to his sick children some time before, using the herbs and other healing arts she had learned over the years. My mother seemed at a loss for something to say in answer and the farmer was just repeating himself and speaking more loudly in order to make himself heard over the growing din from the streets. "They will leave you alone," he promised us. "You won't be harmed, but you must stay inside. Keep the girls in, too."

Then he was gone and Mama quickly shut the door and drew the bolt across it. She checked it three or four times before retreating back to the center of the room.

"Is it bad?" Feiga was asking.

Mama said nothing but quickly began to herd us back toward the kitchen.

The rioting in the street went on for the entire day. Crowds of Ukrainians surged up and down the street, smashing doors and windows at various houses. We heard later that the other Jewish houses on Kozcaczwka Street had their windows broken and that ours, alone, was spared. Other vandalism was done to some of the Polish houses, too, but the brunt of the damage was inflicted on our Jewish neighbors. The Ukrainians pushed their way up the road, heading toward the city itself and we heard later that they did a great deal of damage wherever they went. In some places people who were found on the street were beaten and mauled by the rioters. Things only calmed down a little after sunset though the Ukrainians didn't disperse with the coming of nightfall but continued milling about, shouting and drinking and setting fires along the side of the road.

There were no police in Kolomyia to keep things in check any longer since the Russians had suddenly gone. We were on our own. Fortunately, the Ukrainian man who had hammered at our door earlier that day, when the rioting had just begun, was as good as his word. When we peeked outside that evening we could see a few Ukrainians with sticks standing around outside our house but no one was offering any violence to us. The people of Piadyki remembered my mother and all the kindnesses she had shown them and some at least had obviously chosen to protect us.

But the rioting did not end the next morning as we had hoped. In fact, it got worse as more and more Ukrainians from the outlying villages poured into Kolomyia along our road and stormed past our house, heading into the heart of the city. A few stray rocks were thrown at us, striking the outside but, miraculously, no windows were broken and little damage was done. On the second day of the rioting, Mama said we needed water but none of us wanted to go out to the pump. I think she went out herself but I can't be sure. Maybe someone, one of the Ukrainians, carried the water back from the well for her. At any rate my sisters and I just huddled with our grandmother, listening to the madness raging outside and grateful when Mama finally returned, lugging the bucket of water inside. We were so frightened none of us rose to help and she didn't ask us to.

When night fell a second time the rioting was still going on, only now there was dancing and laughing in the streets, too. Ukrainian women and even their children had joined their angry men. We watched everything from the window for as long as Mama would allow it and were very frightened. Although we had heard about this kind of thing we had never seen it for ourselves or, at least, we girls had never seen it. Mama was not so surprised. There was a history in Galicia, after all, of peasants attacking Jews.

By the end of the second day of rioting, things seemed to finally be quieting down and by the third morning there was even silence on the streets. After a while, Mama looked outside and told us there was no one in front of our house any longer and that the road was empty. We sat still and quiet all that morning, afraid to stir ourselves, afraid to even open the door. Finally, though, Mama announced that we couldn't hide forever and she pulled on her coat and went out onto our porch. After a little bit we girls followed, leaving Bubbeh Shprintzer inside. Bubbeh hadn't spoken for some time now, lost in her own darkness, her own thoughts.

Outside the street was littered with debris, broken sticks, shattered glass, shingles torn from some of the homes. It was as if a storm had come through Kozcaczwka Street, a tornado. But we knew it had only been people – our neighbors from the Ukrainian villages across the bridge.

Slowly Feiga and I followed Mama as she stepped down from the porch and turned around to look back at our house. We left Gusta, our older sister, on the porch. Except for a few places there was no damage on the exterior of the old inn that we could see. But, as we walked down to the road, our eyes still darting in all directions and, most especially, toward the bridge to Piadyki, we could see that many of the other houses on our street had been badly damaged by the rampaging Ukrainians.

Though they had told us it was Jews they were after, they had not spared many of the Polish houses on our street either. Across the road from us, at 61 Kozcaczwka, Janek Kozhanofski our neighbor was outside, too. He was taking inventory of the damage to his property which was very noticeable. When he looked up and saw us standing by the road he seemed to become alarmed and, looking swiftly down the road, he rushed to our side of the street. "Panyi Srulova," he said, addressing my mother, "are you all right . . . are the children?"

Mama replied that we were all unharmed and asked about his family. Without giving an answer he said we must go back inside at once, that it was too dangerous to be outside now. Mama told him the Ukrainians had left our house alone and Mr. Kozhanofski replied that the other Jews on the street had not been so lucky. Speaking hurriedly now, he said that the houses of the Frieds and the Schechters had been attacked and that some men had been beaten badly. Mama was unnerved to hear this and turned to us, saying we must get off the street at once, as Mr. Kozhanofski kept urging, while she would go see if anyone needed her help.

"No, no," said Mr. Kozhanofski on hearing this, "you must go inside quickly, too." He was insistent. "Look," he added finally, lowering his voice, "the Ukrainians have gone, it's true, but there's no telling what will happen now . . . or if they'll come back. The Germans," he paused as though fearing to speak of them, "they're saying the Germans are coming here soon and that the Ukrainians have only gone because of that. The Germans have sent word ahead, promising they'll deal with . . . with all the Jews."

Mama listened to this in silence.

Mr. Kozhanofski continued. “Who knows what they will do? You’ve heard the stories. It’s better not to be on the street when they come. They can’t be far from here because the Ukrainians have withdrawn. Please,” he begged, “go inside now.”

Mama said, “I understand Mr. Kozhanofski,” and turned to us. “You see, it’s better to be inside where it’s safe . . . go see to Bubbeh . . . that she’s all right. Tell her everything is good here, that the Ukrainians have gone and the house is untouched.”

Feiga and I did as we were told and in a little while Mama followed us inside, too. When we saw her coming through the door we rushed to talk with her, to ask questions about what Mr. Kozhanofski had said, but she only shook her head and waved us off. Then she went to an old chair she liked more than any other and sat down heavily on it. I kept watching her as she sat there, her eyes slowly moving about the room in which we were all gathered and then as she looked at the door and back again at us. As she did this her eyes found me. I must have looked very frightened because when she saw me looking at her, she smiled and nodded her head a little, as if to offer me encouragement. But she didn’t look at me for long. She kept turning her head back, again and again, to the door that led outside to Kozcaczwka Street.

Chapter 5

Occupation

THE GERMANS came soon after but not as we expected. The first troops to arrive were the Hungarians. They were allied with the Germans and they came through in early July. Order was restored on the streets by then and we were able to go out safely once more. The Ukrainians we had known from Piadyki stayed away from Kozcaczwka Street after the Hungarians came and everyone was relieved at this. People began going outside to make repairs on their houses and Mama even found time to visit our neighbors, especially the Frieds and Schechters, offering what help she could. Poor Mr. Schechter and one of his sons had been injured in the riots but not too badly and we were glad of that.

There was no more school by this time, not for any of us, and we all just stayed close to home. I found time to see my friend, Wanda Madeira, who lived by the river and we spent a lot of time together whispering, either at her house or in mine, talking about what would happen as a result of the war. I didn't talk a lot about the Germans because I had heard stories about them and did not want to think about this. Wanda was silent about it, too. It was better that way since no amount of talking could have changed what was to come.

By the end of July the first German troops arrived. We watched them marching along the road in front of the inn. They came to Kolomyia suddenly, in a roar of noise from their trucks and motorcycles, long convoys of men and vehicles, raising dust clouds and pouring into the city in what seemed like an endless stream. Wanda was with me on the day they arrived and we watched them advancing up the road from the old inn porch. They seemed so handsome in their crisp gray uniforms, their helmets all shiny and gleaming despite the dust that billowed up around them as it had around the Russians who had entered before them. But these Germans were nothing like the rag-tag Russians who had come to

Kolomyia in 1939 nor were they like the Hungarians who had followed the Russians.

Wanda and I had been talking together when they first appeared on the road and we both stopped at the sound of their approaching engines. When they came into view, we were completely mesmerized. As they paraded past my house they kept their eyes trained on the road ahead and did not look around at anything. We were impressed by such discipline. There were hundreds of them, maybe more, and it was the first time I had seen German soldiers. I thought they were very fine to look at.

But they were not fine at all and there came a time when the very sight of them would tie my stomach into tight little knots and make my arms and legs go weak.

After the Germans came, things seemed to settle down again. It wasn't good for us but, at least for a few months, there was some stability. The Ukrainians, as Mr. Kozhanofski had said, seemed to have been controlled. They did not come rampaging onto our street any longer. In fact we didn't see much of them at all. But everything we were hearing from the Polish people we knew gave us cause for worry. Some of the Poles came to tell Mama that they had heard the Germans had promised the Ukrainians in the area that they would soon deal with us, the Jews, and that this was why the Ukrainians had become so quiet. They were waiting for the Germans to keep their word.

There were rumors, too, that a German unit had already rounded up some 2,000 Jews in Kolomyia and tried to shoot them but that the Hungarian commander in the area had intervened to stop the killing. My brother Samuel came to visit us often now, bringing us whatever news he could get. He still had money at his disposal and many contacts who would tell him what was happening. He and Mama often sat together now, out of the hearing of the rest of us, talking about what was going on in the area. By the worried looks on their faces and their low voices we could see things were not good.

We stayed in the house now whenever we could. There was no school anymore, not for Jews anyway, and so there was little reason to stray from home. By the beginning of August the Germans took over Kolomyia completely from the Hungarians and this was a special cause for concern because we remembered how the Hungarian commander had stopped the killing of Jews before. Almost as soon as the Germans took over they began to make new laws against us. One was that a Jew had to wear an armband with a Star of David so the Germans and others would always know who we were. There was talk of Jews being singled out and humiliated in the streets of Kolomyia and so Mama said we should stay away from there at all costs. But you couldn't stay away all the time.

By the fall of that year the Jewish High Holy Days came around and we prepared to celebrate them for the first time under German rule. Everyone was apprehensive but Mama said we should not give up what was ours. We had to keep the traditional holidays as we had always done. One day Samuel stopped by and Mama asked him to go into Kolomyia for us. She had a chicken to be slaughtered and the nearest kosher slaughterer was there. Samuel took the chicken and another, which he had brought with him, and headed toward the city. He had a worried look on his face when he left us but he knew this was something he must do. Besides, he had gone into the city several times before, after the Germans had come, and he knew his way about. It was not a comfortable thing, to be sure, but the Germans had not interfered too much with our day to day activities. They seemed to be mostly concerned with establishing order in the city and its surrounding area so, aside from the indignities they forced you to undergo at times in the streets, this was fairly routine.

We were all excited because *Rosh Hashanah* was an important time for us, our new year. We always gathered together for a big meal on that holiday and other family members would visit with us. This year we did not anticipate everyone's coming together because of the situation but still it was the time of year for that and so we were looking forward to the evening meal just the same.

We waited all day for Samuel's return but he didn't come back. Mama kept going out onto the porch and looking down the road to see if she could spot him but to no avail. She didn't say anything to us girls and our grandmother just sat in Mama's chair without speaking. For the day before such a holiday, it was a very somber time and Mama, I knew, was worried because she had to start her cooking. You had to cook before sundown because you couldn't light the stove or do any kind of work once the holiday began. But Samuel's delay must have worried her in other ways, too, though she didn't let on to the rest of us.

By the late afternoon we didn't know what to make of the situation. All of us girls were out on the porch with Mama, just watching the road. Finally Mama gave a big sigh and turned to us. "Go into the house," she finally said. Her tone of voice was firm, no nonsense, and we did as she instructed. When she followed us in, she was rubbing her hands together nervously. I asked her what she was going to do as she brushed past me. "I'm going to start the cooking," she answered.

"Without the chicken?" I asked her.

But Mama didn't say anything in reply.

Samuel came back near sundown, bursting into the house, his hair all askew, his face sweaty and flushed. He was breathing hard, trying to catch his breath. The Star of David he had worn on his arm was missing. He couldn't sit down. He was pacing back and forth and Mama came into the room when she heard he was back. She looked like she wanted to rush over to embrace him but something about his manner seemed to cause her to hold back. She just stood looking at him, waiting for him to catch his breath so he could speak.

Finally he did. "It's no good," he rasped, his voice hoarse and choking, "no good. Don't go back there anymore . . . we can't go back there . . . no more."

"What happened?" Mama said, too frightened to say anything else.

"They're rounding up Jews," Samuel told us now, in a rush. "They're rounding everyone up. I was there," he stopped, took a deep breath to calm himself. He seemed to be struggling to get the words out. "I was waiting with the chickens and I heard a shouting, shrieking . . . outside. Some of us went to look. We saw what was happening. The Germans were moving through the streets, beating and arresting people, grabbing everyone . . . anybody with an armband. I tore mine off," he gestured helplessly at the place where his Jewish insignia had been. "I left the chickens and ran. If not, they'd have taken me, too. Don't go back there anymore. No one . . . no one is to go back. Stay here . . . I have to see what we can do. I have to go to Breina and the boys in Piadyki now." He stopped speaking and Mama nodded, understanding.

"Don't go back anymore," Samuel repeated insistently and Mama kept nodding as he spoke. "No more," he said again and again. "Stay here . . . in the house. They aren't bothering you here for now. I have to think . . ."

Mama finally went to him and put her hands on his shoulders. "Go back to your wife," she said softly, her voice very low. "Go to the children. We'll be all right here."

Samuel nodded and backed out of the house. His face was still very pale. Deep circles had appeared under his eyes. We watched him leave and then stood silently with Mama after he had gone.

Finally she turned and went back to the kitchen. In a little while she called us to come in and help. We found her standing over the kitchen table, her face very pale, looking down at her own hands as she pushed the food aimlessly around on the table's surface, preparing our holiday meal without the chicken.

I think that was when my brother Samuel began looking for a way to hide. It was a dangerous time and he did not come to us much after that. He did not want to be on the streets anymore than he had to. Sometimes he would send us messages by some Poles he knew but he no longer sent us money. It wouldn't have done us any good if he had. The Germans organized a *Judenraat*, a Jewish committee, under a well off Jewish businessman named Marcus Horowitz to represent all the Jews in Kolomyia and told him that we Jews were to give up all our valuables including any money we had. The *Judenraat* selected a number of young Jewish men and delegated the responsibility to collect all Jewish property to them.

Two Jewish boys eventually came around to our house, hammering on the door insistently, to collect what the Germans demanded. These two boys, looking very uneasy, told us we had to pack up all our silver and gold along with our money, as well as any furs or woolens we had, and hand them over to them because the Germans wanted these for the war effort.

Mama took us aside and told us to start going through the house, collecting what was asked for but, whispering to Feiga and me, she said we were to hide anything we could where the representatives of the *Judenraat* wouldn't find it. While the two boys were supervising our search, Feiga flirted with them to distract them and I managed to take a handful of gold coins that we had from the days when Samuel was still giving us money and slip out with these to the barn. There I dug a shallow hole, burying the coins, and carefully tamping down the dirt over them. Maybe there were twenty or thirty coins in total, of various denominations. I was too frightened to count them or make a good inventory. I just wanted to get them hidden away and get back inside before I was missed.

By the time I came back, Mama was folding up a Persian wool jacket she owned and two woolen scarves. She handed these over, along with all our silverware and a silver *challah* plate that she used for *Shabbos* and holiday dinners. Though she loved this because she had it from my father's mother, from when they had first married, she just bit her lip and handed the plate and her silverware to the two boys from the *Judenraat* without a word. I wanted to cry. The boys seemed pleased that they had gotten so much in what was obviously such a poor house and did not, I think, even notice the tears in Mama's eyes. Or in ours. They just took our things and went outside. But I can't be angry with them when I think about all this today. What else could they have done? If they had come back with nothing what would have happened to them? Were the Germans the kind to understand?

After this, the Germans forbade Jews to be on the streets without a special pass though, truthfully, none of us wanted to leave our homes by this point anyway. Outside you didn't know what would happen to you. A German soldier or a Ukrainian militiaman could take you at any time and then you might never see your family again.

There were no jobs for Jews anymore and, of course, Jews could not own businesses. Mama was constantly worried about Samuel and about Bertha, now living in Horodenka, but there was little that we could do. It was very hard to get word to them or for them to get word to us. We heard that Bertha was pregnant and then that she had given birth but it was too dangerous to even try to see her or the new baby.

Although Jews could not hold regular jobs, the Germans still allowed some to work as laborers in fields owned by the Ukrainians, or to do construction work for the German military. Unless you had a pass for such things, though, you couldn't go outside any longer. We got food for a time by using those few coins I had managed to hide for Mama on the day when the boys from the *Judenraat* had come, and by trading whatever else we still had in our possession with some of the Ukrainian peasants. Many of these still remembered the days when we had had the inn and how Mama was always ready to tend their sick children. So they came, often at night, with food and milk for us, taking whatever we could offer them in exchange. In this way, Mama stripped down the house of anything that still had value. But we knew this couldn't go on forever. How long, we wondered, could we live off this kind of barter? And yet we made the best of it, afraid to think of what might come after.

I think many of the Ukrainians were sorry to see us in such a situation but they were not sorry to see the Germans taking everything from the Jews in general. Like others of their kind, they thought the Jews had unfairly gotten whatever they had, and at their expense, and were glad to see the Germans taking it all away. But those people who knew us felt sorry that we were being affected, too.

One day around this time we heard a convoy of trucks on the road outside. We went to see what was happening and saw about ten truckloads of people, under guard, rumbling past us. You could tell by the way they were dressed that they were Jews. We went out to the edge of the street to see what was happening. The trucks were moving very slowly, heading north to Piadyki. The guards appeared to be Hungarian gendarmes and the people were calling out to those of us who stood on the road watching. We could hear them asking for food, anything, and Mama told us to rush back into the house and bring out all the bread she had baked the night before.

Although it was *Shabbos*, our Sabbath, and Mama had baked the bread for us, she told us to take it all and toss it to the people on the slow moving trucks and we rushed to do this. No one prevented us from doing it so we stood there and threw the loaves of bread Mama had baked up to the grateful people. Because the trucks were proceeding so slowly it took a long time for them to disappear across the bridge to Piadyki and we were able to give away all our bread this way.

A day or so later two women appeared at our door begging for food. They were young women and Mama asked who they were. They told us in Yiddish that they were Hungarian Jews and had been on the trucks that had passed our house. They remembered that we had thrown them the bread but what they had to tell us was horrible. As Mama and the rest of us stood there and listened, they described how the trucks they were on had traveled north to a little traveled part of the Dniester River and there had pulled up along side the river. The two women told us the trucks were all backed up to the river's edge and then they were flung open at the back and the people who had been transported there were all pushed out into the cold, fast running current. The Dniester is a deep and very wide river, nearly as dangerous in places as the Prut, and the Jews who had been taken there were forced into it with no choice but to try to swim across to the other side.

The two women were so frightened, as they described what had happened, that they had trouble explaining it all. They said nearly everyone in the trucks with them had been drowned. Those who could swim, and were strong enough, rode the current away from the place where they had been forced into the river and struggled back to shore, dripping wet, shivering and terrified.

Mama gave them food and offered them a place to stay with us but they replied that they wanted to go into Kolomyia where there were many Jews, hoping they would find a place to stay there. They said they couldn't go back to Hungary because they were afraid they would only be rounded up again and maybe this time they wouldn't be so lucky. We heard later that others had survived the attempted drowning, too, and that many of them made their way back to the large Jewish community in Kolomyia. We weren't so sure that this was the best choice for them but then where else could they go? The Germans were everywhere. They must have thought there would be safety in numbers and that they could hide among all the other Jews that were there.

The Germans began building a ghetto in Kolomyia in the winter of 1941. By March we heard that it was ready and that all Jews in the region would have to relocate there. We were now to be taken from our home, the only home I and my sisters had ever known, and forcibly transferred to a part of the city the Germans had walled off, a place where Jews were to live all together under the watchful eyes of the German occupiers.

We hadn't heard from Samuel by this point in months, though he had earlier sent word that he was trying to secure a hiding place for his family. We worried about Bertha and Yakuv and their newly born baby in Horodenka, too. But they were too far away from us now and travel was severely restricted by the Germans, especially if you were Jewish. We could learn nothing of what had become of them. Mama said that at least we had not gotten any bad news and that we must pay attention to our own circumstances for the time being. We knew she was right.

One day the Germans sent word that the time had come and that all Jews would now have to move to the ghetto. We were told to gather whatever we could carry, including a day's worth of food, and to go outside our homes the following morning, leaving the keys in the doors, the doors unlocked.

We all sat and cried that night and I wandered through the inn, looking at everything, at the walls, the various rooms, the little furniture we still had left, trying to take everything in, to remember everything as it was. I thought I would never see these things again and, sadly, this turned out to be true.

That morning Mama had us all packed and ready to go. She didn't want any trouble with the authorities. We had prepared only what we could carry, as the Ukrainians who worked for the Germans had instructed. My two little cousins, Aaron and Srulek, were very frightened by everything that was happening to us. They had never been like other children who would run and play and do the things children generally do and were silent most of the time, as though they hoped no one would notice they were there. They used to play together in the back of the *korchma* among the gardens and fields that Mama would plant. They were both very shy and preferred not to be noticed. But now they had to come with us whether they liked it or not. When we all went outside with our packs to wait for further instructions, they came with us and sat nervously in the shadow cast by the old house from the morning sun.

But, while we had been told to be out of our house early that morning, and had complied because we were too afraid not to, we soon discovered that our turn to go to the ghetto would not come until much later on that day. On the road in front of our old inn the press of people, of other Jews coming in from the distant villages, was astonishing. They marched past our house for hours, under the watchful eyes of Ukrainian militiamen who were armed only with clubs and were supervised by a few Gestapo officers who oversaw everyone and everything. The Germans alone had guns.

I watched the sad-eyed, shuffling Jews from the outlying towns as they slowly walked past our old inn, along *Uliza* Kozcaczwka, downcast, silent, carrying whatever they could on their backs. The Germans were bringing in all the Jews from the surrounding area to put them into the newly built Kolomyia ghetto and there were so many we had to wait until the long, dismal parade of people thinned out enough for us to join them.

We sat all morning like this, outside the house we were being forced to abandon, perched on the piles our few belongings made along the edge of the road, watching the sad march of people slowly trudge by, to Kolomyia. Little Aaron and Srulek hid behind my sisters Feiga and Gusta while Mama sat with Bubbeh Shprintzer in front. Bubbeh, blind as she was, seemed to hear everything that was occurring and murmured now and then into Mama's ear and Mama would listen without saying anything, sometimes just shaking her head. Bubbeh didn't seem to mind that Mama didn't answer her.

By noontime the silent, slow moving parade of Jews with their meager belongings was starting to thin. Finally one of the Ukrainian militiamen came walking toward us from the road, shouting at us. I couldn't tell what he was saying but it was clear enough what he wanted. Slowly Mama roused herself and helped Bubbeh stand up beside her, too. Feiga got Aaron and Srulek up and Gusta struggled to stand by herself, using the crutches Meir had made for her so long ago. Gusta could not carry any of her own belongings because of her dependence on the crutches so Feiga and I had agreed to carry her share between us. The Ukrainian guardsman was shouting more loudly at us as he came nearer, waving his stick, so we tried to hurry onto the road under his angry eyes. I turned around and looked one last time at the house in which I had grown up, wondering if I would ever see it again, and saw my sister struggling to keep up with us on her crutches. I reached out my hand and Feiga did the same from the other side. Mama was leading Bubbeh who was moving very, very slowly. But Gusta was having an especially hard time keeping up. The Ukrainian guardsman seemed unsure of what to do with us. He wanted us to catch up with the others in the long procession but we were going very slowly because of Gusta and Bubbeh.

Finally, slapping the baton he was holding against his hand he went off in frustration to find one of the German guards. As we were finally falling into the straggling line of forlorn people, he came back with a German officer. This man came to a halt and watched us for a moment, his hand on the pistol holstered at his side.

"What's the matter here?" he suddenly demanded of us. His face was twisted into an angry mask, perhaps to frighten us or perhaps it merely reflected what was going on in his soul. My mother answered, pointing to Bubbeh. "She's old and blind. And the girl is lame," she said, indicating Gusta. "She can't keep up. We're doing the best we can . . ."

The German seemed undecided for a moment. Then he pulled out his gun and waved it at Gusta. "If she can't walk I'll shoot her right here," he began shouting.

"No," Mama panicked, letting go of Bubbeh, "no, she can walk, she can do it," she said. "I'll show you. Please . . ."

Feiga and I each took hold of one of Gusta's arms and almost carried her into the middle of the street. She seemed to wince in pain from the sudden exertion. The Gestapo man looked at us and frowned. There was a skull and crossbones on his military cap and he kept staring at us until we looked away from him in confusion. We started walking, following the others, Gusta struggling with her crutches, and the German stood there, watching us. When he had satisfied himself that we were keeping up he holstered his gun dramatically and strode off. But he left the leather flap unsnapped so he could take it out quickly again if he wanted to. I decided we must not give him cause to do that.

We began going as fast as we could, Gusta stumbling between my other sister and me, Mama leading our blind grandmother, and the two little boys trailing silently behind us. We were at the end of the line of all the people who had been streaming in to Kolomyia all day along the road, among the last of them in fact, and had all we could do to keep pace with them. As we did so, I saw a Ukrainian I remembered from better days among those others who were overseeing our march. His name, I recalled, was Stefan but I don't remember his family name anymore. He was in his very early twenties and he came from Piadyki, just across the bridge. He had always been polite to us and Mama used to give him sweets when he came to the inn when he was a boy. He still looked like a boy to us now.

He was just staring at us as we struggled along and he seemed genuinely sorry at our situation. He had a stick in his hand, like the others, but he wasn't waving it or beating it against anything the way the other guards were. He was just holding it, letting it hang down by his side as we passed him. He offered me a small smile of encouragement but I was too frightened to smile back. It was not a day for smiling. He could see how hard it was for us to walk with a crippled girl and a blind old woman but still he made no move to help.

I saw his eyes darting around as we walked by him, scanning the other guardsmen and the Germans until he found that German officer who had brandished his gun at Gusta before and threatened to shoot her, and then this Ukrainian boy, Stefan, seeing the German who seemed to be looking right back at him, abruptly turned away from us and began waving his stick at others in the line, shouting at them in as loud and harsh a voice as all the other Ukrainian militiamen.

Still, I thought his heart wasn't in it and believe that to this day. Not everyone who did the Nazis' bidding did it with pleasure.

We walked in this fashion for what seemed like hours, toward the center of Kolomyia. It was slow going but we didn't want the Ukrainians and Germans to think we couldn't keep up so we pushed ourselves, stumbling at times, listening to the bellowed instructions of the Germans and their Ukrainian guardsmen, always delivered in angry shouts and harsh commands, voices that never seemed to let up all the long way into the city. They shouted and berated us for clumsy louts and dullards the entire way, sometimes striking one person or another with their sticks to hurry everyone along. It was late afternoon when we finally saw the barbed wire fence they had erected for us and my heart sank as I realized what it meant, that once inside we would be unable to leave again. This was not to be a new home for us but our prison.

Chapter 6

Surviving the Ghetto

THE SUN was already dipping low in the sky when the guards shut the barbed wire gate behind us. It had taken us that long to reach the inner part of the city and we were among the very last to enter. The guards there were all Ukrainians, like the men who had stood over us during the long march from our home. You could recognize them because they wore armbands identifying them as members of the Ukrainian militia. Ours said we were Jews.

When we entered the ghetto under their eyes we were directed by shouts and wildly waving clubs down a dusty, narrow side street where we were told we would find housing. This turned out to be a small wooden structure with a living room, a kitchen area and two bedrooms. But it was already occupied when we reached it.

Another family had been installed in the little house ahead of us and they came out on the porch and said there was no room for anyone else when we arrived. We didn't know these people so they must have come from one of the outlying towns beyond Piadyki. They seemed to be well off because of how they were dressed – much finer than what we were accustomed to. There was a husband and wife with a daughter, who turned out to be around Feiga's age, and an elderly woman who, we learned later, was this girl's grandmother. They stood crowded in the doorway of the little house, blocking our entry, insisting there was no room inside for us. It was only a small house, they said, and we should go elsewhere.

There was a man there from the *Judenraat* and he directed us to a wooden shed that stood against the house, near the street. It looked like a tool shed or maybe it had been a storehouse or workshop. Whatever its purpose it had clearly been used by the former owner for something other than living space. It had no windows anywhere except for a small piece of plate glass in the door through which you could look inside if you stood on your toes. Or at least I had to do that, being small for my age.

The militiamen unlocked the padlock on this door and opened it for us. They told us we were to live there.

We didn't know what to say but Mama didn't argue and went inside at once. This shed had a hard packed dirt floor and in the middle of it was a roughhewn wooden table that had been used for some kind of repair work. The wood was unfinished and bare of anything but big shard-like splinters. It had several deep gashes and cuts in places where various tools had struck it over the years. Against one wall inside the shed was a long unfinished wooden bench. There were a few rickety old chairs around the table, as well, along with a small wood stove and, in one corner, a cot. Mama led Bubbeh to the cot and told her to sit there.

She did as Mama said without complaint. Since everything was so new she dared not move because of her blindness. The cot was to be Bubbeh's, Mama said.

Looking around the small shed and then at us Mama tried to put a good face on our circumstances. But as she spoke her voice seemed to tighten in her throat. She told us to put down our burdens and help her tidy the place up for Bubbeh. Feiga and I assisted Gusta to one of the chairs and seated her there. She was very tired and still breathing hard and sweating from the exertions of the afternoon. The two little boys, Aaron and Srulek, stood in the doorway, wide-eyed. Mama said they must come in and help us clean out the place, too, and, like the rest of us, they did as she told them. Outside, the militiaman who had unlocked the shed door for us was barking orders again, maybe still directed at us, maybe at others. We couldn't tell and soon we stopped listening.

Mama spread out one or two of the blankets we had brought to cover the dirt floor and at once began unwrapping some of the food she had packed for us, putting it out on the table. She said we had better eat something since we had been on our feet for so long and there was plenty more to do before we could expect to live there in any kind of comfort. Feiga and

I looked at one another but neither of us spoke. We couldn't imagine living there at all.

The place where our new home was situated was at the very edge of the ghetto, not far from the barbed wire fence. Standing outside you could see the open fields beyond the fencing. It was farmed land for the most part. If I strained my eyes I imagined that I could even see our home on Kozcaczwka Street. What had been our home. My eyes ran with tears when I thought of it, and when I looked through the coarse wire fencing that kept us inside. Mama got us settled as quickly as she could. There was nothing else to be done. Mama took an old gasoline tin she found lying in one corner of the shed and said we were to use it as our toilet and that Feiga and I were to take turns, with the boys, carrying it outside to dump its contents. There was also an outhouse nearby that we could use for this purpose as we later discovered.

For food we soon learned that the *Judenraat* issued rations periodically to the ghetto occupants and that someone had to go at such times from each family to the old Jewish *gymnasium*, the *kehilah*, where the food was to be apportioned out. They did not give much, we soon discovered, a small portion for each family when you showed them your ration cards. But you took whatever you could get in such circumstances.

It soon fell to me to perform the chore of going for our rations though sometimes one or the other of the boys would come along to help me. But most often I went alone. Then I would stand in line with our ration card and wait my turn and when I got to the front of the line I would take whatever was given: a few potatoes, sometimes, a cup of wheat chaff for flour (we did not even get wheat), a little tea and sometimes some animal fat. Once I remember getting a few eggs but that didn't happen again. We were always hungry once we were sent to the ghetto and we had to scrounge for whatever we could find to supplement the meager rations allotted to each Jewish family.

I soon learned when the German commandant's headquarters dumped their garbage and began to go there, with other children, to dig out what I could. We scrambled through the piles of leavings and sometimes fought one another over a few potato peels or leftover bones from the Germans' meals. Sometimes there were some discarded vegetables, cooked and uncooked, and these were a special prize I would keep my eyes open for. The cuttings from carrots and some dried and shriveled lettuce that I brought back helped supplement the meals Mama prepared for us back in our little shed.

When I would return, with whatever I could gather, Mama would collect it all and spread it out on the table and look it all over very carefully. She never threw any of it away, no matter how awful any of it looked. She found ways to cook everything, to keep us fed, even making us little pancakes with the potato peelings I brought back. But we were still hungry most of the time because the rations the *Judenraat* provided were just not enough for us all.

Soon after we had arrived Feiga said we should look for Samuel, that maybe he would be able to help us, but Mama said no, we were to forget about trying to find him and that we should not even mention him any longer. Feiga wanted to know why and so did I. Gusta, who was older than we were just looked very uncomfortable. Mama said we should do as we were told but we thought Samuel could surely help us and we kept insisting that we should try to find him. This went on for several days with Mama being increasingly evasive. But either I or Feiga would find ways to bring the matter up again. Finally one day Mama, who was working over some scraps I had brought back to try to put together a meal for us, set down what she had in her hands and said we must lower our voices and listen closely to what she was going to tell us.

Feiga and I exchanged glances but did as we were told.

Mama looked from one of us to the other. The two little boys were outside, playing in the dirt and she seemed to feel that she was free to speak frankly to us. "Samuel is not here," Mama finally said, "so it's no good talking about him."

"Where is he then?" Feiga asked. My heart sank at her words.

"Hiding," said Mama as though it pained her to say it aloud. "Anna, his old housekeeper, is hiding him at Piadyki. She has a cottage in the woods there, you know the place. Samuel's gone there with Breina and the children." Mama now looked at us sternly. "You must never speak of this," she warned. "Not to anyone. No one is to know. Promise me."

We both looked at Gusta who was staring down at her hands. It was clear she already knew and had kept the secret with Mama.

"Promise," Mama said again, insisting.

We did. Mama smiled and said "Good."

Samuel's old housekeeper, Anna, was a Polish woman who lived alone with her grown son. He was what used to be called slow in the head. They had a tiny farm on the outskirts of Piadyki, a very isolated location. Few went by there and Samuel apparently hoped to wait out the war in that place under the care of this woman. Mama told us that Samuel had paid her well for her protection but this could only succeed, Mama stressed, if no one knew. She said that now we had Samuel and Breina's lives in our hands and must remember to keep silent about the matter. I wondered aloud why Samuel hadn't found a place for us as well but Mama hushed me up.

"There was nothing he could do," she said fiercely. "The Ukrainians knew we were on Kozcaczwka Street and they would have missed us if we had suddenly disappeared and then they would have come looking . . . besides," she added slowly, "the old woman said she could only take Samuel and his family. It's better they're alone there and safe than that none of us are."

"How will he find us again?" Feiga asked suddenly.

"He knows where we are," said Mama smiling. "With God's help we'll all be fine and when the war's over he'll find us . . . or we'll find him."

"So it's just us now, Mama," I said. "We're all alone?"

Mama frowned. She seemed to be fighting back tears.

"Help me with these potato peelings, Mutzka," she said.

The routine in the ghetto was the same day after day. There was no school for us and not much to do except look for food and try to keep out of the way of the Ukrainian guards and the Germans so we sat inside the shed or outside against its wall when the weather was clear, trying not to be noticed. I would sit and watch the fields through the barbed wire while the little boys played in the dirt. Feiga, at this time, began a friendship with the girl who lived in the house adjacent to our shed, but otherwise the people living there had little to do with us. They had money they had smuggled into the ghetto with them and used it to buy better treatment from the guards. Maybe that's how they got the house for themselves, too, and how we ended up in the tool shed. Feiga and this girl – Dora I think was her name – spent more and more time together. Since they were about the same age, I suppose it was to be expected. I found myself increasingly alone.

I used to look forward to going to collect our rations and to foraging outside the German headquarters building in the center of the ghetto. There was little else to do to occupy our time after all. Periodically the Ukrainian guards would come round and give us new instructions, to do this or not to do that, but mainly they were looking in on us, to be sure nothing was amiss. We heard rumors, too, of what were called "actions" in other parts of the ghetto, round-ups of able bodied Jews to be sent to work camps. Everyone was afraid of this because we had no idea what became of those who were caught and sent away. One day one of our little boys, I forget which one, did not come home. Mama sent us out to look for him and we scoured the nearby streets but we couldn't find him anywhere. We never saw him again and believed he must have been taken in one of the actions. After that we all stuck more closely together. Mama said we must watch out for one another and we tried to do as she said.

Feiga, by this time, had found a group of friends, some of whom she had known before our days in the ghetto and others who were new. She even found herself a boyfriend. Lonek Baumgarten was his name. He was one of two brothers. The younger was called Lolek and I used to get their names confused. Lonek had done a little business with Samuel in better days and now that we were all in the ghetto together he started coming to visit my sister Feiga whenever he could and she began talking about him constantly. I was younger and couldn't see why she was so attached to this boy but she was and that was that and I soon found myself even more alone than ever because I had no friends my own age and my sister, who was closest in age to me, was preoccupied with other matters. Gusta, of course, mostly stayed in the shed helping Mama and sitting with Bubbeh Shprintzer. Left to my own devices, I soon had a great deal of time on my hands.

One day while walking along the fence, gazing idly across the outside fields and dreaming of what it had been like to run freely in places like that, I saw a commotion not far from our shack. A group of young boys were scrambling along the fence, trying to hide something. I watched them for a time and soon saw a boy come up out of the ground as if by magic. And then I saw a second. I was fascinated. I hid myself and kept watching until, after a time, they dispersed. When it was quiet, toward evening, I wandered over to the place where they had been playing. There was a pile of dried branches and some shrubs there and I began to pull these apart. I don't know what I was looking for but I was fascinated by what I had seen. The boys had been so busy at this spot and there was the magical appearance of two of them.

I found a hole in the ground there, very deep. As I peered downward it seemed to disappear on a slant, heading outward toward the fields beyond the barbed wire. Excited at what I had found, I bent down and pushed my head in. The hole was deeper than I had thought and seemed to angle out at the bottom with no end to it. I caught my breath and looked up to see if anyone was watching. When I was convinced no one was, I slid down into the hole, head first, and began to squirm my way through the damp earth into the darkness. The dirt from the tunnel got into my hair and my ears and even in my mouth and by the time I had dragged myself through and come up again, I was blinking dust and soil from my eyes. But when I emerged and poked my head out I was astonished to see that I was outside the fence. For the first time since I had heard the barbed wire gate shut behind us on that day when we had been brought into the ghetto, I was outside again.

I wasn't sure what I had found and so I turned about and went back through the tunnel, back inside the ghetto, before anyone could see me. But I began to go by the place where the hole had been dug pretty regularly. Soon I realized that the boys I had been watching, younger than I, but not much smaller, were using the tunnel to go back and forth between the ghetto and the outside world. I didn't know who had made the tunnel or why, but clearly these boys were using it for their own purposes even while they kept it a carefully guarded secret. There were not many guards around at this time and no one seemed to notice the tunnel was even there. Or if they noticed it, they didn't care. Where could Jews go anyway? Outside the ghetto there were now only Poles and Ukrainians and the Ukrainians hated us and would turn us in at once if they caught us. Who knew what the Poles would do?

Eventually, I went to my mother with what I had discovered and described the tunnel and where it led. She listened intently as I told her of the use the younger boys were making of it. I said I could go out through the tunnel just like they were doing and find us more food. This was our opportunity to survive, I told her in a rush.

Mama looked pained but listened carefully to my eager words, staring first at me and then at Gusta and Bubbeh. She knew that we desperately needed more to eat, that we couldn't continue to survive on the meager rations we were allotted or the garbage I was sometimes able to bring home. And we certainly didn't have money to buy extra food from those guards who were willing to sell it as our neighbors in the house were doing.

Mama realized, too, that it was becoming more and more dangerous to go to the center of the ghetto because each time you did you risked being grabbed and sent away in one of the 'actions.' You never knew when one was about to take place since there was never any advance warning. The Germans just appeared with their Ukrainian accomplices and grabbed everyone on the street just like Samuel had seen that day in the market.

There had already been several 'actions' since we had come to the ghetto and one of us, one of our cousins, was already gone. Mama was fearful that more of us would be taken. If we could find food another way, she knew, it would be a blessing.

"You must be very careful," Mama finally said to me, after hearing me out.

"I know," I told her, confident with the inexperience of youth.

"Take no chances," she pressed me. "Don't let anyone see you."

"No, Mama," I said. "I won't."

She had made a decision. She smiled weakly and reached over to pat my hand and I grinned, proud of her confidence in me. Mama now took one of the old sheets she had brought with us from our house on Kozcaczwka and prepared a sack from it, something I could sling over my shoulder and use to hold whatever I could find. She sewed on rough strips of cloth to make it easy to wear, a kind of knapsack, and then she tightened the seams as best she could with her needle. When she had finished, she handed it to me with tears in her eyes. "I don't even know where to send you," she whispered.

"I'll find our old friends. They'll help," I promised, eagerly prying the sack from her hands and throwing it over my shoulder.

She was still smiling at me as I left the shed and headed into the street, toward the concealed tunnel. There was nothing more to say and the last thing I remembered as I left were her eyes on me as I ran out the door. I was frightened of what lay ahead but pleased to be leaving the ghetto at last, even if I knew it would only be for a little while.

The world outside the fence felt fresh and free. I came up out of the hole in the midst of a field of corn and stood up, stretching my cramped legs and my arms, brushing the earth and tiny pebbles from my clothing. Crawling through the tunnel in the darkness, I had scraped my elbows but the abrasions on my skin did not stop me for a moment and I began to run, as I had never run before, through the cornfield, down the slope of the land toward the outskirts of the city where our old house stood. But I was careful to stay off the road for now because you couldn't tell who would be out this time of the day. It was early morning and I didn't want to meet any of the Ukrainians, especially those in the militia, as I crossed the fields toward *Uliza* Kozcaczwka.

When I finally reached the street where we had lived I was surprised to see that little had changed. Of course there had only been three Jewish families there, the rest being Poles. I raced past the abandoned Jewish houses and crossed the fields again behind our old inn, not wanting to see it or whether anyone was living there now. But I couldn't stay away. I was drawn to it, like a magnet. Because it was still so early in the day there seemed to be no activity there. Maybe no one was living there now I thought. I walked swiftly past the house and down to the river. I avoided the bridge to Piadyki where the Ukrainians lived and went along the riverbank, touching the tall grass there, nearly slipping on the wet earth and shiny stones that lay close to the water's edge. Here I had played since I was a child and it felt good to be back. I sat down by the water and put my hand into the river, stirring the water's surface. There was a plopping sound as some river creature came up for air and dove again. The insects were buzzing, just as I remembered them. Only the children with whom I used to play were no longer there.

Realizing that this was dangerous I suddenly got up and began to look around. What if some of my old playmates came back? What if they recognized me? Then I thought of my mother's faith in me, letting me go out like this, taking such a chance, everything depending on my skill at finding food for us. Without better food, I knew we would all sicken and waste away. I looked down at my own body and touched my stomach and ribs. I could feel them pressing against the tattered blouse I was wearing. We would all die, I knew, if I couldn't find enough food. Determined, I walked up the embankment and made my way to the house that was just over the rise. It was the Bielinski house and I swallowed hard and went to their door. I knocked lightly, afraid to make too much noise. When there was no answer I knocked again, just a little more loudly. I wasn't sure what would happen.

Suddenly the door swung open and I found myself staring at Mrs. Bielinski. She looked shocked to see me standing there. Then she put out her hand and roughly pulled me inside, shutting the door behind us. "What are you doing here?" she demanded. And then: "How is your mother? How did you get out?"

I answered her in a rush of words telling her all I could of what had happened to us, breathlessly adding that we were desperate, that we needed food.

She put her finger to her lips, silencing me. Then she stood there, as though undecided, looking me over, assessing the frail, skeletal child that stood before her. Abruptly she took my hand and led me into the kitchen. "We don't have much these days," she said as she opened her cupboard and felt around inside. She handed me a small loaf of bread and then some potatoes and a little sack of corn flower. I wanted to cry as I took these and put them into my knapsack. "Don't go back by the road," she whispered. "Be careful."

I was nodding as she spoke, overcome by the sight of such food after so many months without in the ghetto.

"You can't stay here," she was saying. "Mr. Bielinski will soon be getting up to go to work. It's better he doesn't see you. Or Janka or Stasia," she added, naming her children. "It's better as few people see you as possible."

I thanked her and let her walk me to the door. I wanted to stay so badly, never to go back to the ghetto again, but how could I do that? Mama and my sisters and Bubbeh were there, all depending on my return, praying I would be successful in finding us food. And Mrs. Bielinski didn't want me to stay either. It was too dangerous and she knew it even if, in my child's mind, I did not. So I took my leave and went back behind her house, staying away from the street as Mrs. Bielinski had warned me to do.

Still, it was too good to be free like this, too good to cut things short and run back to the ghetto. Besides, the food I had gotten from my benefactress was not a great amount. It wouldn't last very long. Summoning my courage I went to the Kozhanofskis next and knocked timidly on their door, too. From where I stood I could see our inn across the street. It looked abandoned, like the other Jewish homes on the street. Mr. Kozhanofski opened the door and saw me standing there and he, too, expressed surprise. I told him what I had told Mrs. Bielinski and he let me come in just as she had. He sat me down and asked about us, how we were surviving in our new situation. I told him all I could about the ghetto and how scarce food was and showed him what I had managed to get from Mrs. Bielinski. He found a little raw meat and a few more potatoes and added these to my sack. "Things are very dangerous here now," he was saying as he put the things into my bag. "The Ukrainian militia is everywhere. Maybe you're better off in the city, where the Germans have put you. Outside who knows what the Ukrainians would do to you?"

When I left the Kozhanofskis I had a half-filled sack but I still did not want to return to our shed in the ghetto. Being outside was too intoxicating, my first taste of freedom since they had shut us in behind the barbed wire. I thought of the tunnel again, my road out. Would it be safe to go back? Could I avoid discovery? The morning was already advancing and people were stirring on the street. Some would know me and know I didn't belong there any longer. Not everyone could be expected to be as friendly as our old neighbors.

But instead of heading back to the ghetto, I turned my steps toward the river again and crossed the road quickly. I began to follow the river away from the road and my feet carried me to my old girlfriend's house, to Wanda Madeira.

When I got there I could see that people were already working in the sausage factory behind the house. Trying to stay out of sight I made my way to the main door of the house and knocked on it like I used to, when times were better for us. I think it was little Janka Madeira who came to the door that first time, my friend Wanda's younger sister. She was about eight years old at that time while Wanda was my age, fifteen. Wanda also had a little brother, Zbyshek who was no more than four, and an older sister, about eighteen, named Angela, who was married by this time to a local boy, Jaszek Hudema. He just happened to be the younger brother of Rudeck Hudema who had courted my own older sister, Regina, so many years before.

Although Wanda's older sister, Angela, no longer lived with them, she was often in the house, helping her mother to run the little factory they operated. On that day, as I later learned, she and her mother were both in the factory, supervising the sausage making. I could smell the rich aroma of the spices and cooked meats from where I stood on the Madeira porch.

Janka looked pleased to see me as she opened the door and not at all surprised that I was there though it had been a long time since I had come to visit. She had no idea about the ghetto or that we had moved away and were now living behind a fence of barbed wire that kept us apart from other people. I told her I was there to see Wanda and she went at once to get her. When Wanda came to the door I could see the astonishment in her eyes. Without a word we grabbed hold of one other and started laughing and crying almost at the same time. "So good to see you," Wanda was saying and I was agreeing, holding onto her tightly. She quickly pulled me inside and rushed me to her room, slamming the door behind us. We left Janka standing outside and when Wanda realized this she opened the door again and called Janka over. She whispered to her to say nothing, not to tell anyone who had come to visit them, and Janka winked conspiratorially. She was pleased to have been taken into her sister's confidence. Then I sat on Wanda's bed and poured out my story to her. It was the third time I had done this that morning. Wanda listened raptly. She said she could not believe what had happened to us. I said neither could I but that it was all true, that we were now living like prisoners in the ghetto and could barely get enough food to survive. I showed her what I had gathered in my sack and explained how I had gone to the Bielinskis and the Kozhanofskis.

Wanda said they were good people and that she would find food for us, too. I wanted to cry. It had been so long since I had been among our neighbors and I had been so afraid, unsure of how they would receive me when I approached them. But every one of them had acted with kindness. My voice choked in my throat and Wanda stood up and came over to me, taking my hands in hers. "Don't worry, Mutzka," she said. "You have friends here. We won't let you starve."

I spent the rest of the day there, in Wanda's room, resting and talking about our now very different lives. I had much to say and it was like it used to be, we two exchanging our girlish confidences. Wanda had things to tell me about the different children we had grown up with, girls and boys I had lost track of when the Russians came and forced us to go to separate schools. There was so much to catch up on that Wanda wouldn't let me go outside for the entire day. "It's better no one sees you, anyway," she said. "You'll stay here and be safe with me."

Wanda brought me something to eat and drink and we ate together in her room. Toward evening she sneaked me outside and walked with me along the back fields toward the city. I was sorry to be leaving. I loved the sense of freedom I had found again but I knew I had to go back. My knapsack was nearly filled now. Wanda had added what she could to it, more bread and some flour. She said she didn't want to take too much because it was better that her mother didn't find out. You couldn't be too careful she whispered. But she said that, when I came back, I should come straight to her house and she would see that I was supplied with whatever she could spare.

And so I took my leave of Wanda, my true friend, and went back by the cornfields alone, wandering along the outside of the fence until I found the tunnel I had used to escape that morning. Crouching down among the corn stalks I waited there, watching the ghetto through the barbed wire until there seemed to be no further activity going on within, where I knew the tunnel came out, and, when I was sure everyone had gone from that place, I clutched my knapsack tightly to my chest and squeezed my way into the tunnel opening as I had done before, squirming through the dark rabbit hole, spitting dirt from my mouth as I pushed my way through, back into the rock strewn, barren landscape of the ghetto again.

Chapter 7

Like a Terrible Dream

MAMA WAS overjoyed to see me. She had been beside herself all that day, worrying over what had become of me. When she saw what I had brought back and heard what I had done, she was even happier.

We ate well that night. It was like a feast to us, especially with the little bit of meat I had brought. Mama didn't ask any questions about whether it was kosher or not. She was just glad we had it. She cooked up the few potatoes and made pancakes. We had food for the following day as well. For the first time in months we weren't suffering from groaning, empty bellies and I was happy to see Bubbeh Shprintzer smiling again. My sisters, too, were delighted and Feiga ate her meal with us instead of sneaking out to join her friend, Dora, in the house that evening. Our little cousin, Aaron I think was the one who was still with us, ate ravenously as only a little boy can and I took special pleasure in knowing that I had been the source of the food that took away the pain from his eyes after such a long time.

After this I began making regular trips through the tunnel to the outside world. I would spend many of my days outside now, near Kozcaczwka Street, and I always came away from there with food for us. The Bielinskis always gave us some bread or flour and sometimes potatoes when they had these. The Kozhanofskis were also generous. But no one was as generous as Wanda Madeira, my long time friend, who would make sure to find milk for us, if no one else could, and to give us bread and flour and, sometimes, a bit of chicken. She could not give us sausage because her mother monitored the supply. After all, they made these for sale and it was their livelihood. But whatever Wanda could sneak away with she would always get for me and, for at least a month, when I was able to make these trips, we began eating better than we had before. What we got was still in small quantities because I could only carry so much back and it was not always safe to sneak away. Sometimes the guards would come by and sometimes the boys would be using the hole for whatever purpose they had, presumably a purpose not so different from the one that sent me scurrying out into the wider world beyond our ghetto. I was never certain. But for us it was a lifeline to the outside world.

Unfortunately, it was not to last.

One day, I went out as I had many times before and went to Wanda's house to spend the day with her. It was fall by this time, getting cooler in the nights, and Wanda said I should go back sooner than usual or I would catch cold or worse. We walked leisurely back together, toward the ghetto, and took leave of one another as we usually did. This had become almost routine for me and I was no longer afraid. I pretty much knew the schedule of the guards in the ghetto, and when the boys would be playing around the tunnel and how to avoid discovery when using it myself. I was very confident by then, believing that I could come and go from the ghetto almost at will. Wanda left me in one of the fields and went back toward her house along the river and I proceeded by myself, carrying my sack. It was very full this time. I had stopped by many of our old neighbors and they had been glad to give us something. No matter how little, it added up and Wanda had insisted on filling whatever space was left in my sack herself.

I had been walking for only a little while back toward the ghetto when I heard a great deal of noise coming from there. People shouting and dogs barking and the crack of what sounded like gunshots reached me in the fields. I was suddenly afraid and began to speed my steps, worrying about Mama and the others. Suddenly, I saw someone out of the corner of my eye, from behind. I turned and saw a familiar face, one of the boys I had known on Kozcaczwka Street. Franek. I smiled since I hadn't seen him in so long and was glad to have found him again. Half turning to him I wanted to tell him how much I had missed him but I was surprised by the look on his face. He looked terribly angry, apparently with me. Suddenly he grabbed for me and caught the knapsack I was carrying, tearing it away from my shoulders. It fell to the ground and everything that was in it spilled out, milk spreading onto the earth, pouring from its bottle that had cracked irrevocably against a stone. I watched the white liquid spread out on the dirt at my feet in shock, thinking how precious it was, how horrible to see it lost like that, knowing it was too late to go back and beg for more.

I was horrified. I wanted to ask Franek why he had done such a thing but when I saw how he was looking at me I froze.

"What are you doing here?" he demanded. "What are you doing outside the ghetto?"

I didn't know how to answer him. I was still confused from the sounds I had heard coming from the ghetto and from seeing my food, the food I had so carefully gathered for my family, scattered on the ground at my feet. My shoulder hurt, too, where he had yanked my satchel away.

"You have to go back," he was saying even as I stood there looking foolishly at him. "They're killing Jews today," he said. "You have to go back there with the other Jews. What are you doing out here?"

I remembered, then, that Franek was of German blood, not really a Polish boy at all.

"Please, Franek," I murmured, afraid to speak too loudly there, "please," I said. He was holding onto me now, squeezing my arm and pulling me toward the ghetto. "Why are you doing this?" I pleaded, wincing from the pain.

But he had a strange look in his eyes. He didn't remember that we used to play together by the river I thought. He didn't remember how we had grown up together or all the little teasing that had passed between us. He only knew that he was a German and I a Jew. He had been educated by the Nazis. They always looked for Germans wherever they went and had found Franek and his family and had made them Germans, like they were. He wasn't a Pole any longer.

Thinking fast I told him I would go back if he would only let me go, that that was where I had been heading when he had grabbed me. "I was going back, Franek," I kept assuring him. "Just let me go, please." I was practically whimpering by this time.

Something changed in his face as I begged him and I felt his hand loosen on my arm. Finally he just let go of my wrist. "You'll go back?" he said as though he was surprised at his own words.

"Yes," I promised. "I was on my way. What's there for me out here?" I looked down at all the scattered food I had lost but dared not try to gather it up again.

"All right," he said dully, "go back then." He turned away from me, as suddenly as he had appeared and began to walk off, as though he had lost all interest, and I started to run away from him, toward the ghetto, wanting only to get as far from this boy as I could. When I looked back over my shoulder, he was already gone but I kept running without thinking. I didn't want to run into him or anyone else like him again.

As I got closer to the ghetto, the sounds of violence coming from there became greater than before however, and soon I was as afraid to go there as I was to remain outside where Franek, and maybe others by now, might find me. I didn't know which way to turn. I began to run erratically and finally, seeing a haystack, I ran there and buried myself in it. I wanted to disappear from sight so that no one could see me, neither those who were doing whatever they were doing in the ghetto nor those who, like Franek, wanted me to go back there and . . . and what?

From my haystack I could hear the shouting and loud crackling noises clearly. Gunfire, interspersed with the relentless din of barking dogs. I huddled there, deep in the haystack the rest of that day, until the noises died down and the sun was close to setting. Then I came out and looked all around. No one was about. If I was lucky, Franek had not seen me take a detour to the haystack and believed I had gone back to face whatever had been going on inside. Now, convinced I was alone in the field, I slowly made my way back toward the ghetto at last. When I found the concealed opening to the tunnel again, I got down on my hands and knees, wriggled my way back through the close, dirt walls, clumps of earth falling on my hair and face as I twisted and wormed through the familiar narrow passage. When I came out on the other side, the sun was dropping below the horizon. Everything was strangely quiet. I stood up and looked around and then I carefully made my way to our little shed.

When I got there, no one was outside. I looked inside the little window in the door and cupped my hands over my eyes, the better to see into the darkness. Everything was quiet and my grandma was lying across the cot, sleeping. No one else was inside. I tried the door but it was locked, padlocked from the outside.

"Bubbeh," I called, "Bubbeh Shprintzer," knocking against the glass, trying to wake my grandmother to let me in. I was very frightened by the absence of everyone else. My grandmother didn't respond to my calls or knocks. She just lay there, still sleeping. Finally, I went around to the front of the house and slipped quietly inside. I knew you could get into the shed from the house as well and though we didn't get on with the family who lived there, except for Dora, I was sure they would not object to my going to my grandmother this way. When I entered everything was quiet. The occupants of the house were sitting quietly at their table, slowly and methodically eating their dinner. I saw that their food was better than what we were accustomed to, at least before I had begun sneaking out through the tunnel.

Feiga, to my surprise, was sitting with them. It wasn't unusual for Feiga to be with them, of course, because of her close relationship with the girl, Dora. But it was strange to see her there when Bubbeh was asleep in the shed, locked in from the outside. None of these people were speaking, not even Feiga. They just had their heads down. They were eating in silence. At once I went to Feiga and she looked up at me.

"Where were you?" she asked, her voice accusing, seeming to come from far away.

"I went out by the tunnel in the morning," I said. "I heard all the noise here. I was afraid to come back . . . until it was quiet. What's happened?"

Feiga just stared back at me in silence.

"Where are Mama and Gusta?" I asked.

"Gone," Feiga finally said.

The others around the table just kept eating, not looking up. "What happened?" I demanded.

"The Nazis," Feiga said slowly, almost mechanically, "they came without any warning and ordered everyone out. Mama told them Gusta was sick and Bubbeh couldn't see but they said if you don't go out we'll shoot you right here." Feiga's voice was trembling as she spoke. She paused to swallow. "So Mama went out with Gusta, helping her walk. But Bubbeh couldn't follow because she couldn't see and Mama begged them to leave her alone. She's blind, Mama said, she can't see anything, I'll come back for her. But the man wouldn't listen. He just took out his gun and went inside. He shot Bubbeh in the head."

I listened without speaking. I was unable to think. My grandmother . . . I had seen her from the window lying asleep on the cot. But she hadn't been sleeping at all.

"We were upstairs . . ." Feiga was rushing her words now, sobbing between each, "we all hid in the attic when we heard them coming. . . they didn't know we were here. But I heard everything . . . what they did . . ." Her voice seemed to be fading away. It was hard to catch her words.

I didn't know how to respond and ran to her, wrapping my arms around her.

"What are we going to do?" Feiga was saying urgently into my ear, "what are we going to do? They took them away . . ."

We clung together, our bodies trembling in the dim light of the room. The others at the table pretended not to hear us. They just kept looking down at their plates, as though we weren't there. Even Dora, Feiga's friend, was silent.

Suddenly I pulled away from Feiga. "Mama?" I said.

"They took her away," Feiga whispered. "They took them all . . . Gusta, everyone . . . everyone who wasn't hiding." Feiga's voice was strangely flat as she spoke. Suddenly she seemed very far away from me.

Everything came clear now. I understood, at last, what the ghetto in which they had put us was all about, why they had brought us there. I couldn't believe my own eyes and ears but I couldn't deny it either.

"We've got to get away from here," I said to Feiga finally. "They'll come back. They're coming back. They told me in the fields they were killing Jews today . . . they'll come back . . ."

Feiga seemed to freeze.

"No," she said fiercely, "where can we go? There's no place. They'll find us and then it will be all over."

"There's no choice," I heard myself saying. "If we stay, they'll kill us for sure."

"We can hide," she said hopefully, "like we did in the attic today."

I couldn't believe what my sister was saying. "Soon there'll be no place left to hide," I said angrily, "not even here."

"I can't go." Feiga turned her face away from me and I watched it from the side. It seemed to mirror her confusion as she wavered between tears and anger. "I won't . . . I can't," she said.

I could only look at her in astonishment. "Why not?" I said. "There's nothing here for us now. It's just the two of us and I know the way out . . ."

"You don't understand," Feiga said. "You're too young."

"What's to understand? If we stay, we'll be killed. Like Bubbeh."

"If we run away, where can we go? Here there's food at least. And we're young. They can use us. They won't kill you if you can work."

"It's him, isn't it?" I said finally, thinking suddenly of Lonek Baumgarten, the boy my sister had been seeing since we had been brought to that foul place.

"Why should I go and leave Lonek behind?" Feiga burst out, turning back to me. Her eyes were red and frightened.

"Then go find him," I snapped. "Bring him along with us. He can come, too."

"No," said Feiga. She got up from the table and stood there quietly for a moment. Then: "I don't know where he is . . ."

"What if he was taken, too?" I whispered.

"He's hidden money away to pay them," Feiga answered. "They won't take him because he can pay them. He can pay for us all. If you stay, he'll look after you, too, I know it." Feiga's eyes were pleading as she urged me to stay there with her.

"I'm not staying," I said finally. "And you can't either."

We sat out that night on the porch of the house. Neither of us could bring ourselves to go back into the shed where Bubbeh Shprintzer still lay across the little cot. We talked all night and I struggled to convince Feiga to come away with me. I was determined not to stay a moment longer in that place than I had to, but Feiga was intent on remaining, sure that Lonek was still in the ghetto and could protect her with the payments he was making to the Ukrainian guards. "The guards are all corrupt," Feiga kept assuring me, as if by convincing me she could convince herself, too. "They'll sell their own mothers for a little money."

She fell silent when she said this though, thinking of our own mother, taken away on a wagon with our crippled sister and the little boy, our cousin.

We could neither of us sleep all that night. The air was sharp and cool because it was already fall, October by then, I think, so we just huddled together for warmth, each trying vainly to convince the other of the wisdom of our respective plans.

In the morning we were still wide awake as the sun came up. We just sat there, huddled together, afraid of what the new day would bring. I could see that Feigie's eyes were red and swollen. Mine were, too. We had barely moved from our little corner of the porch the entire night.

Once it was light enough to see the fence and what lay beyond it, Feiga pulled on my shoulder. She said we had to go back into the shed. My sister was older than I and now, for the first time since I'd returned to the ghetto, I realized this again. She whispered that we had to be practical so I got up and followed her around to the shed. But we quickly saw there was no way we could force our way in because of the padlock on the door. Then Feiga said we would just have to get in from inside, using the door that led from the house into the shed. We rarely used it because the occupants of the house didn't like us coming in and out that way but no one stopped us this time.

No one was even awake when we crept inside the house again. They were all asleep and Feiga led the way to the interior doorway and unlatched it. We stepped down into the darkened shed and my sister fumbled with the bare light bulb, the only light we had in that space. Once the light was glowing, we could see Bubbeh Shprintzer's body still sprawled across the little cot that had served as her bed.

Feiga looked at me and then at our grandmother. "We have to make the best of things," she said, screwing up her courage. Slowly she edged toward our grandmother's corpse and stood over it. Then she bent down and began to feel along the line of Bubbeh's clothing. I couldn't look as she determinedly reached underneath our grandmother's skirts and groped about. When she drew her hand out again she had a wad of money in it, and a watch. The money was in American dollars. Bubbeh had had it from her children, our aunts and uncles who had long ago left Poland to settle in the United States.

"Which do you want?" Feiga said to me, holding the items out so I could see them. I shuddered and said I didn't want any of it.

"Well you have to take something. Bubbeh would have wanted you to. Here," she said, offering me the watch. But I wouldn't take it.

"I'll need the money," she said abruptly, stuffing the bills into her dress. "American dollars won't do you any good on the outside but here, who knows? Maybe Lonek can exchange them."

Feiga was always the practical one among us and she knew what had to be done. I thought she must be right about the money and was happy to let her have it. These were the only things of value our grandmother still had by this time, though why she had hidden money like this, when we were in such dire need to buy food to survive, I couldn't understand. Perhaps she had thought there would be still greater need to come.

When she had taken what she could, Feiga said it was better not to be found there and led me outside again, carefully shutting off the light behind us. I followed her, afraid to even look back at my grandmother's body.

We were back on the porch, shivering from the early morning chill when the horse-drawn wagon finally came round, trailed by two thin men with armbands that said they were Jews. A Ukrainian guard was with them. He looked our way and then turned his head as though we weren't even there and walked over to the shed door. With his club he broke the padlock clean off. Then he threw the door open and the two emaciated-looking Jewish men went inside. In a few moments they re-emerged, carrying the body of our grandmother between them. There was blackened, congealed blood on her head and flies already buzzing about. The Jewish workers staggered under their burden as they carried it to the wagon and, without speaking, heaved it in.

I saw that the wagon was full of dead bodies and that Bubbeh's now lay atop these. Without any direction from the Ukrainian guard, as though they knew their jobs all too well, one of them snapped at the reins and got the horse moving, the wagon rumbling and creaking behind it. The Ukrainian guard walked behind them, swinging his stick back and forth, keeping beat to the rattle of the wagon wheels.

That was the last I saw of my grandmother. As I watched them disappear, I found myself recalling the times we used to visit her in Horodenka before she had given up her house to Bertha and Yakuv, and I remembered how, blind as she was by then, she used to coddle us girls and make cakes for us and serve these with a little tea. She used to keep the money she got from America in a little tin box in her cupboard and always knew just where it was, even when she could no longer see. Sometimes I would watch her groping for that tin to stuff new bills that had just come by post into it. She was saving the money, I knew, so that someday she could buy passage for us all, so we could join my mother's brothers and sisters across the ocean in America.

But Bubbeh Shprintzer had always spoken about only one thing for herself. She had said she wanted to go to Palestine. She always used to say that she wanted to die there so she could be buried in the land of our people. And now they were taking her body away in a horse drawn wagon to bury her in Poland, in the land that had killed her.

When the wagon and the men were gone I got up and slowly walked away from the house. Feiga followed. "Where will you go?" she kept asking. "What will you do? How will you feed yourself?"

"I don't know," I said. "But I can't stay here. Not now."

Feiga reached out her hand and grabbed my wrist. "Don't," she pleaded.

But I was determined not to listen. I kept walking away from her, toward the opening to the tunnel. Finally, seeing it, I turned back. I could barely see her, through my own tears. "Take care of yourself, Feiga," I whispered. "I hope you find Lonek . . . that everything will be okay . . . please be careful."

Feiga looked like she wanted to break down and sob right there but she was holding back. I was torn. I didn't want to leave her but I knew I couldn't stay any longer and I had tried all through the night to convince her to join me. But Feiga was always headstrong and she had Lonek now.

Finally I could delay no longer. I took her hand and gently pried it from my arm and turned to face the tunnel entrance. No one was around and there would be no better time for this. Feiga whimpered softly as she felt me shake her hand loose and I looked at her face again. "Be careful," I repeated.

"You too, Mutzka," she whispered.

Still feeling her fingers on my skin I dropped to my hands and knees and began to crawl, head first, back into the dark tunnel mouth. In a moment I was in, and the blackness of that place closed over me one final time.

Chapter 8

Escape

ON THE OTHER side of the barbed wire I ran as hard as I could into the fields, hiding myself amidst the unharvested crops still growing there. I was breathing hard, trying to make as little noise as possible, trying to keep my head down. I kept remembering seeing Franek on the way back to the ghetto the day before and what had happened. I didn't want to run into him again or anyone like him. If they thought I was a Jew they would send me back and I was desperate never to go back to that place.

I couldn't get the image of my grandmother out of my mind, lying there as though asleep, dead with a bullet in her head, lying there across the cot in the darkened shed that had been our home these many months. And I couldn't shake the image of my mother and Gusta being taken off by the Germans and Ukrainians to . . . I couldn't imagine where, but I thought it couldn't be good. There had been rumors in the ghetto, rumors of where they took those Jews they periodically rounded up. Some said they were sent to work camps but others whispered that it was far worse than that. I had heard rumors of Jews who had been arrested and shipped to the nearby Szeparowce Forest where they were shot. If you resisted seizure they shot you anyway, didn't they? Hadn't they done as much to my Bubbeh? But she couldn't have resisted, being old and blind. Why shoot her? Because they had no use for her any longer and would have killed her wherever they took her I knew. As I ran, I kept returning, again and again, to what had happened the day before in the ghetto. I couldn't help thinking of my mother and sister and what would now become of them.

There was nothing to be done, though. I couldn't find them or go to them without being taken myself. Nor could I hope to fight those men who had taken them. I was only a child, fifteen years old. I hadn't even been strong enough to persuade my older sister Feiga to save herself with me. Numbed by what she had seen, Feiga thought she could survive there still, counting on her youth to give her life value to the Germans, for their war effort.

What had she remained for . . . to work for them, a slave, until . . .

Until what?

I couldn't think about any of it anymore and just kept running along the hills, trying to stay out of sight. When I grew tired, I just stopped and lay down in whatever inconspicuous places I could find.

I hadn't eaten anything since the day before and must have been running on fear alone.

Feiga and I had huddled on the porch of the ghetto house the whole previous night, unwilling to go back to the shed, afraid to even ask Dora's family to take us in. We hadn't eaten and hadn't wanted to. How could you be hungry when you had seen what we saw? But now, running hard and stopping only occasionally to get my breath, I began to feel hunger and thirst again. I was too afraid to stop to look for food, of course, but I was beginning to feel the need for it again. Still, I had only one thought in my mind, to get to safety . . . and only one place I could think of . . . the home of my friend, Wanda Madeira.

I wandered about and hid for much of that day in the fields between the ghetto and my old home on Kozcaczwka Street, afraid to let myself be seen by anyone. But toward evening I had become really, really hungry. I decided I couldn't put it off any longer and so I set out toward Wanda's house in earnest. I didn't know what I would tell her or even if she would help me when I got there, but I had nowhere else to go.

It was nightfall when I finally summoned up the nerve to approach the house. Outside I saw lights still burning in the windows and so I made my way up to the front door and tapped hesitantly against the lintel. I was afraid to knock too loudly on the door itself and held my breath when I heard footsteps behind the door. What could I say to them? Who would be on the other side?

When the door swung open I took a deep breath and just shut my eyes for an instant, afraid to even look. As I opened them I saw Wanda standing there in the lighted doorway. I had been afraid her mother or older sister would answer, or someone else I couldn't fully trust, but my prayers had been answered. It was my girlhood friend. Wanda looked astonished to see me there in the darkness because I had only come during the daytime before this. She looked hastily over her shoulder and, seeing that no one else was nearby, she stepped outside and shut the door behind her. "What's happened?" she said and, finally, after a whole day of hiding and holding back, I burst out in tears, telling her what had occurred.

Wanda took my hand before I was even finished and pulled me toward the Madeira barn. She had her finger to her lips, urging me to lower my voice. "You must be quiet," she said. "Mama's inside. She can't know you're here. She'll be too frightened. We can't take a chance . . ."

We went into the barn and Wanda told me to go sit in the rear, against some hay, out of sight. The animals were shifting about and their strong odor hit me as I went to where Wanda's fingers were pointing. Then she disappeared and I threw myself into the hay and just started to sob. In a little while there was some noise at the front of the barn and I tried to collect myself, to be quiet as my friend had urged. I didn't know who was coming but when this person walked straight toward me I was relieved to see it was only Wanda again, returning with a plate of food and a small glass of milk in her hands. I took what she brought greedily and ate and drank it as fast as I could. I had known I was hungry but hadn't realized just how far gone I was.

When I was done, Wanda sat down beside me and said we had to figure out what to do. I told her I had no place else to go and begged her to let me stay but Wanda shook her head.

"No," she said, "it's one thing to hide you for a little while when you come for a visit. But I don't see how I can hide you here all the time. Mama or Angela will find you sooner or later. Or one of the workers will. They'll turn you in for sure and then it will be bad for all of us. The Germans will come and take us all away. Or kill us."

"They took my mother and sister," I said. "They shot my grandmother . . ."

Wanda touched my hand. "I'll get you some more to eat," she said.

"No," I whispered. "No thanks, I've had enough. I just need some place to stay, even for a little while. I don't know where else to go."

Wanda said, "Yes, maybe for a little while. I'll see . . . you can stay here for now, in the barn. In the daytime, when the workers are coming in and out you'll have to hide of course, but at night it's okay. No one comes to the barn at night."

"I have no place else to go," I said again, pointlessly but trying to make a point. I was desperate.

"I know," Wanda said. "Stay here for now. Then we'll see."

Wanda was as good as her word and hid me in the barn, bringing me food and something to drink every day after she had eaten. I think she took it from her own plate, pretending to her mother and siblings that she wasn't hungry. I couldn't have asked for a better friend.

In the days, I hid in the loft of the barn or, if no one was at home, Wanda came and let me into the house. Then we would talk together in her room, listening closely for footsteps or doors opening and closing, afraid we would be found out. Once, while we were in the house like this, we got a terrible scare. The sound of the door opening sent Wanda into a panic and for a few minutes she was truly beside herself. As we listened, we heard her sister's voice and Wanda said "Mutzka, you have to hide. Now!"

I didn't know which way to turn and Wanda said "In here," thrusting me into an old wardrobe in the room we had been sitting in and closing the door behind me. I sat there, buried behind the clothing for hours, barely able to breathe and trying to keep utterly silent as Angela puttered about the house the rest of the day, Wanda pretending all was well and trying to distract her older sister, trying to convince her to go off on some errand. When Wanda finally came to let me out I was so grateful to breathe fresh air again but Wanda said this was bad, that I had almost been discovered. She said Angela had walked toward the closet several times and that for awhile it had started to look like Angela would never leave.

"Would it be so bad if she knew I was here?" I asked her innocently.

Wanda's face turned pale. "You don't understand. You're a Jew. The Germans are killing Jews . . . and anyone who takes them in. It's as bad hiding a Jew as being one."

I was embarrassed and ashamed that I had brought such trouble on my friend. After this Wanda didn't want to let me into the house anymore but she was too kindhearted to stick to that for too long. Still, I could see that things could not continue this way.

Once, while I was in the back of the barn, little Janka came wandering in. I don't know what drew her there, whether she was on an errand or something else. Most likely she was just playing around as children do, as I used to do in those idyllic days on the Kozcaczwka. She came walking into the barn and I was sitting there, in full view. She stopped when she saw me and opened her mouth to say something.

I jumped up and said "Hush, Janka. It's a secret. A surprise. No one must know I'm here."

I was very frightened but tried hard to hide it. I winked at her and said, "You must keep this secret, okay?"

Janka's face went from confusion to a big grin and finally she nodded. "All right," she said. "I promise."

Later I told Wanda what had happened and she was visibly nervous about it. But she found Janka and confirmed that she was prepared to play along with us. Again I had gotten by, if only just barely, thanks to good luck and maybe something more.

When I had been there for at least a week Wanda came in one day to say she was going to be gone for a few days. I was upset, not knowing who would take care of me. We didn't want to involve Janka because she was so young and any effort she made on my behalf might be readily discovered. Wanda said not to worry, that I must just keep out of sight and that she would be back as soon as she could. In the meantime she brought me a little food and told me to eat it sparingly, to save what I could. She was going to the mill to grind their wheat into flour. But it wasn't close by.

And so I hid myself as best I could and tried to keep completely out of sight. By this time I had become used to the barn animals and they had gotten used to me. My presence no longer made them skittish and I knew the routine, when the workers came to move them outside and when they brought them back. There were just a few cows and some horses they took out daily for the farm work.

After the first day that Wanda was gone I had used up all the food she had brought me and, by the second, I was hungry. Even worse, I was unable to get anything to drink and so my parched mouth made life in the barn a hell for me. I wanted to sneak out and find food but I was afraid and remembered my promise to Wanda, to keep out of sight until she returned.

By the third day I was ravenous and felt like I would never taste water again. It had rained the night before and the sound of the rain beating on the barn roof that night, and of it dripping down the side afterwards in the morning, made me crazy. I was afraid to leave the barn by myself. Whenever I had gone out before, Wanda had been there to let me know if the coast was clear. But now there was no one to depend on and I was trapped.

Finally, in desperation, I went to the back of the barn and found some loose boards and pushed against them. Scratching my hands on the coarse wood, I managed to make a hole big enough to slip through. I crawled out, looking around to make sure everything was okay. The first thing I saw was a dirty pool of water in some wagon tracks and without thinking I threw myself down and put my face in the puddle, drinking the muddy water. It tasted gritty but I was so desperately thirsty. Then I tried scooping it up in my cut hands. I drank like that until I could taste the mud between my teeth and then I stopped.

Hungry now, I began looking around for something to eat. Near the barn there was an overgrown area, thick with weeds and I half crawled, half walked to these, afraid to stand up for fear I would be seen. Then I began to pull out clumps of the vegetation and chew on it. I was looking for wild carrots but I got mostly grass. I had previously gone with Wanda, when it was safe, into the family garden to pick a few things but I didn't want to risk that now, with no one to make sure it was safe.

The stalks of grass and other weeds I had eaten and the muddy water now made me feel sick and I went back into the barn and hid myself in the deepest part of the hay that was stored there. At least I was no longer famished though now, because of the aching in my stomach, I had other things to think about.

Wanda returned that afternoon and was shocked to see the condition I was in. She was also very quiet and didn't seem to want to say much. When I finally felt a little better I asked if everything had gone all right. She just kept looking at me. At last she could contain herself no longer.

"We can't keep this up, Mutzka," she said.

I didn't know how to respond and just stared at her.

"I can't be here all the time. Sometimes I have to go away. My mother needs me to do things for her and I'm the oldest now that Angela is out of the house. Besides, sooner or later you're going to be discovered. Look at you, grass stains on your mouth. You look terrible."

"Where can I go, Wanda?" I said. "I have nowhere . . ."

"If the Germans find out about you, it'll be the end for all of us. What will they do to my mother, to my little sister and brother? I can't be the cause of that. You have to go."

I could say nothing in reply. I knew she was right, that I was a danger to all of them. My mind was racing, trying to think where I could go. Then it hit me. My brother Samuel. He was safe in Piadyki, wasn't he? Surely I'd find safety with him there.

Wanda was speaking again. "I mean it Mutzka. I can't let you stay here any longer . . ."

I nodded and looked away.

"Tonight I'll sneak you into the house," she said. "We'll plan it out. You'll see, it'll be okay."

I could only nod in agreement.

Later that night, as she had promised, Wanda got me into the house and we sat on her bed in her room talking in low voices about what I must do. Wanda was sad that she had to turn me out but she couldn't see any other way. I think she thought that sooner or later, if nothing else gave us away, little Janka would. Or Zbyschek, who at four years of age, was too young to keep any kind of secret at all for very long. I had been lucky Wanda had let me stay on for as long as she had.

Wanda brought me a pair of her shoes and handed them to me. "You had better put these on now," she said. "You'll need them for walking because those old shoes of yours aren't any good anymore. I looked down at my feet and for the first time realized how shabbily I was dressed. And how badly worn my shoes were. I bent down and took off the ones I was wearing and put on Wanda's in their place. They felt better on my feet. It was a good thing we were so close in size.

Wanda was looking at me as I did this and I looked up finally and said "Can you give me something, something to pretend I'm not a Jew? If they think I'm a Jew, I'll be killed for sure."

Without another thought Wanda reached up and took the necklace she always wore from her throat and handed it me. It was a small tin cross, nothing special. It had no real value but it said to anyone who saw it that the wearer was a Christian. I took it and looked at it for a few moments. Then I smiled gratefully and put it around my neck. It felt strange putting a cross on but I had no choice. "Some papers, too," I blurted out. "Do you have any papers I could take?"

"No," Wanda said quickly. She was thinking that any papers she had would have her name on them and would point right back to her and her family if I were caught.

"I'll need something," I insisted. "I'm going to be out in the street, all by myself, I need something to convince the Germans . . ."

Wanda pointed to a drawer in her night chest. "Look there," she finally said.

I opened it but there was nothing. I looked back at her and she shrugged. But I could see she was torn between helping me and keeping herself and her family from harm. I kept looking and then I saw her report card, with her names and grades on it. It was something at least. I put my hand on it and looked up at her. She shook her head vigorously, "No," she said. "I can't give you that."

"There's nothing else," I said urgently.

Her face was impassive by this time and I couldn't tell what she was thinking. Finally I let go of the report card and stepped away from the dressing table. Wanda turned away, too, and walked quietly toward the door. Without thinking, without saying anything further to her, I quickly turned back and put my hand inside the drawer, snatching that report card and shoving it under my dress. When I looked back, Wanda was still standing by the door, looking into the hallway. As I moved toward her she suddenly turned back to me, her face softer again, half smiling. I felt terrible, having taken her report card against her wishes but I was desperate and knew I had to have something that said I wasn't a Jew.

Wanda whispered, "I think the coast is clear now. Let's go downstairs."

And that's what we did.

Chapter 9

My Brother Samuel

IT WAS early evening when I left the Madeiras' home for good. It was already late October or early November, I'm no longer sure, but the air was quite cool. I thought it would be better to travel by night now because I knew I had to pass that area across the bridge where there would be many who knew me by sight. I was headed for the outskirts of Piadyki where I knew my brother Samuel would be found.

Passing through the area on the other side of the bridge, even at night, was still unnerving. When I crossed over I began to be uneasy. Every step I took seemed dangerously loud, likely to call attention to my presence, and I kept looking around, afraid I would see someone I knew looking my way. But there was no one by the time I was passing through there and the street was blessedly dark.

As I walked briskly through the village I kept touching the cross that was around my neck, thinking about what it meant. Sometimes, too, I took the report card I had stolen from Wanda out of my dress and tried to read it in the moonlight. But it was too dark to see it very well so I just pretended to read it, as though there was anyone there to fool but myself! I guess I just wanted to reassure myself that I still had this precious piece of paper. The name at the top read "Wanda Madeira" and, as I looked at, it I decided there and then what I had to do. From now on, I told myself, if anyone stopped me, I would no longer be Miriam Feuer. I would be Wanda, Wanda Madeira – and Wanda's life, her story, would be mine.

I had been raised with Polish children. Though a Jew, I had grown up among Poles, to my mother's everlasting consternation. In fact, I had even had to learn Yiddish when the Communists came and made us go to Yiddish schools. Polish was my first language and Catholicism, the religion of the Polish people, was not strange to me. Having gone, when younger, to the Krulova Jadviga School in Kolomyia, named after Poland's greatest Queen, and having played all my young life with Polish children in our area, I was no less familiar with their songs and prayers than I was with my own. My mother had often scolded me for this but now, I thought, it would work to my advantage. As I walked steadily through Piadyki I went over all this in my mind, telling myself, over and over, that now I was Wanda, a good Catholic girl, Wanda Madeira.

I still didn't have a really firm idea of what I must do. I was seeking my oldest brother and still hoped he would look out for me as he had always done while I was growing up. But I liked this other plan, this idea of being Wanda. And so I had it in mind when I came to the outskirts of Piadyki and headed toward the farm where I knew my brother was staying. It was very late by then and I was getting cold and tired. When I passed a little Ukrainian church my hand went unthinkingly to the cross I was wearing and I turned my steps there. Everything was quiet. The priest and caretaker must have been asleep. So I went round the back and found a barn with the door slightly ajar. I slipped in and made a place for myself on some straw and put my head down. Before I knew it, I had slipped into a deep, forgetful sleep.

When I woke I had been dreaming. The sunlight was pouring through the open barn door and I thought for a moment that I was back in the ghetto with Mama and everyone. Then I thought maybe I was still in Wanda's barn. But after a moment I was able to orient myself. Looking around I remembered where I was. I got up and brushed the loose straw from my dress and checked to see that I still had the report card next to my skin. I took a few tentative steps toward the doorway and heard some chickens rooting about. They scattered as I came out. I was very hungry and didn't know where I would find food. Finally I plucked up my courage and went up to the priest's house and knocked very gently. An old Ukrainian woman opened the door after a few moments and stood there looking at me. I saw her eyes come to rest on the tin cross at my chest.

She was bent over and her skin was very leathery. I said I was on the road and could I have some food? She just kept staring at me. Finally, she said I might come in. She sat me down at a small table and brought me a piece of buttered bread and a small glass of milk. I ate and drank gratefully as she watched me. She wasn't very talkative and I was glad of that. I wouldn't have known what to say. When I was finished I thanked her and said I would be going on. She just kept looking me over until finally she got up and walked me to the door. I think she stayed there, watching me, as I walked off down the road. Maybe she was afraid I would come back and ask for more.

But I knew the way from there to the little farm where my brother was said to be hiding. I was walking fast now, having had my strength restored by the meager breakfast the priest's housekeeper, for that's what I took her to be, had provided. I knew the woman who had taken my brother in, too, and exactly where she lived. I left the road as soon as I could and went across some fields. Her small plot of land was on the road to the nearby village of Ceniawa. That was the beauty of it, my mother had said, because it was off the beaten track.

When I came to a thick wooded area that looked familiar I knew I had gone in the right direction. I walked up a narrow dirt road that disappeared into a thick copse of trees. Past the trees the road twisted and I stayed on it. I had been to this place before, on errands I had run with Feiga, my sister, so it wasn't unfamiliar to me. I knew my way around. It was just on the other side of Piadyki.

When I found the farm I was surprised at how small it looked since the last time I had been there. It wasn't much, just a small house and barn and a few broken down outbuildings nearby. I went up to the door and knocked, as loudly as I could. I don't know what I was expecting. Maybe that my brother Samuel would come out. But he didn't and I had to knock a long time until I finally got an answer. The woman who had been my brother's housekeeper, Anna, opened the door and stood there, looking at me. She seemed surprised at my sudden appearance. I thought I would find a welcome from her but her eyes only darted about, searching the nearby trees.

"What do you want here?" she finally asked me.

"My brother," I said hesitantly, not knowing what else to say. "I came to find my brother . . ."

"He's not here," said the woman sharply. Then she caught herself. "What makes you think he's here?" she asked me suspiciously. There was concern in her voice and suddenly I realized that maybe I had done the wrong thing by coming there.

"My mother," I stammered, "my mother said he was . . . that I could find him here. Please," I said, "I have to find him."

Her face softened. I think she could see I wasn't going away. Where could I have gone after all? I had come so far and had no other ideas except for the vague one of changing my identity, pretending to be my friend. But I was still only fifteen and had never been out on my own like this. Where do you go when you're on your own for the first time and so young?

"All right," she said at last, "but keep your voice down . . . come with me." She stepped out of the cottage, shutting the door behind her and signaling me to follow her. We went to the barn. Looking all around again, as though to be sure no one was nearby, she carefully opened the barn door. I followed her inside. It was dark in there, until my eyes gradually adjusted. Now I could see Anna fussing at the cows' trough. She had only two old cows in that barn. She was really quite poor I realized.

I saw that she was struggling to push the feed trough aside and there, beneath it, was a flat board, covered with straw. She knocked on the board and we heard scuffling underneath. I stood back as the board started to lift up, the straw falling away. Up out of the ground, slowly, my brother Samuel appeared. He lifted himself out of the hole and stood up beside Anna, looking at me. In the hole I could see three more heads peering out – Breina and the two boys. They were covered with soil and bits of straw and looked terrible.

Samuel was standing over me, and I looked up at him. Anna, the Polish woman, stood aside, very nervous and fidgety. My brother's face was covered with dirt, his hair askew, but he stood there like he used to, broad and solid like a squat bear. I didn't know what to say and just kept looking up at him. Then, all at once, I burst out crying and wanted to touch him, to reach for him but he reached for me instead and took me into his arms. He held me there a long time, not asking any questions as I sobbed against him.

Finally, when I could catch my breath he whispered it was all right and then I began to blurt everything out. I told him all the terrible things that had happened, how Mama and Gusta were gone, that Bubbeh had been shot in the head. I poured everything out. About the Germans and the Ukrainians and the lack of food and their cruelties and the terrible place we had had to live. Then I told him of my escape and how I had hidden with Wanda for more than a week until she told me I had to leave there, too. When I was done, when I could finally stop my onrushing words, I just stood there breathing rapidly, trying to catch my breath. Samuel held me tightly and I lay my head against his shoulders. When I opened my eyes, I saw Anna still staring at us.

At last my brother released me. He started to pace back and forth. From the corner of my eyes I saw Breina and the two boys still looking up at us from the hole in the barn floor. I thought maybe they wanted to come out, too, but they made no attempt to do so. Samuel finally stopped walking and turned back to me. "It's no good," he mumbled, "Mama . . . Gusta . . . What of Feiga?" he asked suddenly.

"She stayed," I said. "She was all right but she wouldn't come with me. She's waiting for . . . for Lonek Baumgarten."

"The Baumgarten brothers are all right?" Samuel asked.

"I don't know," I told him truthfully. "Feiga was hiding with the others when they came and took Mama and Gusta away . . . when they shot . . ." I stopped. I couldn't finish the words and caught my breath.

Samuel looked at me gently, as though to encourage me to tell him everything I knew.

"Feiga was sure Lonek would be all right," I went on finally, "because he and Lolek were paying the Ukrainian guards to leave them alone. Feiga said Lonek would pay for us, too . . . but I just couldn't stay any longer. I was too afraid."

"Anyone who stays now is a fool if there's a way out," Samuel said.

I was grateful that he said that because I wasn't sure, even then, that I had done the right thing. "I don't think Lonek knows about the tunnel," I offered. "But Feiga does."

"Maybe they'll use it then . . . before it's discovered by the Germans."

"Samuel," I said, "I don't know what to do now, where to go. I need a place to stay. Wanda Madeira couldn't keep me anymore so I came here . . ."

Samuel looked at the old woman when I said this. She was watching us nervously from the threshold of the barn door and had a very worried look on her face. She was shaking her head. "I can't keep her, too," she murmured to Samuel now, "there's not enough to eat as it is. And my son . . . what if he sees her?"

Samuel turned back to me. "You can't stay here Mutzka," he said finally. "We haven't the room."

"But it's a big house," I said, looking toward Anna's cottage, knowing it was nothing of the sort. Still, I thought it was big enough for one more, especially a girl like me.

"You don't understand," Samuel said. "We can't stay in the house . . ."

"I know," I said, reassuring him. "But I can stay in here, too, if I have to, like I did at Wanda's house."

Samuel just shook his head as the old woman was still doing. "It's not that simple," he whispered finally. "We're under the ground here. We stay down there all day, in case anyone comes by, and only come out once in a while, in the evenings sometimes, and not for long then either. We shouldn't even be out now. It's dangerous. There's not enough room in there for another." He was looking at the hole in which Breina and the children were sitting. "It's tight enough as it is for the four of us," he said under his breath.

"What should I do then?" I said, looking at my brother.

"You have to make your own way now, Mutzka," he said.

"I could help her," I replied, looking in Anna's direction, "I can work around the house and help out. I can do all the things she's too old to do. And I have this," I added hopefully, touching the cross around my neck.

The old woman was still vigorously shaking her head no and Samuel looked very, very sad. "Not now," he finally said. "It wouldn't be safe. You would endanger us all."

"Where then," I asked him, pleading, "where can I go?"

"Away from here," he answered, "get as far from here as you can. Find a place without Jews, where they don't even know any Jews and . . ."

"But I don't know where to go . . ." I said, starting to sob again.

Samuel leaned over and took my hands. "Listen, Mutzka," he said. "This is a very bad time for all of us. You're young. You don't look Jewish. A girl can get by in a way men can't. Your hair is light. No one has to know what you are."

Even as I listened to him and shook my head, I knew he was right. I had known it since I took the report card and cross from Wanda's house. But still I was afraid.

Samuel was wearing a fleece lined jacket and, as he looked at me, in my thin dress, the same thing I had worn since the day I ran away from the ghetto, he seemed to realize how little I had with me. The nights had turned much colder by this time, too, as it was early November, and I had felt the cold as I made my way to Piadyki. Samuel suddenly reached into his jacket pocket and pulled out a handful of coins, Polish zlotys, and handed them to me. "Take these," he said. "I don't have any use for them here but you'll need them." Then as though another thought had suddenly occurred to him, he took off the jacket, too. "And you'll need this," he said, handing it to me.

I took the jacket and put it on, thrusting the zlotys he had given me back into the jacket pocket from which he had taken them. "What about you?" I asked as I felt the weight of his jacket on my shoulders. "How will you keep warm?"

"I've got the hole," he tried to smile. "We're all pressed together down there. We keep each other warm."

I looked at my brother's face and saw that he was trying very hard to make light of things but he seemed frightened in a way I couldn't remember seeing him before. "You must be careful, Mutzka," he was speaking to me again. "Stay away from anywhere the Germans are. Find a place that's off the beaten track . . . look for some kind of work. That'll keep you going. And don't use any Yiddish. Never."

I nodded silently.

"I wish we could keep you here with us," he was murmuring, "but there's just no room. You'll be all right if you do as I've said. Just keep out of sight. You're a Polish girl now, right?"

I kept nodding, listening to his words.

"Good," he said. Then, glancing at Anna, he added: "Now you've got to go. It's too dangerous being here. This place is out of the way but people still come by. Even I shouldn't be out of the hole in daylight like this. Will you go now, Mutzka? Please?"

"Yes," I said.

"Be careful, little sister," he tried smiling again, taking hold of me and placing a kiss on my forehead. "I wish we could keep you with us," he whispered, "I really, really do . . ."

"I wish you could, too," I said but I knew there was no longer any hope of that.

Chapter 10

"Go to Tluste"

FROM PIADYKI, where Samuel was hiding with his family, I walked, as fast as my legs could carry me, toward the nearby village of Ceniewa and, after walking through it, I turned north. I was fortunate to get rides from two local farmers shortly after I found the main road, riding first in the wagon of one, then in the other. These men didn't ask me many questions and I didn't talk too much about where I was going or where I had come from, either. I thought the quieter I was the better.

The first night after I had left Ceniewa, I hid in the barn of another church but was too afraid to tell anyone I was there. I just slipped in, when it grew dark, and left first thing in the morning. It was getting colder in the evenings and I was grateful to have Samuel's jacket as well as the zlotys he had given me since I could now buy a little food as I traveled east. I was just wandering about without any sense or purpose of where I must go. Finally, in Gwodziec I started talking to some people in the town, asking if anyone knew where I could find work. I knew that I would need to find a place to stay and a way to earn some money because the zlotys Samuel had given me wouldn't last forever. I told whoever I met that I was a Polish girl, alone, and that I had lost my family when the Russians came. No one seemed to have any reason to think differently or, at least if they did, they didn't let on.

There were no Jews in any of these towns. I knew that because Jews all had to wear the special armbands demanded by the Germans and there were none to be seen. There were Poles and Ukrainians, of course. But all the Jews were gone. I didn't want to stay there too long because of the Ukrainians and I didn't have a very firm idea of where I was headed but I began to think of my sister Bertha in Horodenka. Maybe it would still be possible to find her and get help there. Maybe she was far enough away from Kolomyia to have avoided being forced into the ghetto with us and the other Jews in the area. And so I turned my steps eastward, toward Horodenka, the town my mother and grandmother had come from and where my sister must still be living.

I was wandering without thinking of what needed to be done, just hoping to find a place where I could hide. The little towns and villages I passed through all blur together in my mind now as I try to remember. I followed the little roads that ran between the many villages at times but sometimes I just walked across open fields. At night I slept in haystacks wherever I could find them and helped myself to whatever was growing in the fields when I grew hungry. Often, I simply snuck into the church barns I passed, sleeping there and leaving in the morning, saying nothing to those who were living there. Sometimes, though, I would talk with the priests' housekeepers – all the priests had them – and they would give me a little food and something to drink. I mainly went to the Ukrainian churches, since they were the most numerous in the area. I must have looked like a poor, miserable bedraggled Polish girl to them.

It was getting colder each night and I realized I could not continue living in this way. With winter would come the snows. Haystacks and open barns would no longer be enough to keep me warm so when I came to Horodenka I felt a great surge of relief and headed straight for my sister's house. Though I didn't see any Jews on the streets here either, I didn't let that stop me. I was afraid to think about what it meant.

Only when I found the house, a small, old building on a narrow and twisting street that was cobbled to reduce the amount of mud, only when I came to that place and stood outside, under the shadow of a nearby building, and saw strangers going in and out, did I realize what I had already known deep in my heart – that Bertha and Yakuv were gone, too, and that there was no one I could turn to, no one to take me in. I watched the house that had been my grandmother's, which I knew so well, from outside for a while, hoping Bertha would appear, being careful to keep out of sight. I didn't want anyone seeing me and thinking here is Bertha's sister, waiting, another Jew. After a long time – I don't remember how long I waited – I realized it was futile, that Bertha no longer lived in that house, and finally I hurriedly walked away. I didn't know where to go from there, only that I couldn't go back to Piadyki or Kolomyia.

There was a town called Gwozdziec – I remember going there – somewhere between Kolomyia and Snyiatyn. I don't recall how long it took me to get there. I was just wandering about, frightened and unsure of what to do. I was only fifteen, after all, and had never been on my own like this. I was still sleeping in fields and church barns, sometimes appealing to the caretakers for a little food and drink when I had to, and glad of my brother's jacket because it was getting harder and harder to be out on the roads, especially in the nights. Others were traveling like I was, I think, people displaced by the war and the Germans. No one asked any questions. People just passed one another by unless they needed something. But it was rare anyone had much to spare. I had little trouble in getting by and was accepted as a Pole just as Samuel had said I would be.

At some point I found myself in a town whose name I can't recall with great clarity any longer. I remember it now as Czortkow, a city well to the north of my hometown of Kolomyia, but subsequent events make this doubtful. Perhaps I was in so much of a daze at this time that these things are no longer as clear to me as they should be. After all, it was more than 65 years ago. But in this town, Czortkow or some other that was like it, I suddenly found myself near a railway station. Railroads always made me feel at home. Hadn't I come from Kolomyia, the central rail hub for the entire area and hadn't half my neighbors, when I was growing up, worked for the railroad in one way or another?

I had been walking through the street when I found myself passing the railroad station, trying to think of what I must do next, or maybe not thinking of anything much at all since I had been on the road, by this time, for quite a while. After so many days even wandering aimlessly starts to seem normal to a person and I had begun to accept this way of existing. I couldn't change my clothes and had to get food where I could find it. A railroad station usually had a bathroom and that would give me a chance to wash myself a little, to feel more comfortable in the shabby things I was condemned to wear, day in and day out. Perhaps I had simply shut my mind to the larger questions because it was easier than thinking of all that had happened in the ghetto in Kolomyia, or about my brother hiding with his wife and children under the ground in Piadyki, or my missing sister in Horodenka. Whatever the cause, I had become absorbed in my wanderings and had stopped counting the towns I passed through or hoping for any better than I had and was glad at the thought that I had found a public bathroom.

Suddenly, just as I was thinking about cleaning myself up, I heard loud noises coming from the street and, looking up, I saw German soldiers converging on the main street where I was walking, in big trucks. People began running in every direction but other Germans were coming toward them from the side streets, forcing them back toward the trucks. I watched in shock as soldiers jumped off the trucks, waving their rifles and shouting, grabbing at the herd of frightened people in the street. Amidst the shrieking whistles and harsh shouts of the soldiers, everyone was trying to get away. Panicking, I looked around desperately for a place to hide. If you tried to run down the side streets I could see you would only run head on into other Germans coming from there. They seemed to be rounding everyone up and pushing them into the trucks.

Turning around in a tight circle, I saw there was nowhere to run to except that bathroom in the train station and so I rushed toward it. It was empty inside and frantically I hid myself behind the door. I stayed there, shaking and listening to the shrieking and whistles outside, trying to calm myself, to shrink back into the wall so I couldn't be seen. At one point I heard the heavy boots of German soldiers rushing along the pavement outside. They seemed to be getting louder, to be moving toward me. I stopped breathing and held myself still, struggling not to move, not to make one sound. Then, abruptly, a head poked through the doorway and I felt my heart jump into my throat. It was a German soldier and I could hear another outside, shouting to him. I froze and held my breath, afraid he would hear me behind the door . . . or see my shadow. Then, I knew, it would be all over. Time seemed to stop as the German deliberated. It seemed like he would just push the door open and come inside and I knew that if he did he would find me instantly.

Then, as quickly as he had appeared, he was gone, never having looked behind the door where I had been hunkered down, trembling almost uncontrollably. I felt like I was going to slide to the floor in relief when I heard his footsteps moving off. He had apparently decided to heed his fellow soldier's call and return to the street. Perhaps he thought he had seen everything to see in that little bathroom since it was entirely empty except for me where I stood behind him, protected only by that door.

I don't know how long the Germans' round-up went on outside like this, but I stayed there in my place for a long time, afraid to step back out into the daylight of the street.

When I finally did, at least an hour had passed and the streets were quiet again. I emerged tentatively, looking around. There was no one in the street and the Germans were gone. Thanks to that little bathroom in the train station, I had avoided what I later realized had been a German effort to grab workers for their war effort. They did that throughout those early war years, seizing people and sending them off to work camps. Many were sent all the way back to Germany itself, to do the work German men could no longer do because they were at war in the east and because too few women were available in Germany to pick up the slack. Of course, they weren't just grabbing Jews, I realized. They were taking anyone they could find. Even not being a Jew wouldn't have saved me in this case.

After this close call I left the town as quickly as I could, sleeping that night in the first rural Ukrainian church barn I could find. I didn't want to be anywhere near a town where the Germans were so active.

The next morning I approached the first man I saw on the road, a Ukrainian, and told him I was looking for work. I had decided that I had to get off the streets so I would no longer be exposed as I had been the day before. To do that I would need some kind of home, a place where I could live like a Pole. If I couldn't find some place for myself soon I was afraid the Germans would eventually grab me, too, and once they had me, if they ever realized I was a Jew, I would be even worse off.

The man I approached that morning was a farmer who seemed to be in his mid-forties. He was solidly built, wearing peasants' clothing. He looked me up and down as I stood there, practically begging him for work and I saw his eyes come to rest on my little tin cross. When he looked at my face again he half-smiled and I realized the cross had worked its magic for me, just as I had intended it to. In his eyes I was just another Polish girl.

The man shook his head in answer to my question and said there was no work to be had around there but, he told me, if I were to go to the nearby town of Tluste I might have better luck. The Germans, he said, had recently taken a lot of people from there for their war effort and there would be a need for extra hands. "Go to Tluste," he said, pointing me towards a road sign which showed the way and I decided that I would.

It was early morning when I came to the Dniester where the road I was on came to an end. The Dniester is a broad and meandering river, not easy to cross, and the road to Tluste led directly to it. The only way across was by ferry in those days. These were small barges or rafts operated by local people that plied the crossings, carrying travelers from one side of the river to the other. While wide, the Dniester was not all that deep in this part though you never knew where the riverbed would drop precipitously. So it was essential to take passage with an experienced river man.

When I got there the river mist had not yet lifted and there was still a damp morning chill in the air. I huddled in my oversized jacket and strained my eyes across the river, looking for the ferry but could see nothing. The morning sun was still not fully risen and the farther shore was cloaked in early morning shadows. I looked all around and realized I was alone. I just folded myself deeper into my jacket, not wanting to appear conspicuous, hoping no one would think it odd a young girl, alone, was standing at the road's end, looking to cross the Dniester so early in the morning. I especially wanted to avoid any German soldiers who might be nearby because they might be suspicious of my presence at that still early hour.

Suddenly I heard footsteps and, turning, saw a man approaching. He looked like a city man and was wearing a short coat. I averted my eyes as he came closer but continued to watch him carefully, not sure how to act when he reached me. Would he be suspicious of me? Report me to the authorities? I was very frightened, especially after the events the day before in the nearby town. As he came up he gave me a nod and I half-smiled at him, afraid to do more. He stopped in the chill morning and slapped his hands together as if to warm himself. He looked at me as though to say something but I quickly looked away again. I didn't want to talk to him if I could help it. Out of the corner of my eyes I caught a shrug as he turned to more important matters. He started stomping about along the river's edge, looking, as I had been doing, for the ferryman. Finally he started to shout, cupping his hands over his mouth. "Mykia," he bellowed. "Mykia." He kept this up a few times and I realized this must be the name of the ferryman on this part of the river and that this man who was waiting with me must have known him. Crossing the Dniester here, on the way to Tluste and the other cities on the other side, must have been a familiar task for him.

He was still stomping up and down the bank and shouting when, finally, I heard a dull rumbling in the distance and then a soft whooshing sound coming from the river as the placidly flowing water shifted in a series of broken ripples at our feet. Out of the gray mist that lay low along the surface of the river the corner of a wooden barge suddenly appeared, growing larger before my eyes. I hadn't realized before how much of the river was obscured when I looked across it because I could see the far side above the river fog.

Mykia, the ferryman, was tall and very thin with an abundance of thick, bushy hair on his head and unshaven face. He was garbed in old clothing, obviously homemade, of the sort the Ukrainian peasants in the countryside often wore. The man on shore with me was slapping his hands loudly against his arms in time with the slurping sound the barge made as it hove into view. He seemed impatient to be off. The ferryman carefully brought the corner of his raft, and then one whole side, into the shore, guiding it with a long pole he wielded at the rear of the barge for this purpose. The small engine that powered the raft had been turned off and there was nothing but silence in the early morning, except for the sound of his ferry grounding against the river's edge.

Grinning at the man and then looking at me, the ferryman, Mykia, pushed his raft tightly into the shore and then drove his pole into the river mud behind it, to hold the vessel steady so we could board. Then he rushed the length of his barge to our side and opened the little gate to let us on. The barge was enclosed all around with a roughly cut wooden fence to keep customers from falling into the river. I was sure it was a good idea. I stood back to let the man beside me board first but he shook his head and waved me ahead so I stepped uncertainly onto the little ferry and felt it sink and shift beneath my feet, the water giving way under my added weight. The gentleman who had been waiting with me now followed onto the boat and the barge sank and shimmied even more with his added presence.

Then the ferryman, Mykia, stood before me, his hand stretched out. I wasn't sure what the fee to cross was but I reached into my pocket and pulled out one of Samuel's zlotys and handed it to him, hoping this would be enough. He grinned and shoved it into his own pocket and then I saw my fellow passenger hand him a coin as well. I was watching over my few zlotys very carefully and hated to part with any of them because I had so little hope of getting more any time soon, but I had to get across, not least because I wanted to put the river between myself and the Germans who had nearly gotten me in the last town I had left. The ferry was my only hope of that.

Mykia stood at the raft's little gate, looking up and down the road. I suppose he was hoping for other customers but there was no one in sight and finally, shrugging, he closed the gate and went to the rear of the barge and pulled his pole from the mud. He lifted it over the barge and took it to the shoreward side. Reaching out there with it, he used it to push us away from the land. My stomach jumped as the boat broke free and the river took us. Mykia slowly used his pole to turn the barge round in the river's strong current and then he started the tiny motor again and began to drive us back into those river mists out of which he had come.

The water lifted us up and dropped us by turns as the slow river current fought the motor's efforts to push us across. There were only the two of us plus the ferryman and the barge seemed dangerously undirected as it strove against the river's thrust to the south and east. I stood alone and dared not speak, not to my fellow passenger or even to the river man because I was afraid, as much because of the river on which we now rode as because of the Germans I was trying to leave behind. And, while I knew the ride on the river would not last long, there would be no hope of freeing myself from the Germans on the other side of the river if they were to take me. Still, it felt good to be leaving solid land behind, if only for a little while, as though, on that river, frightening as it might have been, I could imagine myself in another place, a place where even the Germans could not reach me. Of course, I knew it wasn't true but it made me happy to think it was, at least for the short space of time it took to make the crossing.

I watched the receding shore from the rear of the little barge as the sun, rising steadily all this time, finally began to burn off the mists. I could now see the land clearly as it dwindled away in the distance, the road I had followed since Piadyki becoming no more than a faint dark spot on that shore. I watched it fade away and only then did I turn round to look at the other side of the river, the shore we were now rapidly approaching. As I did, the muddy eastern bank seemed to loom up suddenly and Mykia, the ferryman, rushed to cut the boat's engine, hastening round to my side of the ferry again with his long pole, probing the river bottom beyond the outer edge of the raft, searching for solid ground.

Chapter 11

The Camp at Lsoftse

WITH THE MEMORY of the Ukrainian farmer's words, "Go to Tluste," still echoing in my ears, I stepped off the barge into the wet muddy ground on the eastern side of the River Dniester. My feet immediately sank in up to my ankles and I had to fight against the insistent suction of the mud to pull myself free. When I looked up, my one fellow passenger had already gone and Mykia, the ferryman, was left alone, standing on his boat, eyeing the road for more customers.

I fought my way through thc black mud to thc road and looked around for signs showing the way to Tluste. I had never been on this side of the river before but I soon found the direction to the main road and, after cleaning the thick river mud from my shoes and feet, I began to make my way in the general direction of Tluste. I passed through a series of villages, the first Uscieczko, right by the river, until I finally came to Rozanowka. This town wasn't very large and was particularly hard going. The streets were unpaved, not at all like the towns I was used to on the western side of the Dniester and everything here was thick with mud. The deep wagon ruts in the roads of Rozanowka were filled with blackened water. I did my best to get round these without falling in but even where the ground seemed dry I would sink in as soon as I stepped down.

I had no thought of stopping, however, because I had my mind set on Tluste where the Ukrainian man had promised I could find work. I knew it was work that I now needed, more than anything else, both to replenish my shrinking supply of zlotys and to ensure myself a place to stay. I had realized from the close call I had had with the Germans the day before that I could no longer wander aimlessly about as I had been doing.

Sooner or later I would stumble into the wrong place and then I might not be as lucky as I had been at the railway station.

I purchased a little bread to eat in Rozanowka but did not stop there long. I wanted desperately to reach Tluste because I had high hopes that I would find a place to stay there. It was still morning when I reached the outskirts of that town and I pressed onward, heading for the central market place. I thought I would find farmers there, anyone who could use an extra pair of hands in their fields or barns. But when I entered the main section of the town I was astonished to see people with armbands like the ones we had been forced to wear in Kolomyia. There were still Jews in Tluste! They hadn't been sent to the ghettos as we had been. I could barely believe what my eyes were telling me. There, on the streets, were Jews walking about amidst the Poles and Ukrainians. They were shabbily dressed, to be sure, but they were free, or at least they were freer than any Jews I had seen since before we had been sent to the Kolomyia ghetto.

I didn't know what to make of it. Looking around I couldn't see any German soldiers on the streets though there were some Ukrainian militiamen here and there. But they seemed to be allowing the Jews to move about. I walked carefully down one side of the street by which I had entered the town, pretending disinterest in everything around me, not wanting to draw attention to myself. There was a heavyset Jewish woman nearby and when I thought the Ukrainian militiamen were looking elsewhere I carefully approached her. I spoke to her in Polish, careful to keep my little cross outside my jacket. She just looked at the cross and then into my eyes and I hurriedly glanced away.

But I wanted desperately to speak with her. "Panyi," I said respectfully, "I'm a girl alone, looking . . . looking for work. Can you tell me . . . a man sent me here to Tluste . . . is there work for someone . . . like me?"

The woman was silent, looking at my face. I thought she wanted to smile encouragingly at me. But she didn't. Her brow was deeply furrowed and she reminded me a little of my own mother in the *korchma*, in the days before the ghetto. She was shaking her head. "There's not much work for anyone, here," she said.

She must have seen how my face dropped at this. She just stood there in the road, where I had stopped her, and cast her eyes all about. I did so, as well, but the Ukrainian militiamen on the street were still looking elsewhere. I was so desperate by then – my throat was tight and I couldn't help swallowing hard when I thought about what I had come through to reach Tluste. I thought my eyes would brim suddenly with tears and I tried to hide my face. I had come so far and hoped for so much in this town. But the woman, a Jew to whom I dared not reveal myself, gave no cause to hope.

"Well," I said, "I heard there was . . . there was work here . . . somewhere."

The woman was still shaking her head. I didn't know what else to do anymore, where else to go. Without work I would be lost. I could not sustain myself on the streets because winter was coming and Polish winters can be especially harsh. My fear must have shown on my face.

"Go to Lsoftse," the woman finally said under her breath. "In Lsoftse you can still find something, child."

I looked up at her and finally saw a half-smile on her lips. "Go to Lsoftse," she was repeating, very quietly, as though she wanted none to hear but me.

"Where is that?" I asked.

The woman pointed along the road I was on. "Follow this street. You'll see the sign. You can read can't you child?" she asked me gently.

"Yes, panyi," I replied.

"Good, then that is the way you must go. Quickly, don't stop," she warned, ". . . to Lsoftse. The sign will show the way."

Then she was pulling her skirts up above her shoes and hastening away from me, down the cobbled road in the direction from which I had come. I wanted to run after her, to take her hand, to thank her, to look once more into her eyes and speak to her, Jew to Jew. But I just remained rooted to the ground where I was, watching her until she had disappeared around a nearby corner. The Ukrainian militiamen were looking at me by then and suddenly I realized where I was. I hurriedly turned away and headed down the street, looking for the sign that would show me the way to Lsoftse.

When I finally found a sign it read: "7 kilometers to Lsoftse." It was posted on the road on the outskirts of the town. Seeing it, I decided not to stay even a moment longer than I had to in Tluste. Something in the woman's demeanor had made me decide that I must waste no more time there than I already had and I just started walking briskly along the road. Such travel was no longer strange to me but I felt a strong compulsion to leave Tluste by this time and decided to act on it.

I had gotten into the habit by then of looking for the Ukrainian churches in whatever town I found myself in, because I knew I could find safety there. The Germans and Ukrainian militia would not take me for a Jew if they saw me in the churches and, because of my cross, I always found a welcome. Although I was familiar enough with the Catholic liturgy of the Poles, I had no similar acquaintance with the Ukrainian rites but, because I told everyone I was a Pole, this did not seem strange to any of the Ukrainians who took me in.

And so, almost as soon as I had left Tluste behind me, I began looking for another Ukrainian church. I had been on the road since early that morning and I was very, very tired by this time. It was not unusual for me to tire on the road and sometimes I would just seek out a haystack in one of the fields I was passing, or some little clearing, any place I could lay my head down and sleep for a few moments. But this time I was uneasy at the thought of doing this. It was already getting quite cold and I didn't know if there would be snow soon. Or if the Ukrainian militiamen in Tluste had noticed me talking to the Jewish woman. Maybe they had become suspicious? Maybe they would follow me to Lsoftse? So I just kept moving, pushing myself to reach the town the woman had told me about.

I saw the town first from a distance and it looked unusually inviting to me. It was a cluster of small houses at first which increased in number the closer I drew to them. I must have been very, very tired by then because all I could think about was finding a place to rest. As I approached I could see that this town wasn't very large and that there were many Poles on the streets. That was a good thing, I thought, because I would more easily blend in. But of course, I might have been better off among Ukrainians or even Jews than among Poles because these were the people I was trying so hard to be like and they might recognize any errors I made sooner than non-Poles. This never occurred to me at the time.

I stopped the first person I saw as I entered Lsoftse, a Polish woman, and asked her the same question I had been asking for a while now, if she knew where I could find work. She directed me to a little Polish church and I went there. I knew enough of the Catholic rites to pass as a Pole. I knocked on the door of the small house that stood by the church and told the elderly woman who answered that I needed work and a place to stay. She looked me over, seeing my dust covered face and oversized jacket. I suppose I didn't look like much to her. She said there was nothing. Still, I was desperate by now. I had come so far. I said, please, I'm all alone. My name is Wanda, Wanda Madeira, and my parents have been lost. The Russians took them away, I said. They took them to Siberia.

I had composed this story in my mind and used it on and off in my travels from the first, but now I had reached the end of the line. If I could not find a place to stop, a place to finally settle at Lsoftse, I didn't know what I would do.

The old Polish woman just kept shaking her head as I poured out my tale to her. She didn't seem to want to hear it. Still, I wouldn't go away. I stood in her doorway talking quickly, telling her whatever I could to keep her from shutting the rectory door in my face. By this point I must have sounded terribly desperate. Finally, she scratched her chin in frustration and said: "No, nothing here. But you can try the other church."

"Another church? Where?" I asked.

"It's a Ukrainian church," she said pointedly. She must have thought I would be disconcerted by this.

"How can I find it?" I all but begged her.

She gave me directions and finally I left her as she was closing the door behind me. I heard its heavy slam as I walked back to the street but I didn't care because I had what I needed, directions to another place where I might find the shelter I needed. I followed the road she had directed me to, hoping she had got it right.

The little Ukrainian church was just where the old woman had said it would be. It was smaller than the Polish church, reflecting the fact that this was more a Polish than Ukrainian town. But I recognized the Greek Orthodox cross on the steeple right away, and the rounded cupola near its pinnacle. Greek churches have distinctive markings and the crosses they display are much more elaborate than the Catholic symbol. The church itself was a small affair, built of dark, weathered wood. There was a little fence around it, running along the edge of the road. In the back I could see the priest's house and a small barn. I plucked up my courage and opened the small picket gate and walked in, following the pebbled path around the side of the church to the little house. There I stood a moment and then knocked boldly on the door. It was already late in the day and it would be cold by nightfall, I knew. I didn't want to think about another night in the open, looking for a sleeping place or a bite to eat.

A woman answered the door. All these churches had caretakers to look after the priests but these were Ukrainians and, unlike the Catholics, the Ukrainian priests could marry. The old woman was wearing a dark dress and had a more sophisticated look to her than many of the caretakers I had encountered. She had intelligent eyes, too. She just looked at me and I quickly said I was looking for work and could she use someone like me? I spoke in Polish and then in Ukrainian since I was able to speak fluently in both tongues. The woman just looked me over without answering. Finally, she said, "What is a little Polish girl doing wandering about like this, asking for work?"

I didn't know how to answer. I was usually quick to respond, quick to tell my story, but this time I was tongue-tied.

"Well, come in," she said, seeing as I had no words to answer her with. She was looking at my clothes, at my dirt encrusted shoes.

"You'll want something to eat and drink," she said.

I was so grateful I didn't know what to say.

This woman took me into the kitchen and made me sit down. Then she brought me a little milk and some bread and I tasted it gladly. I hadn't had much to eat or drink the entire day for I had been on the road since early that morning and the simple food was welcome. When I was done I looked up and saw the woman still staring at me. Her eyes were on my filthy shoes. "Why is a Polish girl looking for work in an Orthodox church?" she asked me abruptly.

"I'm all alone," I said, launching into my prepared story. I explained that my family had been sent east by the Communists and that I was now an orphan.

"All alone like this?" said the woman, shaking her head. "Well, that won't do. How have you been getting by?"

"I . . . I've been walking east," I said, "from town to town. Looking for my parents. I need work. I have no money left . . . no place to stay."

"Did you try the Polish church?" the woman asked. She had a kindly, if very tired, looking face. Her dark hair was streaked with gray. I thought here is someone I can talk to.

"The people at the other church said I should come here," I told her. "They had nothing for me . . . no place I could stay."

"What can you do?" asked the woman.

"Anything," I blurted out. "I can do anything. I can clean and cook and . . ."

"Can you tend cows?" asked the woman.

"Yes, yes I can do that," I said. I was thinking of the dairy my brother Samuel had run and how I had often gone to visit him in Piadyki when I was younger. I knew how they got the milk from the cows and how to give them their feed.

And what I didn't know, I was sure I could learn.

"Well," said the woman, tapping a finger against the side of her face, "I could use some help in the barn . . . I'm not as young as I used to be . . ."

"I can do whatever you need," I said to her hurriedly. Then: "I need the work."

"We can't pay much," said the woman firmly.

"It's all right," I answered her. "I just need a place to stay for a while, and something to eat . . ."

The woman had folded her hands in the apron that she wore stretched across her lap. "My name is Katrina," she said quietly. "I'm the priest's wife here. He's a good man . . ."

"I'm Wanda Madeira," I blurted out, "from . . . from Piadyki."

"That's right by Kolomyia, isn't it?" asked the priest's wife.

"Yes . . . the next town over," I said.

"I see," said the woman. "Well, you can call me Katrina if you like. And I'll call you Wanda. Is that all right?"

"Yes," I said, pleased. "Yes. It's my name so why not?"

Katrina laughed. "Well, we'll have to break you in with the cows then, won't we? But first let's see about a place where you can sleep. Then we'll find some clean shoes for you. The ones you've got look like they've seen their best days."

And so began what was to be my first extended stay anywhere since I had fled the Kolomyia ghetto. Katrina, the priest's wife, was as good as her word and found me a pair of old shoes I could wear in place of the ones Wanda had given me and which I had utterly ruined on my journey, both from so much walking and from all that mud I had trudged through before reaching Lsoftse. The new ones were clunky work shoes but they were more suited to my needs now than the light footwear Wanda had provided. Katrina also set me up in a small room with a bed and, after this, she showed me around the premises, telling me what my responsibilities would be.

During my stay with Katrina I would rise early each morning, with the sun, and go out to the barn to see to the cows, feeding and milking them and then lugging the pails full of their warm milk back into the house where she would meet me. She always had a nice little breakfast prepared which she would share with me. I didn't see her husband, the priest, much. He was an older man and very busy with his parishioners, but Katrina was always around. She also had an elderly serving woman whose name I no longer recall and a laborer named Vasil to do the heavy work around the house and barn. They were all Ukrainians but they never objected to the fact that I was a Pole, as they thought, or that I didn't attend church with them.

I got in the habit on Sundays of going off by myself. I would tell them I was going to the Polish church so they didn't think anything of my absences. And sometimes I even went. But mostly I would wander off by myself, to explore the town of Lsoftse or just to find a place where I could sit by myself. I tried not to think too much of the situation I was in or of the people I had left behind but it was not always easy to banish them from my thoughts. Sometimes it was just better to be by myself, where I could cry unseen.

I think I was there for more than a month during which the weather turned bitterly cold so that I was happy to have found such a place to live. There were no German soldiers about and the Ukrainian militia was not to be seen much either. I couldn't account for that, but I was certainly grateful. I helped Katrina, the priest's wife, in whatever ways I could and learned a great deal about tending cows from her. Vasil did all the heavy work, shoveling the cows' droppings out of the barn and bringing in the hay and feed for the horses. But I was the one who was solely responsible for milking and feeding the cows.

One morning, after I had been there for about a month, I heard a distant siren as I awoke. I hadn't heard it before and was unsure what it meant. It blew several times, insistently, and that made me curious. After I had attended to my chores I asked Katrina, while eating the warm breakfast of eggs and porridge she had prepared for me, what the siren was for. She looked up at my question and said "Oh that's from the work camp. They keep the Jews there."

I took my fork from my mouth and laid it on my plate. "A work camp?" I said.

"Yes, for the Jews." She continued eating.

"Where . . . where is it?" I asked.

Katrina stopped chewing and looked at me strangely. Then she shrugged and told me where the work camp could be found.

I hadn't been to that side of Lsoftse since I had come to stay there and had never seen the camp she spoke of. I'd had no idea it even existed.

"They use it for the young ones," Katrina was saying as she chewed on a bit of sausage. "They keep them there as laborers. For the farmers in the area."

"They do farm work?" I asked.

"Yes. Sometimes road work, too. Whatever the Germans need. I'm surprised you haven't noticed the siren before."

"No," I said. "I never did."

That day was a Sunday and when the rest of the household went to church, I pretended I was going off to the Catholic church on the other side of town as I always did. But as soon as I was out of sight I veered off the road and cut across the fields, heading to the place where Katrina had told me I could see the work camp for myself. When I came out on a hillside I saw it. It was a large compound surrounded by barbed wire. The gates were open and I could see people going in and out. I walked down slowly, anxious to take a look. As I got closer I could see there were only young people there, none much older than I was. They seemed to be able to move about freely and I was fascinated and couldn't take my eyes away.

Suddenly I heard a voice calling, someone said "Mutzka."

I turned, astonished to hear my name for the first time in almost two months. Coming toward me from one of the small crowds of people outside the gate was a dark haired girl about my own age. I looked at her face. She was grinning.

"Mutzka," she shouted, "what are you doing here?"

I didn't know how to answer though I had recognized her at once. It was Celia Bieber, a friend of mine from the Jewish school in the days the Russians had been running things. We had met at the Jewish *gymnasium* in Kolomyia.

"Mutzka," Celia kept repeating, "where did you come from? Have you come to join us here?"

"What . . . what is this place?" I murmured, keeping my voice low as she drew near. It was the first thing that came to my mind. I didn't know what else to say.

"It's a work camp. It's where the Germans sent us. Are you here now, too?" She was looking at me intently as she spoke, searching my face.

I looked around and could see Ukrainian guards at the gates nearby and others moving about inside and outside the barbed wire. "No," I shook my head quickly. "I didn't even know this place was here . . ."

She was still looking at me, at the cross around my neck, and then at the jacket I was wearing. I hastily stuffed the cross inside my jacket.

Her face grew pale. "Mutzie," she said, "what are you doing with a fleece lined jacket like that? Jews aren't supposed to have such things. If the Germans see it they'll give you plenty of trouble. You have to take it off quickly." She reached out to grab me, to take hold of my jacket but I backed away. "No," I said, "you don't understand . . ."

"Mutzka," she kept repeating, "the jacket . . . take it off before they see you."

"I can't," I said, "it's my brother's . . ."

"You should come inside," she whispered urgently. She had an almost conspiratorial look in her eyes. "We have it good here now," she said. "All young people like us are here, and they give us plenty of food. I have a boyfriend inside, too. You'll like it in the camp with us. It's not like things were before, in the ghetto."

I didn't know what to say to her. I just kept backing away, looking at her grinning face, the barbed wire fencing running in a long ragged line behind her.

"Come on," she kept insisting. "Come inside and stay here with us. The work's not so hard and there's plenty to eat. They need us for the war. They have work for us. Only take off this jacket before anyone sees you . . ."

"All right, Celia," I said. "But I have to go back to where I've been staying first. I have to tell them . . ."

"You'll come back then?" she was asking me brightly, excited at what I had said, at my promise to return. From the tone of her voice I could see how pleased she was to have found an old friend and how eager to have me join her there.

"Yes, yes, of course I'll come back," I smiled. "But I have tell the people I'm staying with first."

"Where? Where is that?" asked Celia.

"Outside town," I lied. "Not far. I'll come back as soon as I let them know . . ."

"That's wonderful," said Celia. Then: "But you must take off the jacket. If the Germans see a Jew with such a jacket . . . ."

She didn't finish her thought.

"I'll come back tomorrow," I said, suddenly pulling myself away from her. "Maybe in two days . . . I have to tell them . . ."

I wanted to get away as quickly as I could.

"Wonderful," said Celia. "I'll find you a place in our bunk then. I can't wait to introduce you to Otek, my new boyfriend." She pointed her finger toward a group of young boys near the gate and indicated a small, thin looking fellow. "There he is, over there," she said.

I smiled at her but I kept backing away. Then I was turning about and heading up the hill again. I didn't look round to see what my friend was doing but I was praying, as I hurried over the hill, that she wasn't planning to mention me to anyone else inside the camp.

When I was helping Katrina in the kitchen later that afternoon I was very quiet and kept to myself. I couldn't get my mind off Celia and the work camp. All those Jews there, living under the Germans. Katrina kept watching me as I worked. She had noticed that I was unusually silent. At last she stopped what she was doing and asked why I was keeping to myself like this.

"I don't think I can stay here any longer," I suddenly blurted out to her. I don't know what made me speak so bluntly. I was just afraid. I had come so far, fleeing the ghetto, avoiding the Germans and the Ukrainian militia. And now here I was, only a short walk from a work camp for Jews.

"Why not?" Katrina asked me thoughtfully. "Why can't you stay here? Is something wrong?"

"It's the work," I said quickly, lying. I was trying to explain what must otherwise have seemed unexplainable to her. Surely it was clear enough to her that I had no place else to go, and no one could have been kinder to me than this woman who had taken me in. "The work here is just too hard for me," I offered. "I can't take care of cows anymore. I can't carry the milk or lift the hay. I'm too small for this kind of thing. I'm . . . I'm not used to such hard work."

"You never complained before," said Katrina, looking at me intently.

"I didn't want to trouble you." I put my head down. "But . . . but it's gotten where it's just too hard for me. I need something more suitable."

"All right," said Katrina. "I understand . . ."

I looked at her face and she seemed very sad and much, much older than I had ever seen her look before. I noticed then that there was a pallor to her skin and a certain looseness that I hadn't noticed earlier. I knew she was prone to coughing fits and that she was sometimes so sick that she had trouble getting about or doing anything heavy, but it had never hit me before like this. I must have been a welcome companion for her.

She gave me a faint smile. "What will you do?" she asked.

"I'll look for something else."

"I see . . . well perhaps I can help."

"How?" I asked. "How can you do that?"

"I have a brother," Katrina answered slowly. "He's much younger than I am. A priest, too, like my husband. His name is Kosar, Father Antonio Kosar, and he lives with his wife and two small sons near Tarnopol in a town called Podhajce. Maybe you would prefer caring for children than for cows?"

I just looked at her.

"He and his wife need someone to look after the boys each day because she's a school teacher and my brother has his own heavy responsibilities in Podhajce," Katrina went on. "Does this interest you?"

I just sat there, continuing to stare. I didn't know what to say. Finally I answered: "Yes, I can look after children. Is it far . . . from here I mean?"

"Not so far," said Katrina. "But you can't walk there. I'll arrange a ride for you."

I didn't know how to thank her. Katrina wiped her hands on her apron and took out a pen and some paper and sat down at the table, carefully writing out a letter to her brother, the priest in Podhajce, introducing me to him and saying that I was a Polish girl and an excellent worker and that I would be well suited to care for his sons. When she had finished she blotted the ink from the paper, carefully folded the letter in her big hands and gave it to me. "Vasil must soon go to Zloczow in the north," she said. "I'll see he takes you with him, as far as Tarnopol at least. From there you can walk to Podhajce."

"Thank you," I said, taking the letter from her and holding it in my two hands. "Thank you." I felt like crying.

"You'll need to be ready then . . . as soon as he's ready to leave. It will be early in the morning because it's a long ride," she added, ". . . before the siren sounds at the Jews' camp."

"Of course, I understand. Thank you again," I whispered.

It was all I could think of to say.

Chapter 12

Podhajce

IT SNOWED the night before Vasil was to leave for Zloczow and a thick layer of white blanketed the ground as I went outside to the barn. I had risen early and packed my few things, eager to be off. Vasil was already there, grinning at me, as he hitched the horses to the priest's wagon. Katrina came out of the house and joined us soon afterwards. She brought a satchel and handed it to Vasil. There was a small bottle of milk and some bread inside. "It will keep you both for the day, I think," she told us.

Zloczow was not so far away but it would take Vasil the better part of the day to get there though I would only be going with him as far as the outskirts of Tarnopol. Vasil took the food and stowed it in the wagon and then drove the horses out of the barn. I climbed up onto the wagon next to him as Katrina stood, watching us both. She made a small gesture with her hand, a wave, as the wagon lumbered clumsily past her, toward the road, and I did the same, offering a faint and very grateful smile. I did not know, then, that I would never see Katrina again.

Vasil directed the horses northwards as I settled in beside him, holding tightly to the edge of the seat. The road was so uneven I could feel every jolt and worried about falling off. But I was grateful when we finally left the town of Lsoftse behind.

A Ukrainian, as most of the country people were, Vasil was in his thirties. He wasn't much of a talker but what little he had to say to me came easily for him. He had no objection to Poles that I could see though I didn't know how he felt about Jews and didn't want to test his feelings. He knew me only as Wanda Madeira and, while the last name I had adopted was Spanish, not Polish, because Wanda's father had emigrated from Spain, the fact that I spoke Polish flawlessly and even looked Polish, with my dirty blonde hair and the little cross on my neck, seemed to convince everyone that I was exactly what I pretended to be. Except for my recent meeting with Celia outside the work camp in Lsoftse, I had come to feel secure in my new identity. Besides, I had that report card which I had taken from the real Wanda and now I had the letter from Katrina, too, identifying me as a Polish girl, recommended for employment in the household of the priest at Podhajce.

Vasil pointed out the towns as we passed them and, while he didn't have much to say about any of them, I was glad of even that small bit of conversation. Although I had kept largely to myself during the month or so that I had spent in the Ukrainian church at Lsoftse, I had always been friendly to Vasil, the priest's hired man and he had always been kind to me. Near lunch time, he pulled back on the reins and took out the milk and bread Katrina had given us, sharing it with me. This was a better way to travel, I knew, than the way I had come to Lsoftse more than a month before, even if the wagon bench on which I sat was hard and uncomfortable and there was no escaping the cold wind in our open wagon. I wrapped myself in a blanket that Vasil offered me from a place beneath his feet and this kept me as warm as could be expected in the Ukrainian winter.

I think the trip to Tarnopol took only a few hours but I may have dozed off for a time because it was afternoon when I found Vasil shaking me, pointing ahead of us. He told me that we would soon be passing Tarnopol and that, if I wanted to find the priest in Podhajce, I would need to follow a different road than the one he had to take. I wasn't happy to part from him but I knew I had little choice. Katrina had arranged for me to work in her brother's household and work was not easy to find, not the kind of work where a Jewish girl pretending to be a Pole could easily lose herself. Behind me was the work camp at Lsoftse and my friend Celia and all the other Jewish youths who were being kept there to work for the Germans. I couldn't help thinking that I had seen only young people going in and out of the camp. Where were the older people, the ones like my mother, or the crippled ones like my sister, whom the Germans had taken from the ghetto at Kolomyia?

I thanked Vasil for having taken me so far and waited until he drew the horses back, stopping the wagon, and then, taking my little satchel of things, I dropped the blanket in which I had wrapped myself and climbed down and stood in the road. Vasil pointed to his left, where a road turned off. There, he said, is the way to Brzezany. "You have to go toward Brzezany to reach Podhajce," he said.

He asked if I would be all right and I assured him I would. I told him I was a very experienced traveler by now and he chuckled and clicked the reins across the horses' backs once more and they began to move forward. I stood in the road watching him go and only then, when the wagon was a ways off did it hit me. I was utterly and completely alone again. I touched the letter from Katrina that I was carrying in my pocket and also the report card I had from Wanda. These were my passports to safety now. I touched the little tin cross on my neck, too. I was starting to feel like it was my lucky charm.

The road to Brzezany lay to the west and so I began what would prove to be another long and tiring walk. There were a number of villages and small towns and I walked through them as quickly as I could. I still had a few of Samuel's zlotys left and I knew I could use them to buy some food if I had to. But it felt like those days before I had crossed the Dniester and come to Lsoftse all over again. I went through town after town, asking people I met for directions whenever I seemed to be losing my way. I said I was looking for Podhajce and many people were helpful, pointing out the way for me. By evening I was in a small town and went through the streets until I found an elderly Polish couple and approached them, telling them my situation, that I was traveling from Lsoftse on the road to Podhajce but that I had nowhere to stay. The old woman took pity on me and said I could spend the night with them. This was a blessing because it was now winter and much too cold to try to sleep out in the fields. They put me up in a little cot in their kitchen, near the stove for warmth, and in the morning the old woman made me a little *mamaliga*, a corn meal porridge, with some milk. It fortified me and, when I took my leave of them, I felt much invigorated. The elderly man told me the direction of Podhajce and I set off toward it.

I think I was on the road for two more days, following it south from the outskirts of Brzezany, just as the couple who had taken me in had indicated. I don't remember how I spent those nights. I may have begged shelter from others or, perhaps, just slept in open barns I found along the side of the roads again, though, because it was winter, this would have been very hard. Now, more than sixty years later it's difficult to recall all the details perfectly. But I know that by the third day after I had left Vasil outside Tarnopol, I found myself approaching a hillside with an array of fine looking white houses rising up along the sloping ground.

I had gotten a few rides from local farmers to get there, and done quite a bit of walking besides, and I was very tired. But when I saw the houses on the hillside, I just stopped in my tracks, I was on foot by this time again, and stared at them in wonder. The sight before me was the most lovely I had seen in a long while. By this time of course, from all that I had heard from the people I'd met on the road, I was sure this was my destination.

The approach to the town on the hill consisted of older streets and houses, much more rundown. This was the old town of Podhajce, Starymsto as it was called. It was the place where the poorer people lived, including the mainly Ukrainian peasants. But the town, itself, was mostly Polish and, as I would learn in time, Jewish as well. It was, with its well-kept white buildings, perhaps made whiter at this time because of the snowfall that had covered the ground, a delightful and inviting sight to my very tired eyes. I had been on the road for about four days in all, I think, and believing I had come to the end of my travels was a great relief for me.

Of course I had to find the Ukrainian church which, I knew, would be in the outskirts of Podhajce, where most of the Ukrainians lived. And so I walked into Starymsto and began asking people in the streets for the Orthodox priest's house. It wasn't hard to locate and I followed the directions I got, which led toward the beautiful new town on the hill, until I came to the end of the old town where the Ukrainian church was. It was a small affair, but it had a nice size house next to it and a large field that led back beyond the town into the countryside. Here the priest and his family would be able to raise their own food, just like the local farmers who were their parishioners. Near the house stood a fairly respectable looking barn. There were other buildings, all in good condition, too.

I opened the little gate. A path led away from it and split in two, leading both to the church and the priest's house. I followed the walkway that went up to the house.

There was an old, weather beaten porch that went round one side of the house and I stepped onto it and went directly to the front door. There was no one around. I listened carefully for sounds from inside the house but could hear nothing. I put down my bag of things and tentatively tapped on the door. For a moment I felt frightened. But then I thought of my kindly employer in Lsoftse, Katrina, and summoned up my courage, knocking harder. Still, there was no answer. I backed away from the door and walked round the porch, looking to the side of the house. As I did this I heard the door opening behind me and turned quickly. I didn't want it to seem as though I were snooping about.

In the doorway a tall, blonde woman stood staring at me. She was the most beautiful woman I think I had ever seen until that time. I just stopped in my tracks and my mouth fell open. She was looking at me with the most piercing eyes I had ever seen.

"Yes?" she said. "What do you want?"

Her voice was as compelling as her eyes. I stammered and reached into my pocket, drawing out the letter and handing it to her, my hands trembling slightly. I watched as this magnificent woman, truly the vision of an angel, carefully unfolded the paper that I had carelessly carried, tightly crumpled in my pocket. When she had it opened and read it she looked up and seemed to be taking my measure. Then she looked down at the letter again. At last she spoke: "You're Polish?" she asked.

"Yes," I answered, "my name is Wanda . . ."

She cut me off with a wave of her hand. "You're recommended by my husband's sister, I see, to care for our children. We have been looking, of course, for a girl to do this.

We've had several, but they haven't been very good. And you, a Polish girl . . . what can you do?"

"I'm very good with children," I blurted out. "I can cook and clean for you . . ."

"You'll have to do all of that," she said. "And more. I work all day at the school and my husband has his responsibilities. I can't use you if you're prissy about things. Or if you don't know how to keep a house . . ."

"Oh, I do," I said, "I've got lots of experience."

She cut me off again. "You'll have to get on with the boys, of course," she said, "but I don't know . . . a Polish girl. You Poles are not used to working like Ukrainians. Still, Katrina speaks well of you." She waved the letter at me and I reached my hand out to take it back but she held it beyond my reach. "Well, have you worked for Ukrainians before?"

"In Lsoftse," I said, thinking of Katrina.

"Yes, yes, I know that. I meant elsewhere."

"I've always lived among Ukrainians," I said. "My mother had an inn . . ."

"Where?" she said.

Kolomyia," I said, in barely more than a whisper.

"Where are your parents now?" asked this tall and stately lady. "What's happened that you're on your own like this?"

"The Russians," I said. "They took my parents while I was away from home and sent them east. I was at school and when I came home they were gone. I've been alone since," I lied.

"The Communists?" she sniffed. "Well, they're a rough lot. They don't care much for priests either. You're a Catholic?"

"Yes," I lied again.

"Well there's a Catholic church nearby, on the way into Podhajce." She seemed to sneer when she spoke the town's name. "You'd do better adopting the Orthodox rite though."

I shrugged, afraid to say too much.

"Well, you can go to the Catholic church, if you like. Let's see if Katrina's right about you. You said you can cook?"

I nodded.

"Good, then you'll make the boys breakfast. That will be a good test, to see if you can get on with them and if you know your way about a kitchen. Well come in, girl, what are you standing around for?"

She turned away from me without another word and went inside, leaving the door to the house open behind her. I took up my satchel and followed. The vestibule and the room it led to were both dark because the curtains were all drawn. There was a musty smell about the house but there were many nice things inside, including a fine porcelain bowl on a stand near the outer door. This priest and his wife did not live badly I thought as I looked all around, seeking to find where the stately looking lady had gone to. In a moment I heard clattering and knew at once that the noises came from the kitchen. Holding fast to my few things I moved slowly in that direction, toward the sound of clattering dishes.

Chapter 13

Eggs and Curtains

HER NAME was Lala. She was the wife of Katrina's brother, the Ukrainian priest in Podhajce, and I had never seen a more beautiful woman. Or one who was more cruel. On that first day she put me to work in the kitchen, telling me to prepare eggs for her sons and I fumbled nervously about her stove as she stood behind me, watching in silence. When the two little boys came in they reminded me, in an odd sort of way, of Aaron and Srulek, my little cousins who were lost in the ghetto I had left behind. I pretended they were there with me again and, though Lala introduced her sons to me as Bohdan and Daniel, I to me they were my lost cousins again and I always treated them that way. Bohdan, the older, was about six years of age when I first arrived there and Daniel was about four. Both were dirty blondes and favored their beautiful mother in features and coloring. They liked the eggs I prepared for them, too, and, though I was very nervous as I served them, their welcoming attitude and appreciation of my small effort paid off. Lala, the lady, decided I could stay.

Their father, Antonio Kosar, the Greek Orthodox priest of the Ukrainians in Podhajce, came in later and I found him to be a very fine gentleman. He was tall and trimly built, somewhat slight for a man, especially next to his statuesque wife who was nearly as tall as he. Father Antonio had a full head of dark hair and his overall coloring was also darker than Lala's. They made an impressive couple, both fine looking, youthful people. In fact, I thought Father Antonio was too young to be a priest since all the others I had met along my way had been much older men. He must have been Katrina's baby brother or at least one of them, I realized, and this made me think of him in a new way. Like Katrina, he was kind and gentle, as good to me as Lala was harsh.

They gave me a small room in their home and accepted me as nanny for their sons but my duties were not to be limited to the boys alone. My mistress soon put me to work doing many more things than a nanny is expected to do. Besides caring for the boys at home, whether she or Father Kosar were away or not, Lala turned me into her all around help. She had me preparing all the meals, scrubbing the floors, doing the laundry and even helping their serving man, a big Ukrainian named Micken, who did the heaviest work in the household and had responsibility for caring for the priest's horses, pigs and cows.

Father Kosar's house was situated on a sizeable piece of property where he could grow food and raise animals for his own upkeep. He didn't own the house or the land, of course. These belonged to the Church. But they were his so long as he was the priest there and so he was as much farmer as priest, though he wasn't suited to the farm life. He was much too gentle, too cultured to be a simple farmer and his wife, Lala, had the management of affairs there.

Father Kosar was often away, either in the nearby church or off on various travels. Sometimes these took him to the homes of his parishioners and sometimes to other towns. He was often away on religious retreats and seminars and he supplemented his priestly duties with teaching the local children in the Ukrainian school. Lala, too, served as a teacher in this school and was often away from the house, though she didn't travel beyond Podhajce while I was with them. So I had my work cut out for me. While the boys were so young, especially, I had to watch over them all day long, as well as feed, bathe and dress them. But since I was only fifteen I was not so far removed from childhood myself and so I wasn't particularly stern with them. In fact, we played quite a bit together.

Their games reminded me of my own not so long ago on the banks of the Kozcaczwka River in Kolomyia. It made me sad to think about these things because of all that I had lost, but happy, too, in a way because it reminded me of the better times I had known while growing up. There hadn't been too many things since the Germans came to our land that had made me think of those happier times.

The boys and I became fast friends which was a good thing for me. They had had other governesses before and none, I eventually learned, had worked out. Since Lala and Father Antonio were very attentive to the needs and wishes of their sons, my unfortunate predecessors soon found themselves on the street. But the fact that the boys took a shine to me assured me a place with the Kosars in Podhajce which, more than anything else, was what I now needed.

So my time with the Kosars began well enough. Although I could see that Lala would be a difficult mistress, since she had nearly as much contempt for Poles, which is what she believed me to be, as she had for Jews, I didn't worry too much about this. Her little boys had so quickly become enamored of me that, despite her tendency to fly into a rage with me over the smallest of things, I was sure I would be all right. I made Bohdan and Daniel happy so she was willing to overlook my "Polish" background. The boys, of course, reminding me of my own lost little cousins, made me happy, too.

Only at night, in my small room, did I sometimes find myself thinking of the awful things I had seen and then I would toss about and cry on my pillow, unable to find rest or sleep because I was thinking of Mama and Gusta being taken away by the Germans, or of Feiga, whom I had had to leave behind, or of my own Bubbeh Shprintzer, lying dead on the narrow cot with a German bullet in her brain. And sometimes, too, my mind would race to images of Samuel, my brother, hiding with his wife and children in an excavated cell beneath the floor of an old woman's barn on the outskirts of Piadyki while I lived safely among Ukrainians in Podhajce.

My days were busy in the Kosar household, from the moment I awoke and must see to the children until the entire family was ready to turn in again at night. I was always on the go, keeping the house clean, preparing and serving their meals, doing everything that needed doing. Lala Kosar's idea of a nanny for her children was much broader than I could possibly have imagined. I rarely had a moment to myself. Still I tried whenever I could, to get away. Since I was there as a Catholic and a Pole, Sunday became my only time for a little freedom, as it had been when I had lived with Katrina and her husband in Lsoftse. Then I could go off, while the Kosars attended church with Father Antonio administering to his flock. Because I was not an Orthodox Christian, they didn't expect me to be in church with them. Of course, this didn't mean I was entirely free because, as a Catholic girl, I was still expected to do what Catholic girls did. And so I would go off to the nearest Polish church and sit there in the pew and practice the prayers and rituals I already knew, watching others from the corner of my eyes to make sure I had things right.

In this way I found a friend in Podhajce, a Polish girl about my own age named Banushka. I don't recall the first time we met. It may have been in the church on a Sunday but I recognized her right away as someone I had seen near the Kosars' home. In fact, she and her family lived near our Ukrainian church so she was actually a neighbor.

Perhaps it was she who had actually introduced me to the Catholic church in the area. I no longer remember perfectly, but whichever came first, our meeting or my finding the church, it soon became a kind of ritual that I would go off to the church on Sundays with Banushka and her family. She had an older brother, Janek, who was only a little older than I and he was very friendly and welcoming, too. Her parents began to treat me as one of them, perhaps because they felt sorry for a Polish girl living under the roof of Lala Kosar who was so contemptuous of Poles. They never said anything about this, of course, but I could sense their sympathy for me and that they knew of Lala's feelings towards Polish nationals.

Banushka and I became very close friends, just as I had been friendly with Wanda and, later, with Celia Bieber. Of course, Banushka and her family knew me as Wanda now since I had kept that name when I came to Podhajce. It certainly wouldn't have done to have reverted to my real name after all I had been through.

The Catholic priest was a big man, made all the more impressive in his white priestly vestments which were embroidered with gold filigree and blue ribbon-like borders. He was a broad, imposing looking individual with a florid, round face and a balding pate. But he was kindly to all his parishioners and, since I soon became a regular with Banushka's family, he got to know me, too. He would always give me a friendly smile when I would come in with them. Most times we sat up front, not far from where he could see us.

At first I was uncomfortable about this, because I wasn't sure of what I knew, if I was good enough to pass as a Catholic under the scrutiny of a genuine Catholic priest. But I soon fell in with the patterns around me and kneeling and genuflecting at the proper times became second nature. Though my knees often hurt because of the hard scrubbing on my hands and knees that I was forced to do in the Kosar home, where I would wash down the floors almost daily, I was young enough so that this work did not take a heavy toll on me at first. And so I was able to jump up and down as Catholics must when in church before the icons and relics to which they give reverence. And the priest, whose name I can no longer remember, soon considered me one of his flock.

On days other than Sundays though, Lala always managed to keep me busy. After I had been there for only a little while, she called me to her one day and I followed behind her, wiping my raw wet hands on the apron I was wearing. She turned to me as we walked and said I was to run an errand for her. I listened expectantly as she patiently explained that she wanted to buy some nice things for the household and that she would send me to a good place for these. I began to take off my apron as Lala kept talking, telling me to gather up some eggs and a little cheese and a few other items of food from our pantry and that she would then tell me where I was to take them. I was excited to be getting out of the Kosar house since it was so oppressive being there, especially when Lala was at home.

When she finished speaking she just stood there, looking at me, and I reddened and rushed to the kitchen where I pulled together what Lala had told me I was to take for trading. When I returned she was still standing there, frowning, as though she had been counting the minutes it had taken me to gather the items she had specified.

I had what I needed in a small basket and so I went to take my jacket, the same fleece-lined coat that my brother Samuel had given me the last time I had seen him outside Piadyki. When I had it on, I stood at the door, waiting for Lala's further instructions.

"So," she asked, when she saw that I was ready, "you're eager enough. But where do you think you are to go, since I haven't told you yet?"

I hung my head and mumbled, embarrassed. I was so eager to be off that I had given myself away. Lala was nodding, as if to say Poles were all shiftless, glad to escape work whenever they could, and that I was the proof of it.

"I just wanted to be ready," I said to her by way of apology.

"Good," said my mistress. "Then you won't mind the walk. I want you to go into the main part of town, where the Jews live, and knock on all the doors there and see what you can get them to trade. They can't get food easily on their own these days. They can't even go out on the streets anymore, so they'll be glad for whatever you bring. They'll give you whatever they still have that's of any value for a few eggs and some milk or a little cheese. See if you can get them to part with anything silver or some curtains – we could use new curtains here – or whatever else looks good. But don't let them take advantage of you, girl. Being a Pole you aren't likely to be very good at bargaining with them, but they're at a disadvantage because they can't get enough to eat any other way. So bargain hard, girl. I'll be looking over what you bring back, remember, so don't be a little fool and let them pawn off anything worthless on you."

I stood there in silence, not knowing what to say. Lala tilted her head and looked more closely at me. "What's the matter? Are you afraid to go into the Jews' area? There's nothing to worry about. They won't hurt you. They're more afraid of you than you are of them. The Germans have seen to that. And as long as you keep a sharp eye on them they'll be too frightened to cheat you. Now go on and don't come back until you've gotten some nice things for us. Remember, I'll be checking what you bring back. Do you know how to find the Jews' area?"

I nodded, still not speaking.

"Then why are you waiting around here? The Jews won't come to you."

I turned and ran out of the house, gripping my food basket tightly. I had jumped at the chance to leave the house with my mistress' permission but hadn't dreamed that it would mean this.

The Jewish area was in the newer part of Podhajce, on the hill that overlooked the older part of the town where we lived. I walked through the streets, climbing the steeply sloping ground where it rose from the plain of the old town and looked at the houses. No one seemed to be on the streets and, though the houses were all fairly large and nicely situated, they had an almost abandoned look to them, as though they were no longer being kept up. Of course, they weren't, not anymore. I didn't know which house to go to but I chose at random and began approaching one door and then another, carrying my basket and knocking timidly. After I had knocked on a number of them, one door finally opened and I felt a wave of anxiety sweep over me. My hands trembled and I felt as though I should turn and run away. But I stood there, staring at the people inside, Jews, like me. But not like me because to them and to everyone in this town I was something else, a Polish girl, Wanda Madeira, who was not as they were. I was free to come and go while they were prisoners in their own homes. I didn't know what to say as I looked at the elderly man and lady who were standing in the doorway, staring back at me. Finally, I lifted my basket up a bit and said: "I have food here to . . . to trade for my mistress who lives in Starymsto . . . if you have anything of worth to give in return."

I was embarrassed at my own words. I should have been able to say to them here, here is food for your table, for your hungry bellies, because I could see in their thin faces and their eager, yet fearful, eyes that they were desperately in need of what I had brought. But I was too afraid of Lala Kosar to do that. And so I stressed again that I had come to trade and would only relinquish what I was carrying in exchange for something of worth.

Their faces showed that they did not see me as anything other than a Polish girl and I, to my embarrassment, did not give them any signal, any reason, to think differently. I just swung my basket about where they could see it and their eyes followed my movements.

"What have you brought?" asked the old man.

"I have eggs," I said, "and some cheese and a little milk."

"What do you want?" It was the old woman who spoke this time.

"What have you got of any value?" I asked.

"We don't have much left," said the old man.

My heart was breaking but I didn't know what else to say to them. I was only fifteen.

"My mistress said I wasn't to give anything except for a good trade," I explained.

The old woman turned away and went back inside. I was straining to see within but it was dark, the curtains had been drawn. I wanted desperately to follow her, to say I'm like you, a Jew, too, but I knew I couldn't, that everything I had, my safety, my life, depended on my keeping my secret. Even telling these people could ruin everything and then my brother's advice would have been for nothing. Don't speak any Yiddish, he had said. Don't live where Jews are. Pretend you know nothing of Jews. And so I kept quiet as I stood in the doorway and tried not to think about the circumstances of those who were within.

In a little while, the old woman came back, holding a small silver candle stick. It was dented and tarnished. She held it up in the light of the day for me to see it. The old man watched, blinking, as I appraised it. I shook my head, no, and started to turn away.

"Wait," said the old woman. "Give us an egg, even one egg, for it."

"I'm sorry," I mumbled, "I can't. My mistress wouldn't approve. The eggs are hers."

"What does she need?" asked the old woman.

The man beside her was silent, his head down.

"Curtains," I said brightening, looking inside and remembering what Lala had said to me.

The old woman said, "Let me look inside the basket."

I held it up and she peeled back the cloth. She counted the few eggs I had placed there and also the other things. Finally she looked at me again and turned to go back into the house. I heard her moving about and saw the room inside growing lighter. She was taking down the curtains. The old man, her husband, had his hands out for the basket but I shook my head and backed away. When his wife returned, she had the curtains in her hands. They were white brocade and she had folded them neatly. She offered them to me. I handed the basket reluctantly to her husband and took hold of the heavy folded curtains. They were in good condition.

The old man was frantically counting the items in the basket and then he looked at his wife.

"I'll put some blankets over the windows," she said to him to ease his worry.

I said, "Give me the silver candle stick, too."

I don't know why but I was thinking of Lala. What if the curtains didn't please her? The old man shook his head no, but I was insistent. I said I wouldn't leave with the curtains alone and saw the fright return to their faces. "Here then," the old man said hurriedly and pushed the candle stick at me, depositing it on the thick pile of curtains I was struggling to hang onto. Then he shut the door on me and left me there, alone. I turned and walked away, back to the street.

The curtains were unwieldy in my arms but I struggled with them all the way back to Starymsto, making sure to keep them from falling and becoming soiled. I was worried about how Lala Kosar would view what I had gotten, if she would agree that I had done well or if there would be recriminations as there so often were.

But as it happened I needn't have been concerned. She was delighted with what I brought back and was soon sending me to the Jewish area again and again to dicker for more. It would become one of my responsibilities, to trade with the Jews of Podhajce for whatever they still possessed in exchange for a few meager items of food that might last them a day or two at most. But I never went back to the same houses twice as I was too ashamed of what I was doing.

Chapter 14

Visitors

I HAD OTHER chores that kept me occupied in the Kosar household besides bargaining to take from the Jews of Podhajce what little they had left to their names. One day, Lala told me to go out to the barn and help Micken, the farmhand, with the pigs. When I found him in the barn he said, "Do you know how to butcher an animal?"

I shook my head, afraid to say much because I didn't want to reveal what a city girl I really was.

"Well, you can't eat them if someone doesn't kill them first so give me a hand here." He was chasing about in the pig pen, the foul smelling muck splattered across his overalls and chest. Suddenly he had one of the pigs in his hands and was struggling with it as it squirmed madly about, as though it knew what Micken had in mind.

"I've never done anything like this," I started to say. Then I added, "I've done it with chickens."

I had corrected myself because I knew most Poles from the countryside would have known about these things as well as any Ukrainian. Among Jews, of course, the ritual slaughterer, the *shochet*, is a specialized profession and you couldn't just kill an animal yourself so most ordinary people didn't have any familiarity with such things. Butchering had to be done in certain, prescribed ways. But other people were not so finicky as Jews were and I had to keep up the pretense of being Wanda Madeira. Besides, hadn't Wanda's family had a sausage factory at their home? Wanda would have known about such things or, at least, she'd have been less nervous than I was. Of course, no one in Podhajce knew the real Wanda Madeira so they wouldn't have known that the real Wanda knew things that I didn't, but, since I was supposed to be her, I thought it important to preserve her image in myself as much as possible.

"Well you don't have to know a lot about how," Micken was saying between quick breaths as he continued to hang onto his pig. "It's very simple. I'll hold him down and you hit him on the back of the head with that mallet over there. I usually have help with this from one of the neighbors' men. But there's no one today, so it's got to be you."

I moved across the barn floor toward the mallet he had indicated as Micken half carried, half dragged the crazed pig to a stool. There he threw it down and pinned it with his body and then he turned to me. "Hurry it up," he gasped. "I can't sit on this beast forever."

I grasped the mallet and walked back toward Micken and the pig. The mallet was heavy but not too much for me.

"Stand behind . . . there," he gestured with his head.

I went where he had directed me.

"One clean blow should be enough. Here," he tried to show me the place to hit by pointing at it with a free finger. "You don't want to have to hit them too many times. It gets messy. Can you swing it hard?"

"Yes," I whispered, afraid to say anything else.

"Good," he said. "Now's the time then."

I looked at him and at the pig. It had finally tired itself out and seemed to be just lying there, breathing heavily, twitching. It looked like it was trying to catch its breath so it could start its struggle to break free again.

"What are you waiting for, Wanda?" Micken snapped in exasperation. "Before he gets his wind back. Please!"

I raised the hammer over my head and tried to mark the spot on the base of the skull. Suddenly the pig began to squirm once more, as though it sensed the movement of the mallet. "Now," Micken said. "Now . . ." He was starting to have trouble hanging on as the pig tensed its body for a sharp push upward.

I brought the hammer down suddenly with all my strength. The thud of it, as it struck, reverberated through my arms as the mallet head made contact with that of the animal and its skull gave way with a crunching sound. The blood burst out around the mallet but the creature's movements only increased as it squealed and wriggled wildly.

"Again," shouted Micken, "hit him again. Quickly." I did so in horror, a second blow of my mallet striking behind the maddened creature's skull. I was terrified. That second strike was not so strong as the first and the pig was utterly crazed now. Without waiting for Micken to shout at me for another, I administered a third strike with the hammer. The creature's skull was shattered and he went limp under Micken's straining arms. The farmhand released the now flaccid beast and straightened up. He took a look at what I had done and nodded. "You did all right," he said, ". . . for the first time. I'll do the butchering; you can go back to the house if you want."

I nodded and dropped the mallet on the ground and, turning, ran out through the muck and straw that covered the barn floor. I had passed another test, another measure of my newfound Polish identity, but I was sick to my stomach about it. That night, I knew, I would be cooking parts of this very animal whose skull I had just crushed so brutally.

The meat from the pig lasted us a week and I ate it along with everyone else. This sort of food was forbidden to Jews and, except for that time years before when Meir had brought such meat into the *korchma* and angered Mama, I had always tried to avoid it. But food was food as far as I was concerned. You did what you had to, to stay alive. Hadn't we done that in the ghetto, too? And it had certainly been necessary since I had gone on the road. I wasn't about to throw away my safety, indeed my very life, over a little pig meat, even if it sickened me because I had been the one to kill it. I was afraid that showing even a little squeamishness about eating the pig might raise questions in the minds of my employers and so I made a great show of enjoying the meat even though I was sick at the thought of it each time I put a piece in my mouth and, by week's end, had concluded that such meat was the most hideous in the entire world.

It wasn't long after the pig meat was gone that Lala, the lady of the house, became all excited about something. She went round sprucing things up and was especially hard on me, monitoring my cleaning very closely and demanding that I do things I had already done over again. Finally she told me what was going on. We were expecting visitors she said, important visitors, and she wanted everything just right. It was too bad we didn't have any of that pig left she added. But she would have Micken procure some other meat.

Father Antonio was nervous about our visitors it turned out and very much on edge as Lala and I bustled about making everything ready. I did most of the work but Lala stood over me, saying pick this up, clean that, get those things from over there. It was very hectic, especially because I also had to worry about the boys. But my employer decided to send them to bed early, before our guests were due, so that took some of the burden off me. It was the most I could hope for because she kept at me, not giving me a moment's rest. I could see that she was as nervous about the evening as Father Antonio was.

When our guests arrived I was in the kitchen, busily taking the last of the food from the oven. I heard the excited bustling outside and went to the doorway of the kitchen to peek out, to see what all the fuss had been about. I froze in my place when I saw the visitors who were standing there, exchanging formal greetings with my employers. There were four of them, four tall men and they were in uniforms. Three wore the gray military gear of German officers and the fourth was in the black uniform of the Gestapo.

I felt the room begin to swim round my head and I grabbed at the nearest wall to steady myself. Our guests were Germans. They were the very people I had been fleeing since I ran away from the Kolomyia ghetto. I didn't know what to do, whether to run from the house then and there or to try to hide in my room. I could flee to the church I knew but how would this help? Wouldn't they come looking for me? How could I hide anywhere in Podhajce? Maybe, I thought, I could go into the Jews' area which had not yet been fenced in with barbed wire as had been done at Kolomyia. There I would be safe at least for a time, hidden among other Jews. They would never think to look for me there!

I was beside myself. Had the Kosars realized who I was? Had they turned me in? Was it only a matter of moments now before I would be taken . . . and sent away to . . . to where? I could only imagine, fearing the worst, remembering the killing of my grandmother. What could I do now? It was all over, wasn't it?

"Wanda," a harsh voice was speaking, indeed shouting at me. "Wanda. Where are you girl? Bring our guests something to drink at once . . ."

I realized it was Lala Kosar's voice and that she had been talking to me all this while though I hadn't heard. Yanked back to reality I looked at her and saw her scowling face staring at me as she came toward me. "Where is your head, girl?" she was asking. "How long does it take for my words to penetrate that thick skull of yours? I said three times for you to bring out drinks for Major Kleinecke and his companions. Do you mean to embarrass us by being so stupid?"

I backed away toward the kitchen. Lala seemed satisfied that she had frightened me sufficiently to return to my duties but in fact I felt only great relief at her words, seeing at once that she had no idea of what had really unnerved me. I now realized that the German officers were there not for me but for some other purpose and that, for the moment at least, my secret was safe.

I rushed to grab some liquor, I don't recall what kind, and brought the bottle out, cradled in my arms. I approached the table where all were now seated and looked at the four Germans rather timidly. One of them, the Gestapo man, was grinning. He lifted his empty glass and I dutifully filled it. He smacked his lips and showed the glass to the others at the table with a big wink as I moved around the table to fill each of the other glasses in turn.

When they all had their drinks in hand, the Gestapo officer raised his glass to Father Antonio and his wife and said a few words of thanks. I was too nervous in their presence to even listen to what was said. It was a toast of some sort and then they all drank down what I had poured for them and the Gestapo officer showed me his empty glass again without speaking and I rushed to fill it, along with the others.

This Gestapo man was a tall and handsome individual with close-cropped blonde hair. Though his very nearness to me unnerved me terribly I couldn't take my eyes from the smoothly chiseled features of his face. When I looked away at last, I saw that my employer, the priest's wife, couldn't either.

Lala glanced menacingly at me and I lowered my head and withdrew. I heard her speaking ingratiatingly to the Germans and, in particular, to the Gestapo officer as I went out. "These Poles," she was saying, "are so stupid. It's hard to find any who know how to behave. I must apologize for her . . ."

Father Antonio interceded. "She's not so bad," he proposed. "She's better than the last one, and the boys like her . . ."

That was all I heard as I left the room. The rest of that evening went by in a haze. I wanted to stay as far away from the Germans as I could, afraid something would give me away, but I had to keep going out there with the different courses and stand there and serve them until they had taken what they pleased. And I had to be on call even while in the kitchen, responding to Lala anytime she wanted something or other.

She was especially taken, I could see, with the handsome one, the Gestapo man who was, clearly, the leader of these Germans. They deferred to him in everything throughout the evening and he led the discussions. I couldn't hear much of what they were saying, just drips and drabs as I moved in and out of the kitchen. The Gestapo officer spoke a good Ukrainian though his fellow Germans did not. Once when I was carrying something back to the kitchen he suddenly said something to me in German: where are you going with that, girl, or something to that effect. I was so frightened that, even though I understood because German is so similar to Yiddish, I pretended not to have heard him and kept walking.

Lala said, "She's Polish. She doesn't know any German. Only Polish . . . and Ukrainian, which she speaks badly, of course, like a Pole . . ."

"I thought perhaps she had a little German," said the man who had spoken to me. "You never know about these people."

"I told you she isn't very smart," Lala laughed.

The German suddenly called out to me in Polish, telling me to come back in. Realizing that I couldn't pretend not to have heard him this time, I did so. I walked over to him with my head down and stood there, by his side, as he looked me over.

"She's very young," he was saying to the others.

"An orphan," said Lala, "sent to us by my husband's sister in Lsoftse. We took her in as a favor but she's good with the boys."

The German officer was looking at my face. Then his eyes dropped to the tin cross I wore round my neck. He asked me a few questions in Polish and I answered with as few words as I could. I didn't want to spend a lot of time talking with such a man.

Finally he said, "Do you know how to shine boots?"

I nodded, afraid to tell him no.

"Good," he said and extended one of his legs out from beneath the table. "Show us what you can do, girl."

I looked around, terrified, but I saw there was no help for me from the priest and his wife. They were sitting at the table smiling although I thought Father Kosar's grin more of a mask than the real thing. I pulled at my apron and got down on my knees before this man and looked at his boot. It was high up, midway past his calf, and very, very dusty. I took the edge of my apron and began to rub off the dust. I did this rapidly as he watched me from above. At times I could feel his breath on the back of my neck, he was leaning so close to me. The dust of the road was thickly encrusted in the creases of the leather and it was hard work getting any of it off.

"Spit," said the German suddenly.

I looked up astonished.

"Use your spit," he said, nodding at his boot.

I didn't know how to respond.

He bent his head down and spat on the toe of his boot. "Like that, see?" He took the hem of my apron and began to rub at the spot of saliva he had placed on his own boot. I saw that it loosened the dust somewhat and that a little effort could then bring up the underlying shine of the leather. "Understand?" he was asking me, handing me back the hem of my own apron.

I nodded quickly and took the apron and began to rub at the boot as he had done. When the spittle was gone I rolled my tongue about in my mouth and, pursing my lips, spat as he had done on another part of the boot. Then I began rubbing furiously, afraid to stop. I rubbed his entire boot like this, up and down, using my own spit as the necessary cleaning fluid.

When I had finished the boot, this man pulled it away from me and examined my work. Satisfied, he shifted in his seat and pushed out his other leg, giving me that boot to do as well. I could not say no and immediately began to spit and rub the dust from it, too.

"Even a Pole can learn," Lala said, laughing.

When I was done I feared the other Germans would extend their boots but no one did. I got up, clutching my wet, soiled apron and, after looking at Lala who seemed to show no more interest in me, I quietly withdrew. That's how the evening went, with this German officer doing most of the talking and his companions silently nodding or adding a little something here or there, sometimes in German, more often in a heavily accented Ukrainian. I waited, after dinner was done, for a discreet amount of time, and then reappeared in the doorway. Lala signaled that I was to take the dishes out and I rushed to do it. The German officer whose boots were now shiny from my efforts ignored me for the rest of the evening and, when they finally got up to leave, everyone seemed pleased with how things had gone.

The Gestapo man was especially gallant as he took his leave of Father Antonio and his wife, taking a very long time with Lala's offered hand, holding onto it with both of his as he spoke pleasantly of the evening and the dinner. Lala looked at me and, with her eyes, directed me to the Germans' outer garments which were hung nearby. I rushed to bring them in. Each officer took his coat and hat from my hands without seeming to see me. I was glad of that.

"Major Kleinecke," Father Antonio was saying to the Gestapo man, "it was most kind of you to grace our table like this."

The major smiled and waved one hand dismissively. "It was our pleasure, I assure you Father. And such a lovely wife . . . you are a most fortunate man." Turning his attention to Lala again, he said, "Madam, I hope this will not be the last of such invitations. It's hard operating in a foreign land, as you can imagine, and especially in time of war. You make it all so much more tolerable."

Lala smiled at him and flushed a little, finally taking her hand away. The major turned to me for his own coat and hat and I handed them to him, the coat first, which he drew onto his shoulders, and then the cap. He took it out of my hands and placed it briskly on his head. A skull and crossbones were emblazoned on the hat band. I stood looking up at it, staring. Unlike the others, he seemed to see me very clearly, returning my stare. Hastily I lowered my eyes, not wanting to encourage his interest anymore than I had already done. Finally, he turned away and moved to the door with his companions.

"A most interesting evening," he was saying to my employers, "really, most interesting," and he followed the others out the door into the chill night air.

After they were gone Lala seemed to be floating, smiling at Antonio, moving about the room as though she could not contain herself, talking to him and to herself. She did this until she finally saw me watching. Then she stopped in her tracks and said I was to hurry and tidy things up and then take myself off to my room. "There's nothing more for you here," she finished, brusquely turning away.

I did as I was told, with as much speed as I could muster, because I didn't want to stay in their presence any longer than I had to. I was still confused about what had occurred, and nervous. The Germans I had spent months evading, ever since I'd run away from the Kolomyia ghetto, had now found me – though they didn't seem to know it. What would they do? What would I do?

I had left Lsoftse, where I had had a very good situation, out of fear of discovery when I had stumbled into Celia at the work camp, and come all this way to Podhajce only to find myself now face to face with those I feared most: the very people who had taken everything from us and locked us in a ghetto, behind barbed wire and walls. The very people who had taken my mother, my sister, my cousin . . . who had killed my grandmother. Where could I go from here? Could I even go anywhere at this point?

As I mulled all this over later on in my little room, I was unable to settle on a new course of action. If I stayed where I was, I knew it would be as though I had wandered into the wolves' den – or worse. But if I fled, where did I have left to run to? And what would my flight reveal to these people now? Working all this over in my mind, there was one picture I couldn't get out of my head, though. I kept seeing that Gestapo officer, the man Lala had called Major Kleinecke, staring back at me from his great height, the cap I had handed him resting unevenly on his close cropped blonde head, the silver skull and crossbones on its band leering down at me from the place where it sat just above his eyes.

Chapter 15

The Seamstresses

IT WAS only a few months after I had arrived there that Father Antonio received some terrible news. It was bad for me, too. Katrina, the lady who had taken me in in Lsoftse and who had looked after me and finally sent me to safety in Podhajce, had died. I had known she was not well but had had no inkling how bad it might be. The winter months had been harder on her than she had let on and I was greatly saddened, both because she had been so kind and because I hadn't gotten to know her better when I was in her company.

Father Antonio was distraught when he read the letter he had received about this. He said he had to go at once, that he must attend his sister's funeral and he went out to find Micken to prepare a wagon to take him south to Lsoftse. Lala told me to pay attention to my chores and see to the children. It did not seem to occur to her that I might feel anything at the loss of the old woman who had taken me in and recommended me to her. She was only concerned to make sure that Father Antonio would have everything he needed on this trip. She told him to take his time, to do what he had to do and not to worry about his responsibilities in Podhajce. "We'll see to things here for as long as you're gone. Don't let anything distract you from what you must do," she told her husband gently. I was surprised at such kindness from her but I had been aware for some time that how she treated me was not the same as how she dealt with others, particularly her husband.

Father Antonio smiled gratefully at her words, though with deep sadness in his eyes, and left with Micken that very day. It was extremely important to him to be in attendance at Katrina's funeral and they had a long day's wagon ride ahead of them. I took care of the boys, getting them off to school, and then I turned to my chores. Lala, after Father Antonio was gone, was especially harsh with me, shouting at me constantly and making me crawl around on the wooden floors, scrubbing them down with unaccustomed effort. She said she wanted the house to shine as it never had before and my knees were rubbed raw before I was done that day. I also had to see to the farm animals because Micken was gone with Father Antonio so the heavy work he usually did now fell to me. At least there was no butchering to be done.

Towards evening, Lala was busying herself about the house, straightening things, checking over what I had done. I saw that she was wearing one of her Sunday dresses, too. And that her hair was arranged with more care than she ordinarily took. I wasn't surprised, then, when there was a knocking at the door and the German, Heinz Kleinecke, came inside at Lala's invitation. It hadn't been that long since the first time he and his fellow officers had introduced themselves to the priest's household and they had come by once or twice since. But it was surprising to see the major here alone and in the absence of Father Antonio himself.

Major Kleinecke took the priest's wife's hand and kissed it in that aristocratic way he had and Lala blushed, asking for his coat and hat. These she at once handed to me so that I again found myself with the major's garments in my hands. Lala then said I was to serve the dinner. Now I understood why she had been so attentive to every detail earlier in the day and why she had had me prepare such an abundance of food for the evening even though Father Antonio was to be absent.

I hurriedly brought everything out to the two of them as they sat alone at the table, no longer encumbered by the presence of the priest or the other German officers, and watched as Lala, deep in conversation with the major, seemed to hang on his words. These two seemed to find great pleasure in one another's company, I thought, and was grateful that, because of this, neither seemed to notice that I was even around.

I found myself furtively glancing at the major's boots whenever I past by him, afraid he would demand that I spit polish them again. But I was fascinated by the deep shine they now had. Apparently the major had other, more skilled polishers than I for there was no dust on them this evening or, as I could readily see, any reason for him to pay much attention to me.

After they had eaten, Lala told me to leave everything and just go to my room. "You can clean up tomorrow," she said, almost as an after thought. And that's what I did.

The next morning the major was gone but the dirty plates weren't. Lala hadn't even removed them from the table and so I busied myself with them, until the boys had awakened and then I tended to my two charges as well. After they had gone outside I went back to gathering the soiled plates and stacking them in the kitchen. Lala entered quietly behind me while I was at the counter and stood there, just watching me as I worked. When I finally realized she was there I turned and looked up at her. She said, "I'll expect you to keep your mouth shut, Wanda. You understand?"

I nodded. I didn't want any trouble and was glad the German officer was interested in Lala and not me – for many reasons. But Lala seemed to think her threats were what were needed to ensure my silence.

"You're to say nothing about anything you saw last night. Father Antonio has enough on his mind. I expect you to be discreet because . . . if you're not . . ." She didn't finish her thought.

"I didn't see anything, ma'am," I said. "I'm here to do whatever you need. It's not my business what goes on . . ."

"Good," she replied. "That's very good. I'll expect you to continue in this way or else you'll be out of here. And then what will you do, eh?"

Father Antonio returned after three days and never suspected anything was amiss. He seemed deeply saddened by the loss of his sister and I felt very sorry for him because of that. He was always kind to me, from the very first day that I had arrived. He was, in fact, one of the gentlest men I had ever met. I couldn't have been the one to tell him about his wife's actions even if I'd wanted to. I didn't want to be the source of anything that would cause him anymore pain.

Heinz Kleinecke, the local German commander, returned often, mostly alone, and mostly when Father Antonio was away. Sometimes he still brought his companions with him but only if the priest was to be present, too. When Father

Antonio was off on a religious retreat or away on other duties, Kleinecke always came alone. Then he would bring my employer little gifts, sometimes small jars of perfume or some fine material that she would coo over or chocolates. She especially liked the chocolates. He always came after the boys were put to bed and my mistress always hurried me off to my room right after dinner. One time I remember Kleinecke was actually there the next morning and took a quick breakfast from me, before the boys were up and, when we heard them stirring, he hastily finished what I had set out for him and left, Lala seeing him off at the door.

When she came back she glared at me but said nothing and I simply looked away. I had no interest in stirring this pot after all. The Kosars were providing me a safe haven while the war raged around us and it wasn't my concern how they amused themselves or dealt with one another.

One of the gifts Kleinecke left Lala was some very fine cloth. I don't know where he got it but he always seemed to have his hands on the best of everything. But Lala wasn't sure what to do with this as she wasn't much of a seamstress. When she asked me if I could do something with the material for her I told her I couldn't, that I knew very little about such things. This wasn't entirely true as we had always done a lot of our own sewing and knitting in the old days in Kolomyia and I had watched Gusta at work many times. But I didn't want to take on any more responsibilities and the risks of incurring my employer's anger that came with them. They paid me very little, true enough, and I could, perhaps, have asked for a bit more if I had taken on this new job, but I didn't have that much confidence in my ability to please her and it didn't seem worth it just for a few more zlotys in my pocket which I wasn't in a position to spend anyway.

But one day Lala, herself, solved this problem. I learned of this when there was another knock on the door. It was early in the day, before Lala had gone off to teach as was her usual practice, though Bohdan and Daniel had already been sent outside. Lala told me to answer the knock and so I went over to the door and opened it. To my surprise, two girls were standing there, a little older, I thought, than I was. They were very drably dressed and looked a bit frightened. Lala called from the middle of the house, asking who was there and I said it was two strange girls and should I let them in? She shouted yes and came running to the door herself.

As the girls stepped tentatively into the house Lala came up to us and stood there, looking them over. Without saying anything to either of them she told me to take them to the work area in the kitchen. The girls had a few things with them and they carried their packets as they followed me toward the kitchen. Lala came in behind them. She had the cloth that Major Kleinecke had given her in her hands and spread it out on the kitchen table, speaking loudly about its finer points, but to the air, as if the two strange girls were not there. But it was clear to me her words were for them.

"You can sew I hope," she finally said, turning to look at them where they stood huddled together in one corner of the kitchen. "This is what I want." She began showing the girls what they were to do with the material, pushing it this way and that, explaining what she expected. The two girls, both very pale, listened solemnly. One, the younger, tried to smile at my employer but Lala wasn't interested in such niceties. She just kept talking, giving her instructions, and then, having finished, she abruptly turned away and left us alone together.

I looked at the two girls and offered a smile but only the younger girl returned it. I asked if they had had breakfast and both shook their heads no. All right then, I told them, I'll get you something and put out a little butter and some bread. The girls devoured this as though they hadn't eaten in days. I realized that, of course, they had not. They were Jews.

Lala had arranged with Kleinecke for these two girls, sisters, to come to our house several times a week to do work for her as her personal seamstresses, doing the kinds of things my own sister, Gusta, had been trained to do before the Germans had taken her. I did not speak a lot with them. They were too frightened of everything in the house and I wasn't anxious to be seen getting too close to them. I wore my hair in braids in those days, like a Polish girl, and I had my cross so they had no reason to think I was a Jew, too. Still I felt sorry for them. Lala treated them as if they were two additional pieces of furniture in the house during the times they were there with us and had me relay most of her instructions to them after that first day. She also kept them banished to the least frequented parts of the house, usually the kitchen, so they wouldn't be seen by anyone else who might come in.

But I made a point of giving them food whenever they came to us and I always handed them a packet of food to take with them when they left. Father Antonio had said I was to do that, after he saw them for the first time, but I always gave them just a little more than he told me to. It was all I could do under the circumstances. They seemed very, very sad and frightened so much of the time. I tried to make them feel at ease but I couldn't do much because Lala was always watching me and I didn't want her thinking I was becoming too close with them.

The sisters only came to us four or five times in all and mostly did knitting with wool Lala had also gotten from Herr Kleinecke. She was, in fact, riding high thanks to her relationship with the German officer. He seemed to be the highest ranking German in the entire region and could get just about anything he wanted done. Everyone was in fear of him but he was always ready to accommodate Lala. It was nothing for him to allow a couple of Jewish girls to leave their homes and come to work in the Ukrainian priest's house and the fact that he was prepared to do this for us made Lala feel even more important and pleased with herself.

Kleinecke also continued to visit us during this time and always had something of value for my mistress when he came by. This never failed to delight her so that she was certain she was now more important than any other Ukrainian in the district. The major did nothing to suggest otherwise and often stayed overnight. In fact, he became a regular fixture at our home, even when Father Antonio was around, though at such times he directed most of his attention to the priest.

He would speak of many things with Father Antonio including the way the war was proceeding, since the Germans were then finding it hard going in the east where the Russians had stopped them at Stalingrad, and of general affairs in the district. At such times, the major seemed to virtually ignore Lala and she would just sit and listen quietly as her husband chatted with the German officer. But I think Father Antonio was, himself, growing tired of these visits because he did not seem especially enthused, as Lala inevitably would be, when they got word that Major Kleinecke planned to stop by.

After a few weeks, the two Jewish girls no longer came to the house and when I asked my employer what had happened she simply shrugged.

"Major Kleinecke says he can no longer allow anyone to leave the Jewish area," was all she would tell me.

I felt very sorry about this and hoped my mistress would send me into the Jewish area again, like she used to do, to trade for goods, thinking I might find some way to make contact with them again. But I dared not ask her to do this and she never suggested it. In fact, all traffic with the Jewish area of Podhajce soon came to a complete halt. It was as though that part of the town had simply dropped off the earth's face. No one spoke about it and no one went there any longer.

I, of course, had not gone there in quite a while, myself, but I now found that I missed the two sisters, girls I had longed desperately to reach out to but had feared to even speak with, except for the most peremptory of conversations. Once they had stopped coming, though, I realized how much their presence had really meant to me. Although I had kept apart from them, I had secretly looked on them as my sisters, too, perhaps replacing those I had lost. But in all the time they had been coming to the house I had never even once asked their names.

I didn't know who they were or how to find them again once the war finally came to an end and the world returned to what it had been. It never occurred to me, of course, that it might not.

Chapter 16

The Fields of Starymsto

LALA TOOK it into her head, around this time, to object to the free time I had found for myself on Sundays. She couldn't keep me from going to church, of course, because Father Antonio would not have approved. But she insisted that I must return directly after church each Sunday, from here on in, because, with the end of winter, the cows had to be taken out to pasture. That was to be added to my jobs, she said. I was to finish up at church as early as possible and return to the barn to drive the animals into the fields.

The Ukrainian church owned a number of fields in the surrounding area and I was to make use of these, taking the cows out in the late morning and driving them back before evening. With spring this became my new routine and I had to excuse myself from Banushka and her family and race home, each Sunday morning, as soon as the priest ended his service so that I could see to my mistress' cows.

I wasn't happy about the added work but at least, while I was driving the cows, I could be alone to daydream, imagining that everything was back the way it had been in Kolomyia, before the Germans came, and before the Russians. I got to know the cows very well because of this and they came to know me, too. Whenever I went to the barn they would become excited at seeing me as though they knew why I had come, to take them to their favorite pastures. On other days, of course, Micken did this, but on Sundays he was excused and this task now fell to me. The cows, at least, appreciated me for it.

It was not long after this that we had two more visitors. They appeared one day at the door. No one had told me in advance of their coming but their arrival was no surprise for my mistress. The two people at the door were a stout couple, a balding man and a very broadly built woman. When they came in, Lala, my employer, made a great fuss. She told me to take their bags and I struggled with these but the elderly man reached down and lifted the heaviest of them. Lala was embracing the stout woman and they looked oddly mismatched, the tall and stately blonde woman who was my employer and this heavyset old Ukrainian woman who had the look of a peasant written all over her. She was, as it turned out, my mistress' mother, Anna, and the balding man, who was called Vladimir, was her father. They had come from their home in Czortkow to stay with us for a week or so.

I was quite surprised to think that such a handsome looking woman as the priest's wife should have come from two such ordinary looking people. But who can explain how bloodlines travel from generation to generation? Lala's father was a very kind man, always polite to me and helpful. He didn't have a mean bone in his body. But Anna, his wife – well it was very soon apparent to me where Lala's sharpness and cruelty came from. The old woman quickly took up her duties as my supervisor and began to follow me about, questioning everything I did. She was never satisfied with anything and constantly demanded that I do whatever I had only just finished over again. I was grateful for the times when I could get out of the house, for the times I spent with the cows in the fields or with my two charges, Bohdan and Daniel, overseeing their play in the fields beside the church grounds.

In the evenings, Lala would sit with her parents in the living area and her father would puff on his pipe while she and her mother would talk about little things. Father Antonio sometimes joined them but, more often than not, he would absent himself, explaining that he had to prepare a sermon, or read some of the school examinations in fulfillment of his pedagogical duties. Lala and her mother did not seem to miss his presence. When I was needed, to bring them this or that, I would listen to their conversations and tremble when I heard them speaking of the Jews. Lala's mother had even less love for Jews than Lala had, if that were possible.

The two of them were always talking about the Jews who lived in Podhajce, how much they had, how they had come by such wealth and the Ukrainians they had had to rob from in order to secure their property. Lala's mother, especially, would crow about how the Germans would fix everything. Then Lala would laugh and say that this was already being done and she said it as though she knew some secret arrangements to which few were privy. Then the two of them would put their heads together and Lala would whisper into her mother's ears and then they would laugh loudly and the old woman would say "good for them, then, they deserve what they have gotten." If I were nearby at such times, and the old woman caught sight of me, she would glower at me and I would turn my head and hurry off, eager to be away from her and her daughter.

I think that Lala's father was embarrassed by such conversations but he kept silent and never interfered between the two women. And in the meantime I made the best of it, despite the old woman's clear dislike for me, too. I thought it was because I was a Pole since I knew that Lala had no love for Poles either but one day, while I was cooking soup in the kitchen, the old woman came in behind me and began snooping about, looking over my shoulder. When she saw how I was making the soup she remarked that I had dropped some white beans in the mix and asked why I did that.

"That's how the Jews cook soup," the old woman muttered. "Why do you make soup like a Jew?"

She looked at me intently and I trembled inside. But I put the best face on it and said, "It's how I learned . . ."

"Well it's the way the Jews do it," she sniffed.

In fact it was how my mother always made soup because it clarified the broth but how could I admit that? I just pretended her words didn't matter to me but she kept clucking her tongue behind me and stayed there in the kitchen a long time that day, murmuring about the Jews and saying intermittently, "Are you sure you're not a Jew, too?"

I kept on with my work and pretended she wasn't there.

It was a good thing the little boys in my care thought so highly of me. Neither Lala nor Father Antonio seemed interested in the old woman's suspicions because, I'm certain, they needed someone whom the boys liked and I filled that bill. I always made it a point to play with the boys, to win them over, realizing that they were my guarantor of continued employment in the priest's house. And where would a Jewish girl in hiding be more likely to find safety than with a priest?

Still, I was glad when the visit of Lala's parents finally ended. The old woman and her husband prepared to leave though she still had not changed her feelings about me. She still looked at me with suspicion and glared harshly at me whenever I entered the room. But no one, not even her husband, gave any credence to this and they left as they had come, with no one saying a word to me until the morning of their departure and then I was told to help them with their bags and we put them on the wagon they had come in and then they were off. I certainly wasn't sorry to see them go.

During the time that they had been with us, maybe about a week in all, Major Heinz Kleinecke had stayed away. Lala was restless because he hadn't been by and as soon as Father Antonio prepared to leave for a religious retreat in Lvov, which was not long after this, Lala contrived to send word to him again. Then his visits began once more. He would come by for dinner in the evenings and I would try to make myself scarce. He continued to bring Lala little gifts. Sometimes he brought her soap, which was hard to come by as the war went on, and sometimes more cloth or chocolates.

She had a number of fine dresses made from the cloth though the Jewish seamstresses were no longer available for such work. One day she was so pleased with one of her new dresses that she gave me one of her older ones, a hand-me-down that was not in very good condition and somewhat too large for me. But she insisted I wear it and so I did, rolling up the sleeves as best I could. It was better than the worn old clothes that I had had until then and so I thanked her for it as she went about the house in her new attire that she had obtained courtesy of Major Kleinecke.

Father Antonio never seemed to question where she came by all the nice things she had. He was a bookish man and very involved in the affairs of his church. Perhaps, too, he simply preferred not to know. He certainly loved his Lala very much and doted on her in every way. Whatever she asked for he would try to obtain and he was only happy, it seemed, when she was.

After he returned, from Lvov, Herr Kleinecke's visits ended again and it wasn't long before Lala was moping about. Father Antonio didn't understand what made her so unhappy but he did everything he could think of to please her. He would bring her something to drink in the evenings and talk to her in gentle tones. She listened to him and took what he gave her but she could not rouse herself to smile at him. I suppose she was just thinking about her missing major, perhaps worrying that he had found some other woman in Podhajce on whom to lavish his attention. I don't know why she should have worried about such a thing, of course, because I doubt there was anyone more beautiful in the entire town than she was – not at least from what I had seen, anyway – but people will worry even when they don't have cause to. And when you don't know what is going on, that is the time when you are likely to worry most.

As the weather warmed I became more and more pleased to be taking the cows to the pasture on Sundays. It was a time when I could feel free again. I didn't even mind having to run out of church, leaving my friend Banushka and her brother Janek behind. There was another Polish girl who was Banushka's friend and soon became mine, as well. Her name was Gienia. I told Banushka and Gienia about how awful it was for me in the priest's house, with such a cruel mistress, and both urged me just to leave. I replied where can I go and they said there are plenty of places, you don't have to be a slave to that woman. But I was afraid. I didn't want to tell them that there were complications in my situation, that, since I was really a Jew, there was no better place for me. How could I tell them that, after all? I had no idea how they would respond since many Poles disliked Jews as much or more than the Ukrainians did. And even if they did try to keep my secret, how could I be sure of their discretion?

Still they kept urging me to leave the priest's house so after a while I stopped telling them the dreadful stories because it became harder and harder for me to explain why I stayed. Escaping their company to take the cows to the pasture now became the perfect excuse for me to cut short our discussions. The fact that I had to rush out of the church was out of my control since I had to do what my employers demanded and so I began spending less time with Banushka and her friend, mainly confining our contacts to the time we spent together in church when there was little time for talking.

One day I took the cows out on a Sunday in this fashion. It was a very warm, sunny day and I opened the barn door and, with a little switch in my hand, tapped the cows' rears lightly to drive them from their stalls onto the road. There was little traffic on the roads in those days as you can imagine. There were few automobiles and most vehicles that there were had been impounded for military use in any case, which meant they were deployed at the eastern front where the Germans were still fighting the Russians. The road we were on wasn't even a main road either so you hardly saw anything more than a farmer's wagon trundling by. I drove the cows across the road to what I knew was a favorite pasture of theirs. There were Ukrainian farmers about but it was a very lazy Sunday, no doubt because of the new warmth in the air. Spring was well along or maybe it was even early summer. I don't have good fix on the exact time of year.

As I proceeded with the cows toward our usual pasture I saw something unusual going on ahead of me. There were lines and lines of people all strung out and German soldiers with machine guns walking through the pasture. One of them suddenly appeared in front of me and said, "Halt. You can't come here today. Go back."

I was shocked because this was church land and I always pastured the cows in these fields. Yet clearly something was going on ahead. I tried to ask the soldier what was wrong but he pointed with the muzzle of his gun at the cows and repeated "You have to go back. Now."

The cows were not happy and neither was I. Sunday afternoons had become a time I treasured and here was this soldier telling me to take the cows away. If I couldn't pasture them here, where could I go? And what would my mistress say? I tried to argue with him but he got very insistent, waving his gun around and shouting and so I used the switch in my hand to strike the cows and turn them around.

They weren't any happier at being denied the pasture than I was but there was no arguing with this German. As I turned the cows about I kept looking over my shoulder though, in the direction of the pasture where I could see all those people lined up. I was close enough to see that there were men and women and even what appeared to be children in their midst. But all I could think of was that they were on church land and what right had they to be there when the cows needed to eat?

As I walked back toward the road so we could cross back to the church I saw one of our neighbors, a Ukrainian, and he smiled and asked after the cows. I said that I wanted to take them out to the pasture but that the Germans had turned me back and that there were many people down there and that I didn't know what was going on.

"Oh, it's the Jews," said the farmer. "They've gathered all the Jews from the town and brought them there."

"What for?" I asked him but my heart was already pounding.

"They're going to shoot them all, I suppose," he said.

"Even the children?" I blurted out.

"All of them," he said. "Why not? It's about time."

I stumbled back with the cows, seeing nothing in front of me but that crowd of people lined up in the pasture. The farmer's words kept pounding in my ears. "Why not? It's about time." When I reached the church grounds I flicked the switch against the cows' rumps, trying to speed them along. But Lala was outside. When she saw me she glared angrily and demanded to know why I had brought the cows back. What was wrong with me, didn't I have any sense of responsibility? Did I think the cows would give milk if they weren't properly fed?

I said the Germans were in the fields and that I had been turned away.

"What are they doing in our fields?" she wanted to know.

"They've brought the . . . the Jews," I said. "They're all lined up . . ."

Father Antonio came out as I was speaking and Lala turned immediately to him. "Did you hear, Antonio?" she said. "They're killing the Jews in the fields today."

Father Antonio stopped in his tracks and went pale, but Lala was already running to the barn. “Where are you going, Lala?” he said.

“To get a horse,” she called back. “Come with me. I want to see this.”

“Lala,” he said, “stay here. Don’t go down there . . .”

But she already had a horse out and was cinching up the saddle. “There’s another in the barn,” she called over her shoulder. “Take it and ride down with me.”

“I will not,” Father Antonio said. “And you mustn’t either.”

“Well, I’m going,” she said as she climbed into the saddle. “I want to see how they do it.”

“Please don’t,” Father Antonio was saying, his voice cracking as he spoke. But she was already riding out to the road.

“Lala,” he called after her, “stay here. It’s not right.”

“You can come along, Antonio – if you want to,” she shouted back at him.

“No,” he said as he watched her ride off across the road. “I’m going into the church to pray. And you should, too.”

Chapter 17

Who is a Jew?

WHEN LALA returned in an hour or so she was excited beyond words. She leaped off the horse and ran toward the church, calling for Father Antonio. He came out, still visibly shaken, his eyes reddened and wet, as though with tears.

"You should have seen it," Lala was saying to him, "they lined them all up beside a long trench . . . they made them dig it out themselves . . . everyone . . . and made them remove their clothes, every one of them, even the women, and one by one they went down the line. And they shot them. They killed them all, all the Jews, Antonio," she finished almost breathlessly. "They kicked the dead ones, the ones who hadn't fallen in as they shot them, into the pit."

Father Antonio stood there, looking at his beautiful wife, torn between his admiration for such beauty and what I was certain was his horror at her words. He was shaking his head all the while she was speaking. "May God forgive us," he finally whispered. But I don't think Lala heard since she was going on and on about what she had seen. I left the cows and ran off. I don't know who finally tended to them, whether Micken or Father Antonio himself or if they even had a chance to go to pasture on that day. I just kept thinking of the Jews I had seen in Podhajce when I had gone there for my employer to trade for their nice things. And of the two Jewish sisters who had come to us as seamstresses. Was it possible that these people were all gone now, all of them lying dead in the pasture where I used to take the cows? I could not believe it . . . or imagine it. I could not even think about it.

But word soon spread through the street that it was true and that the old Jewish area in Podhajce had been emptied of its occupants. All those people, we heard, had been taken out and shot. They hadn't been penned in a ghetto like Kolomyia but it had been as bad for them. And now they were wiped away, as the rain dissolves the footprints we leave behind in the moist earth. Who would remember all of these people, or know they were ever alive? Even their children were gone, the ones whose task it should have been to remember.

I remained in my room and cried that night. I didn't want to come out and see Lala gloating or even hear Father Antonio gently chiding her for her bloodlust. I couldn't bear the thought that he loved a woman like that.

The next few days were very hard but I lost myself in my work. Was it possible I was now the only Jew left in Podhajce? If so, I knew I must be especially careful as they would not look kindly on me if I were discovered. But it wasn't long before Father Antonio came to me and said we had to talk. I was terrified. What if he suspected? What if he knew? I followed him into his study and sat there with my hands folded unobtrusively in my lap.

"Things are changing very fast now, Wanda," he said to me. I looked down at my feet, afraid to meet his eyes.

"There are new rules from the Germans," he went on. "Everyone must have proper identification, certifying who they are. Now that there are no more Jews in Podhajce," he said this last with a catch in his throat, "it's important that everyone be identified, that their ancestry be attested to."

I listened quietly, unsure of how to reply.

"Do you have any papers, Wanda?" he asked me gently.

Finally I looked at him. "I have my report card from school," I whispered.

He was shaking his head gravely. "No, that's not enough, Wanda. You must have a *kenncarte*. It's what the Germans issue to everyone, based on their ancestral records. It will say where you're from, your bloodlines, and attest that there is no Jewish ancestry in your background. Do you have that, Wanda?"

I knew the moment of truth had come. I was very, very uneasy. "No," I said at last. "My parents were taken away by the Communists . . . I'm alone."

"Where are your birth records?" he asked gently.

"In Kolomyia," I replied, unsure of how he would receive this because it was well known that Kolomyia was a very Jewish area.

"Then you must get them," he said, leaning back in his chair. "You must go there, if you have to. There isn't a lot of time. Major Kleinecke has been asking about you. If you don't have papers, you can't remain with us and you'll have to leave."

I was trembling, beside myself, but I struggled to keep everything under control.

"I can't go back," I said finally. "Everything's changed. My parents are gone. I don't know who to see."

"What church did you go to there?" he asked me, his eyes narrowing as he scrutinized my expression.

I remembered the big church on *Uliza* Sobieskiego, the one I thought Wanda Madeira, the real Wanda, used to go to. "Kosciol Parafialny," I said. It was a Roman Catholic church that was well known in our area and I was sure it was the one Wanda had attended.

"Then you must go back there," he said softly. "There isn't much time. If you don't . . . if you don't get your birth records from the church then the Germans won't issue you a *kenncarte* and . . . and you won't be able to stay here with us any longer . . ."

I could see that his hand was trembling, too.

Finally he nodded and made an effort to smile at me, indicating that our talk was done. Slowly I got up and went outside. Now I had a real problem, I knew. How could I go back there, to the church, and ask for what I knew I had no right to, what the church officials would know, at once, I had no right to, as well? The real Wanda Madeira lived in Kolomyia and would be known to them, of course. And if I went back, in any event, how could I avoid being discovered for who and what I really was?

The next Sunday in church I whispered to Banushka about what had happened with Father Antonio, while the prayers were going on. "I don't know what I'm going to do," I said to her. "I can't go all the way back to Kolomyia. It's too far and I'm afraid." I dared not tell her anything more than that.

"Tell the priest," said Banushka firmly. "He'll help, I'm sure of it."

I swallowed hard when she said this. If I did that and he made an inquiry, what would the church in Kolomyia tell him? It was Wanda's church after all. And Wanda lived there still. They would know at once that an impostor had requested the birth certificate.

But the more I thought about it the more it seemed that this was the only way left to me. I knew I couldn't go back to Kolomyia myself. That was too dangerous. Yet, if I did nothing, I would surely be turned out by Father Antonio and his wife. And if I were? Then what would Major Kleinecke think of the matter? Wouldn't he conclude that I was not who I said I was?

At once I determined to follow Banushka's advice and begged her to help me out. She agreed to approach the Catholic priest with me so, at the end of the prayers, we both made our way up to him, before anyone else could do so. As I've said, he was a big man with a very round face but he was kindly and when I explained my problem to him, kissing his hand and calling him "holy father" as was the custom as I looked up into his concerned face, I could see that he was moved. He said that I was not to worry for he would send to the church I had named in Kolomyia at once. If it was at all feasible he assured me he would get my birth certificate for me.

It all sounded so simple except that I knew it wasn't. I knew that, living a lie as I was, I stood now on the very brink of exposure and that that could cost me much more than my job in the Ukrainian priest's house.

The days passed slowly now. Almost everyday Father Antonio would take me aside and ask what I was doing about our "problem." I told him that I had asked the Catholic priest to intervene and Father Antonio seemed relieved at first. But his relief didn't last very long. He came back to me the next day, and then the day after that, and asked what I had heard from the other priest and when I had to tell him nothing as yet, he would look concerned and walk off in deep concentration. Lala's attitude toward me was, if anything, harsher than before. She was continuously upbraiding me for little mistakes I made or for doing something or other that she disliked. It was becoming a burden even to remain in that house. But, of course, I had no alternative.

The next Sunday I went to church as usual and sat in the front row with my friends. I was unusually earnest in my devotions and really poured my heart out. I was very concerned about my situation and hoping to get some indication from the priest. But, though he looked my way a number of times as I prayed so fervently, he never said a word to me and when I left the church, my heart was weighed down with worry. All that following week I did my best to avoid everyone. Father Antonio didn't ask me anything but I felt like he was watching. Major Kleinecke had not been by for some time and I knew that Lala was becoming uneasy about this and that she seemed to hold me responsible. Her cruelty did not abate and she slapped me numerous times for the tiniest of mistakes. Even the two boys seemed to fear her wrath by this point. But Father Antonio loved her a great deal for it seemed that no matter how cruel and hard she could be, it was never enough to alter her image in his eyes.

The following Sunday I didn't go to church. I was sure by this point that the news was bad and I hid myself in the fields instead, thinking about the choices before me. Once the parish priest knew that I was not who I was pretending to be he would no longer welcome me into the church. Perhaps he would even report me to the authorities. And even if he didn't, without the birth certificate, I would have no *kenncarte* and then the Germans would conclude that I was a Jew because only Jews could not get proper documentation of a Christian heritage. I was in a terrible panic but I didn't know what else to do. If I ran away it would be an admission that I was an impostor and a Jew. Besides, where could I run to? The Germans were everywhere and now that they had begun eradicating the Jews I would stand out in a sea of gentiles as I never had before. I found myself praying nightly that Heinz Kleinecke would not soon return to us and, since this was what happened, perhaps I was at least partly responsible for Lala's loss, just as she imagined.

By the next Sunday I felt I could not remain in such a state of fear and uncertainty much longer and so I decided to go back to church. I met Banushka and her family that morning and we walked together to the Catholic church just as if everything was perfectly normal. Of course for them it was, even though I was dying inside as I ran over in my mind all the horrible things that would result from the news from Kolomyia which the priest might very well have received by now. I walked hand in hand with Banushka as Janek, her brother, followed behind us. He was a tall, thin boy with sandy colored hair. He was always very friendly toward me and was so on that day, too. But he couldn't know what was going on inside my head.

In church the service dragged on and on and I tried to lose myself in the liturgy as I had learned to do and had often done in the past. But I was too distracted, too worried about the situation and whether the priest had learned my secret. I noticed that he kept looking at me, as the service proceeded, and I looked away, afraid to meet his eyes, afraid of what I would see there. When the prayers finally came to an end I finally looked up and saw the priest looking at me. I started to leave with Banushka and her family but the priest raised his finger and beckoned me to him. I wanted to turn and run but I knew I couldn't. He was looking right at me and summoning me to follow him and so I excused myself and left the others and went toward him. He turned and went into his office in the rectory and I followed dutifully. In the office he was sitting at his great desk.

"Where have you been, little girl?" he said to me sternly. "I looked for you last week but didn't see you in church . . ."

I shrugged and made some excuse or other. I didn't really know how to explain my absence and must have sounded confused and embarrassed – as I was.

"Why didn't you come to church last week?" he asked me again. "It's not like you to miss the service."

I was silent.

"Well I have your birth certificate here," he said, lifting a piece of paper from the surface of his desk. "It arrived last week, but you didn't come for it. I thought you told me it was important . . ."

I looked up at his face, not believing my ears. "You . . . you have it?" I stammered.

"Since last week," he repeated with a smile.

Then he leaned across the desk and handed the paper to me. I took hold of it at once and began to read: Wanda Madeira, it said, born in Kolomyia . . . I couldn't believe my good luck. My hands were shaking, but there it was. They had sent the document without ever questioning if I was the real Wanda or not. I could only thank him. My words came tumbling out as I got up and rushed to his side, kneeling before him, taking his hand and kissing his ring. "Thank you, Holy Father," I said, "thank you so much."

He withdrew his hand and patted me on the head. "Well I expect to see you in church more regularly," he chided me gently. "Go on now, go home to Father Antonio and show him what you have. There should be no further problems now."

I leapt up and ran from the rectory, all the way back to the Ukrainian church compound, clutching that precious piece of paper to my heart. I was afraid to let it go, afraid the wind or something worse, would snatch it away again.

Chapter 18

The *Kenncarte*

THE THEFTS began around that time, I think. Someone or other was getting into our barn and stealing eggs, and even some of the chickens. Lala was furious about it. She said that no one should be allowed to steal from the church and that, since everything we had was the church's, every theft from us was a sacrilege. But now that I had my birth certificate I didn't care much about her petty annoyances. That document meant I had 'proof,' at last, of who I was and that I was Wanda Madeira from Kolomyia.

When I showed it to Father Antonio he seemed to sigh in relief. He said he would go down to Gestapo headquarters with me as soon as possible and help me get my *kenncarte*. Lala was annoyed that he said he would take me himself, but the Ukrainian priest said that that was the best way to put the matter to rest once and for all. He said you couldn't leave it to a young girl like me to handle for herself. By then I was sixteen years old, but I still felt extremely dependent on my employers. Although I had been on my own for nearly a year by that point, I was still grateful that Father Antonio was willing to get involved and help me resolve my status with the Germans. I didn't relish going to meet with the Gestapo officials alone.

"Wanda Madeira," said the major, making a great show of reading the paper in his hand. "Wanda Madeira. What kind of a name is that?"

He was sitting behind a desk, leaning back in his chair, his booted feet propped on the desk's edge. "Madeira, Madeira," he kept repeating. "It's not a Polish name." Looking up from the paper he fixed me with one of his intense stares.

Father Antonio was standing beside me and leaned toward Major Kleinecke at these words. "She's been with us for some time now," he insisted. "She worked for my sister before this, in Lsoftse, near Tluste. My sister was the wife of a priest, too."

"Your sister can't vouch for her, though, you said?" asked the major with interest.

"She died," said Father Antonio. He dropped his gaze as though remembering. "She died shortly after Wanda came to us."

"I'm sorry for your loss," Kleinecke said. But he did not sound sorry, or that he could care about much of anything. His voice was cold and hard and the spare office in which he had received us seemed cold and hard, too.

We had come to Gestapo headquarters as soon as Father Antonio had been able to get away from his other responsibilities. He had assured me that everything would now be all right as we made our way to the Gestapo building, but now we were finding that Major Kleinecke was not so eager to accept my story, even with the birth certificate I had secured from the Kolomyia church in hand.

I was nervous about this and thankful Father Antonio hadn't made me go to the Gestapo alone.

"My father was from Spain," I finally said to the major, offering a half truth by way of explanation, "but he died. My mother's Polish though," I added.

"I thought you said your parents were sent to the east by the Bolsheviks," Major Kleinecke said impatiently.

"Yes," I stammered, "my mother was . . . my father died."

"The child has been through enough because of this war," said Father Antonio, intervening. "She's an orphan and her church has the evidence of who she is. Isn't that enough?"

"We need to be sure," Major Kleinecke replied, taking his feet down and pulling himself forward, closer to the desk. "We can't issue papers if there's any question."

"What question?" asked Father Antonio. "I've vouched for her, and so does my wife. And my sister has vouched for her – I've shown you her letter. And now here is the girl's birth certificate, secured for her by the local Catholic priest. Would she have all this if she weren't who she says she is?"

Major Kleinecke was tapping the paper in his hand against the desk top, his eyes down. I tried desperately to read the expression on his face but couldn't.

"You know us," said Father Antonio, continuing. "Lala and I aren't strangers to you . . ."

The Gestapo officer raised his head and looked intently at the priest.

"I've cooperated with you in every way," Father Antonio continued, beneath the major's gaze. "You have no reason to deny this request now. Besides, we can't get along without her. How will Lala care for the boys without someone in the house to look after them? What will I tell her if we lose the girl?"

The major took a deep breath and seemed to want to say something but caught himself. He shrugged. "The birth certificate seems to be in order," he said in a noncommittal tone.

Father Antonio remained silent and I held my breath, trying not to look into this man's eyes. Kleinecke was still tapping the paper, which had somehow become folded along its pre-existing creases. He was marking time with it against his own fingers now. He looked from Father Antonio to me and then back, again, to the priest. "She's not much to look at," he murmured at last, "even for a Polish girl."

Father Antonio tensed at his words. "I love my wife," he said flatly.

"I know," said the major. He was looking up at the priest and frankly appraising him. "It's obvious to anyone with eyes that you are passionately in love with her, Father," he said. "She's certainly a beautiful woman . . . worth any man's admiration."

Father Antonio shifted uneasily. We had been standing there in the major's office for quite awhile by this time. Although he had taken his time in even agreeing to see us, the major had not proved particularly hospitable once we had been ushered in. He had left us standing there in the middle of the room while he reviewed the paper he had been handed. All business, he had merely acknowledged the Ukrainian priest with a nod at first while ignoring me, and then he had devoted his full attention to the paper in his hand.

Still, it was clear he wasn't keen on giving us what we wanted. I think he had had his suspicions with regard to my background, even from the first, though he had looked away because of Lala. Of course, I was certain Lala would never have spoken up for me herself. Hadn't she even opposed Father Antonio's taking me down to the Gestapo? Still, I served a purpose for her and, as long as I was silent about what had happened between her and the major, she had no reason to want to turn me out. If she thought I were a Jew, perhaps . . . but a Pole? She had no love for Poles, to be sure, but at least they weren't Jews.

Major Kleinecke had not, himself, been back to the house in quite a few weeks and Lala Kosar had been growing increasingly concerned over his prolonged absence. Now he sat at his desk, studying me closely. Did he wonder if I would denounce him, or if I already had? Did he think Father Antonio would have come here with me to get my official identity papers if he had known of the major's evening visits with his wife? All I could think about was my own situation but I was vaguely aware that much more was going on between these people than their concern, or lack of it, for me.

"You're away from home a great deal, Father," Major Kleinecke finally said to him. "Is that wise?"

"I have my duties, Major," Father Antonio replied.

"As do we all," said the major. "Now, however, I suppose that's mostly done here. You're very fortunate to have such a fine home and family. Such a wife . . . I left mine in Germany. The way this war's going . . . well, I don't know when I'll have the chance to see her again."

"Perhaps before your next assignment?"

"We'll have to see. The news . . . well, it looks like this is going to be a long war. I think I'm going to approve this request you've brought me, Father. But I can't promise for the future. I feel as if I owe you something at least."

"It's not what you owe me, Major. It's what we each owe to God."

"Yes, well that's a discussion for another day, isn't it? We do our duty . . . you in your way . . . me in mine. In the end we aren't so different."

"I pray for others' souls . . ."

"War is what it is, Father." Kleinecke hit the desk's surface with the flat of his hand as though to put an end to the debate. "We're both soldiers in a cause that's greater than we are."

"There's only one such cause," answered Father Antonio.

The major shook his head impatiently and tossed the paper carelessly onto his desk. "Accept what I've given you, Father. The girl will have her *kenncarte* and I'll certify this area free of Jews before moving on. What's one more Polish girl in the grand scheme of things anyway?"

Lala took the news of the major's reassignment very badly when Father Antonio brought it to her. He stood there, his shoulders hunched, as his wife turned pale at his words. "Lala," he pleaded, "it's for the best . . . for everyone."

But she was distraught and, for days afterwards, moved about the house with heavy steps, her voice raised at the slightest infraction by the boys or by me. Father Antonio made it a point to busy himself elsewhere now, either in the church or with his parishioners, not wanting to bear the brunt of her anger.

But I was not so fortunate.

One day when Father Antonio was returning from church I brought him water to clean his hands, a custom he followed whenever he entered the house. I always carried the water in a fine china bowl which the Kosars kept near the entryway for this purpose. I was wearing one of my employer's old dresses, one she had handed to me when she was still enjoying the major's favors, receiving new rolls of cloth and other fine gifts from him nearly every week. This hand-me-down dress was too large for me and, though I had tried to mend it, I wasn't an expert with needle and thread and hadn't had a great deal of time to attend to it in any case. The sleeves were wide and too large and I had had to fold them back so I could wear the dress comfortably. But, even so, they tended to come loose at inopportune times, constantly requiring that I stop and carefully fold them back during the course of the day.

As I grabbed the bowl for Father Antonio and poured water into it, the sleeves had come undone again but, fearing my mistress' anger if I didn't bring the water to him as soon as he entered the house, I didn't stop to fold them back as I should have but rushed to meet him, instead, the bowl of water in my hands. As I did so, the large sleeves flared out as they often did and one caught on a door latch as I hurried into the narrow vestibule, snapping my hand back and causing me to lose my grip on the bowl. It flew from my hands and crashed to the floor and shattered, spilling water everywhere.

When Lala saw what had happened she was beside herself with fury. She rushed at me and spun me about, shouting "look what you've done, look what you've done now!"

I tried to explain, crying, telling her my sleeve was too long and had caught on the door but she wouldn't listen. All I could do was stand there as she screamed into my face. Father Antonio, trying to quiet her down, was unable to make himself heard.

"Now you've destroyed a perfectly good bowl, a bowl that's worth more than you are, you stupid girl," Lala was shouting at me. "What's the matter with you? That bowl can't be fixed . . . it was . . . it was priceless."

I went down on my hands and knees to gather up the pieces, trying desperately to dry the floor with the edges of my skirt while, above me, Lala just continued to howl about the shattered bowl. "You're to be punished this time," she was saying. "Oh yes, I know what you've been doing, what you've been saying against me . . ."

I was distraught and didn't know how to respond to her. I had kept her secret and couldn't be blamed if Father Antonio had his suspicions. Or that he had cared enough to accompany me to Gestapo headquarters to help me get my papers. But Lala's anger seemed boundless. All the pent up fury that had accumulated in her soul from the time that Major Kleinecke had seemingly lost interest in her now burst forth and tumbled out onto me. Violently she yanked me to my feet and as I looked round for help, any kind of help, I saw Father Antonio flee the scene. He could never bear to see Lala in a fury or to confront her in her anger.

She held me fast by the wrist and slapped me hard on the face and then she struck me a second time across the mouth.

"You're to be punished now, you little Pole," she railed at me so forcefully that I thought she would blow me right through the door by the power of her voice alone. "For a week you'll sleep outside," she was saying, "on the porch, you little fool. That's right, no bed or room for you now. You think it's hard here do you? Well now you can live on the porch like the little animal you are. Then tell me how hard it is for you here."

I was crying. My face was sore and swollen where she had twice struck me across the mouth. All I could do was desperately blubber my apologies to her and try to explain, but the words wouldn't come as she continued to shake me violently with all the suppressed anger that had been growing in her heart since Major Kleinecke had ceased visiting us.

And so began my banishment from the Kosars' house and the surprising discovery I was to make because of it, concerning the thefts from our barn which had been troubling us.

Chapter 19

Barn Thieves

THAT NIGHT I slept on the porch. Lala was unyielding, refusing to relent, and Father Antonio was simply unwilling to intervene on my behalf. He could never bring himself to confront this woman whom he adored so completely and so I took my things and carried them outside, setting out a rickety chair for myself and curling up in a blanket against the chill night air. I was very sad but felt that there was nowhere I could turn. I had no other place to go to and, as a Jew in hiding, I dared not expose myself too much.

But I was very uneasy as I sat there in that chair, the sky darkening above me. It wasn't because I hadn't lived outside on my own before. I had, in fact, traveled and slept in the open extensively from the time I first ran away from the Kolomyia ghetto until I had at last found a position in the priest's house in Lsoftse, thanks to Father Antonio's gentle sister. But this was the first time I had been thrust outside again since I had found a home of sorts with Katrina. And I was still fearful because of the recent killings that had taken place in the nearby fields. Everything had changed in Podhajce because of those killings and I missed the security of the little room and bed I had been provided with in the Kosars' home.

Now, instead, I found myself shivering and alone in the open air as the sky continued to darken and the evening winds blew in, rustling the tall stalks of corn which covered the adjacent fields. Micken and the other hired workers had planted the church's crops there and these were now in full growth and would soon be ready for the harvest. Not far from where I was I could see part of the barn where the animals were kept. That was where the nightly thefts had been occurring. Knowledge of this only added to my concern as I watched the air all around me slide into an inky blackness with only the bright swath of silvery stars shimmering above me for light.

I knew Lala had lately been incensed by all the thefts and that she had little or no concern for me in the event the thieves returned as they seemed to do most nights and I began to shiver as I thought of this. To take my mind off my troubles I started to fiddle with my hair for want of anything better to do.

I always wore it in braids in those days and had little time to care for it because my employers kept me busy from sun up until the evening. Alone in my own room at night, I did as I pleased of course, and that was when I usually tried to comb it out properly. It was no easy task and there, in the dark, with the night wind blowing in across the fields, it was harder still. I kept at it, though, to take my mind off my situation. Because my hair was so long I had to worry about lice, too. It wasn't easy to wash it in those days unless you had ready access to water and Lala wasn't free with either my time or access. And so I carefully pulled each braid apart there on the porch and went through the strands, tugging, twisting and separating each in turn.

I don't know how long I sat there. Maybe I began to fall asleep. I know my eyes became heavy and my head nodded, though I was continually waking again, with every sound or rustle in the nearby fields. It was that strange rustling which seemed to become more and more insistent that finally caused me to come fully awake. I was sure I had heard something and I sank down deeper into my chair in fright, afraid to do anything but cast my eyes from one side to another, searching out the source of the strange noises I was sure I had heard. As I sat there, unmoving, I was sure the noise I was hearing was growing louder. In the evening's blackness it seemed to me that there was movement in the field right in front of me. I was sure I could see figures flitting among the shadows, in the darkness, dark spots against the darker backdrop of the corn rows.

I was too frightened to move or let on in any way that I was awake. I just sat there, watching, listening to the rustling undertone. I was sure it was voices I was hearing but I couldn't make out what was being said. I began to think of the childhood stories we had been told in Kolomyia, about the night creatures who frequented the edges of the wilderness, floating in with the shadows to steal away human children. I was no longer a child but I felt like one that night, listening to the muted, indecipherable whispers of the fairy folk who I imagined inhabited a world just beyond our human one.

I don't know how long I sat there listening, frightened, a little girl in a nearly grown woman's body, but I'm sure I could not have stayed awake the whole night. I don't recall falling asleep after I first began to hear the voices and see the shadowy movements in the fields but I'm sure I must have. The hours wore on as I shivered on my chair, praying that the strange creatures who had intruded there would let me be. And then, the next thing I remember is that it was morning and the sky was a rapidly brightening gray.

I opened my eyes and watched as the sun came up, as I had done so long ago with my sister Feiga in the Kolomyia ghetto after the killing of my grandmother, and impatiently counted the minutes until I could go back inside the house. When I finally heard rustling behind the porch door I got up and cautiously looked about but could see no evidence of anyone or anything amiss and gathered up my blanket and pillow and went back to the house and timidly knocked on the door. After what seemed like a long time, Lala opened the door and stood there staring down at me. She seemed no more mollified now than she had been the day before, when she had decreed that I was to take my things onto the porch, and I began to think that I would be better off to remain there for the rest of the day. Still, the night was gone and so were our otherworldly visitors and so I went silently inside under her stern and watchful gaze.

As I prepared breakfast that morning for the family I heard Lala shouting angrily again and my heart sank. She was furious about something and I didn't want to get in her way or do anything further to draw her attention. But as Lala and her family sat down to breakfast and I brought their sausages, bread and coffee, I could hear her angrily berating Father Antonio again over some matter or other.

Finally I realized she was complaining about the thefts again, as she had on many mornings before this. The thieves, it seemed, had gotten into the barn that night, as before, and stolen some chickens and a little milk. It had happened while I was out there on the porch and she was beside herself.

I began to think of those shadowy figures I thought I'd seen moving among the corn stalks, and their voices, almost human, which I thought I'd heard while praying. It was as though I'd been lost in some dreadful dream. As Lala went on and on about the losses we had again sustained, I realized there must be a connection between these things, the thefts and my voices. I was afraid to speak up about this but the more I listened the more certain I became that what I had seen and heard were the thieves themselves. Perhaps they weren't even human, as I had feared in the middle of the night sitting alone on the open porch, but I knew it was more than likely that they were and so I had to say something. Finally, summoning up my courage, I did.

Lala listened to my words with her teeth clenched and her eyes burning like hot coals as I recounted the story of the shadowy figures in the fields and the buzz of strange, otherworldly voices I had heard for much of the night. She wasn't at all happy that I had intruded into the morning conversation but what I had seen was too important to her to be simply ignored.

When I finished, Lala asked me coldly why I hadn't said anything about this earlier and I stammered that I hadn't thought much about it until I'd heard her describing the thefts discovered again that morning.

"You could have been more alert," she snapped.

But Father Antonio reached over and patted her hand. "She must have had a hard time sleeping outside all night," he said in a gentle voice meant, I thought, to encourage us both. "Perhaps she didn't realize what she'd seen."

"It doesn't take brains to see a thief," Lala snapped.

"I was sleeping, on and off," I explained. "I don't even know what I saw, only these shadows and the sound, maybe, of some voices. I didn't see anyone steal anything."

"You wouldn't see that, you silly girl," Lala said. "Do you think the thieves would simply announce themselves? What good is having you out there on the porch if you're going to sleep the night through and pay no attention when the thieves come?"

"You didn't say I was to keep watch," I protested.

"How impudent," Lala said. "Do you think you've no responsibility to this household when you see something amiss? Where do you think the food we feed you comes from? Does it come from the sky?"

Father Antonio tapped a finger on the table and looked away uncomfortably.

"I don't know what I saw last night," I said honestly. "There were shadows, that's all. Maybe the sounds of someone talking. I can't be sure. But they didn't come near the house and I didn't see anyone go into the barn."

"Well someone did," answered Lala. "Micken has already taken a count of the missing eggs. And this time there's a chicken missing, too. Who would steal like this from the church lands? Who would be so disrespectful?"

"Times are hard, Lala," Father Antonio said. "There are many who are hungry. The church has enough to spare for them."

"Then let them come and ask us, like honest folk," Lala said. "None of this stealing and skulking about. Well, I'll put a stop to it."

"What do you have in mind?" asked her husband.

"I'll set a trap for them," she replied.

That day Lala had Micken rig up a string from the barn door to the house with a little bell on the end of it. If anyone opened the barn door it would trigger the bell and we would know at once that we were being robbed. Lala supervised the running of the string so that it was high above the ground, not easy to see or even reach. She was afraid the thieves would catch on and cut the cord before entering. That night I slept out on the porch again because Lala was intent on ensuring my punishment continued. This time, though, she and Father Antonio remained awake for a long time, listening for the telltale bell. But it never rang the entire night and I neither saw nor heard anything. Still, the following morning, when

Micken came to the house to perform his chores, he found that we had again been robbed. The barn door had never moved but still there were chickens and eggs missing, as there had been the previous morning.

Lala was beside herself. She went up and down the length of the barn but could not see any evidence of entry. If the door had been opened and shut, the bell would surely have rung because the line from barn door to bell was still intact. But the thefts couldn't be denied. On the third night the same thing happened and we found evidence of loss in the barn in the morning, even though the barn door again had seemingly never been breached. Micken scratched his head and said he had no idea how the theft had occurred but Lala was certain he had failed to adequately tie the barn door to the bell in the house and made him take it all down and restring it. She watched his every step as he did this and even intimated that she wasn't sure that he, himself, was innocent of the thefts. Micken assured her that he was not the culprit and for a fourth night I slept on the porch, watching everything for as long as I could stay awake at Lala's instructions.

This time I thought I saw those shadows again and signs of movement in the fields but again there was no sight of a human being and, again, when we woke the following morning we found that more had been taken from the barn. Lala was furious and tore through the place looking for signs of a break-in but, as before, there were none. After she went in the house, I made my own inspection of the barn, remembering my days in the barn at Wanda's house. I went round the back and carefully inspected each of the boards that made up the barn wall. Just as I'd thought, I soon found evidence of boards that had been removed and replaced. That was how they were doing it, I realized. There was nothing supernatural going on at all. The thieves were human beings like we were only they had realized the barn door was rigged and were avoiding it. I couldn't help laughing to myself and carefully covered up the loosened boards so no one else would notice and went back into the house.

By the fifth night, Lala no longer seemed to be angry at me and was devoting nearly all her energy to the thieves who were making a fool of her. When she was done angrily berating

Micken for his failure to get the cord and bell right, she turned on her own husband and began to accuse Father Antonio of ignoring the matter. She followed him about the house, demanding that he take some sort of action. Father Antonio seemed pained and it was clear he didn't want to see her continue in this way. It was always hard for him to bear the constant brunt of her anger because he was so deeply devoted to her. At last he said he would personally attend to the matter, promising her he would find a way to end the depredations we were enduring each night.

She seemed to accept him at his word and finally grew quiet. Later on that day Father Antonio called me to him and quietly asked about everything that I had seen. I didn't have much more to tell him than what I had already offered but I tried to answer all his questions as carefully and as completely as I could.

"You didn't see anyone in the fields?" he pressed me after I had finished recounting everything I remembered.

"No, Father," I assured him. "Only shadows . . . and some noises. I thought there was someone there but I couldn't be sure."

"You saw this only the first night?"

"Mostly," I said. "I thought I saw something later, too, but not so clearly."

"Do you have any idea how many there were?" he asked me.

"How many, Father? Do you think there are many of them?"

"They're taking a lot of food out of the barn nearly every night now. There must be quite a few of them. And they must be very hungry."

"Who do you think they are, Father?" I asked.

He just grew quiet and said, "Wanda, tonight when you go out on the porch I want you to take some food from the kitchen. Do it quietly. Say nothing to my wife. Put out some milk and bread, too, and whatever else we can spare. Do you understand?"

"I think so, Father," I whispered.

"They must be very hungry," he mused aloud again, ignoring me now. "It's not so much of a hardship to give them what they need, is it? We must do what we can." Then, turning to me again, he said: "After you've left the food, I want you to come back inside and go to your room. You don't need to sleep on the porch any longer. Don't worry about Lala. I'll explain it to her. Just make sure you leave the food at the edge of the porch where it can be easily seen."

"Will they come and take it?" I asked.

"Only God knows," Father Antonio said. "But I think they will."

"Father," I asked him, "who are they? Who do you think it is who has been stealing from us?"

He looked at me searchingly. There was a glint in one corner of his eye, as though from a tear. "I think you already know the answer to that, Wanda," he said.

That night I did as Father Antonio had instructed me and in the morning, when I awoke, I raced to the door and checked the large bowl of milk that I had placed outside. It was completely empty. The bread and meat I had left beside it were all gone, too. I hurriedly took the evidence away and returned to the kitchen before Lala had wakened.

Later, at breakfast, Father Antonio ate quietly and did not look up as I came into the room. Lala was speaking rapidly to him, telling him that Micken had found no evidence of theft from the barn that morning. She was pressing him to tell her how he had managed this.

"I did what needed doing," was all he would reply and continued to chew. But after a while he added: "I kept watch. Nothing happened so I sent Wanda to sleep in her room so she wouldn't scare them off if they were out there. Now let's see how matters go tonight."

Lala looked at him in silence. She had no more questions but seemed content to let the matter rest.

Afterwards I continued to do as Father Antonio urged me, putting out whatever extra food we had that night and on each night thereafter, always clearing away the evidence the following morning before anyone else was awake. Sometimes, when Lala would send me out to the barn to bring back eggs for the household, or vegetables from the garden, I would take a little extra and add this to the offerings we placed on the porch each night.

The barn thefts declined. They didn't end entirely but they became less frequent and I made it a point to do what I could to hide the evidence of any lost food from thefts which did occur. Father Antonio continued to urge me, on the sly, to put out as much as we could spare and we kept this entirely between ourselves.

I don't think Lala ever learned how Father Antonio had ended the nightly losses we had been experiencing. If she did, she never let on. Perhaps she was just glad the problem appeared to have been solved. She was a very proud woman and didn't like the idea of being victimized, especially by vagrants and robbers.

Whatever the explanation for her loss of interest, she let the matter lie and never insisted that Father Antonio explain what he had done in any more detail than he had first offered and I continued to leave food for the mysterious raiders lurking about in our cornfields in the nights. I found myself wondering, as I did this, though, just where these people managed to hide themselves during the daylight hours and how many of them there actually were.

They always seemed to take whatever we left and it seemed as though we could never leave enough. I thought that, perhaps, there were some among them whom I might even have known. Maybe even those two sisters who had been our seamstresses. I imagined that perhaps I was once again providing them with food as I used to when they had been allowed by Major Kleinecke to come to our house and work for my mistress. But I never saw anyone in the fields after that, not even shadows, though the food I left was always gone by the time the sun rose each morning and the frenzy of the day's activities returned once more to the little Ukrainian church and buildings in which we lived.

Chapter 20

A New Arrangement

THINGS SETTLED down for a while. Eventually we got the official word that Major Kleinecke was gone, transferred to some other jurisdiction. The rumors we heard had the war going badly for the Germans in the east and I thought it was possible Kleinecke had been sent there. If so, I knew he would have a much harder assignment than he had enjoyed in Podhajce and I couldn't help my feeling of delight at the thought of this. Whatever the case, however, Lala was very depressed by his departure. Father Antonio did everything he could to cheer her up and even tried spending more time at home but Lala was in a bad way and there was little he could do to restore her spirits. Unfortunately, she continued to take her anger and resentment out on me.

Life in the Kosar home became all but unbearable for me. Even after I was allowed to move back inside the house, Lala continued to vent her anger and disappointment at Kleinecke's departure on me. She was constantly berating me and sometimes she struck me. I could not go to Father Antonio because he loved her so much he could not imagine the things she was capable of doing. Even when he witnessed her tirades or overheard the rants she directed against me, he seemed to want to pretend nothing had occurred. Finally, matters became all but unbearable and one day in church I confided my situation to Banushka and her friend. "Why do you stay, then?" Banushka asked. "You have your *kenncarte* now. You can go anywhere."

"I don't know where to go," I said to her. In truth, it had never occurred to me until that moment that the *kenncarte* fundamentally changed my situation. Without it I had been a prisoner of the Kosars, a person with no one to vouch for her but the priest and his family. But with the *kenncarte* I was no different than any other Pole. I was no longer a Jew according to the Nazis' own records. In Podhajce, where no one knew me as anyone else but the Polish girl Wanda Madeira, the *kenncarte* was like gold for me.

Banushka said: "Why don't you come live with us for awhile? I'm sure my parents will put you up. And we have the room."

"With you?" I said. The thought opened new possibilities.

"Of course," Banushka answered. "You can get a job now that will pay you much more than the Ukrainian priest is paying you. I've always wondered why you stayed with them when you seemed so unhappy."

The more I thought about it the more I realized the truth of Banushka's words.

The next time Lala flared up at me I was ready. "I've decided to move out" I announced suddenly as she was in the middle of one of her harangues, shouting at me for this or that breach that she claimed I had committed. My words stopped her in her tracks and she just stood there in silence, looking at me. I summoned up my courage and added: "I'm going to find another job and move away from here. I'm no longer able to endure this."

"What?" Lala muttered. "Endure this, you little . . .?"

But I didn't wait for her to finish her thought.

I went determinedly to my room and packed my few things. Then I walked into the living area and said good-by to the boys and left the house. The little boys watched me go in tears. I was sorry to be leaving them as I had grown fond of both, but I could no longer accept the constant cruelty of their mother.

I moved in a few houses down, where Banushka and her family lived and they were very pleased to have me. They already knew me as their daughter's friend from church and they made me feel at home from the first. The very next day I went out looking for work and it wasn't long before I found it at a local dairy. I had a lot of experience with cows by then and, of course, I remembered my brother Samuel's dairy operation in Piadyki. The pay was much better, too. I was astonished that moving out had never occurred to me before or at least that I hadn't thought to leave the Kosars as soon as I had the Nazi-issued identity card in my possession.

Life with Banushka's family was initially much better than anything I could have hoped for and for the first time I had some money in my pocket. Because I was only living a few doors away, I still saw the Kosars each day and especially their boys and they always seemed to want me to come by. But I would not. I went from my new home to work and back again and said no more than hello to the boys in passing. To my former mistress, Lala Kosar, I had nothing to say.

This went on for something like a week until one day as I was leaving the dinner table in Banushka's house, after having thanked her mother for the fine food, I found myself in a darkened hallway of the house, on the way to my room. Suddenly I was aware of a presence in the darkness beside me and looked around. It was Janek, Banushka's brother. We had been friends in church and he had often accompanied Banushka and me as we walked back and forth on Sundays. As I've mentioned, he was about two years older than me. Since I was sixteen years old by this time, I imagine he was about eighteen. But I was a very young and naïve sixteen year old, for all my experience on the road alone. Janek, it seemed, was not so inexperienced.

Without warning he suddenly pushed himself against me and I could feel his hot breath against my neck, his hands on my body as he sought to wrestle me into kissing him against a wall. I was in his home and knew that resistance might leave me unwelcome there. But I had no interest in becoming Janek's plaything while I was living there. I struggled to push him off and he kept saying that he wanted to be close to me, that he had noticed me from the first and things like that. I said he must leave me alone, that I was a good girl, but he laughed and said all of us were good girls but even the good ones would some day learn to love a boy.

I said I would choose whoever I wanted when I was ready and he whispered hotly "does that mean you won't choose me?"

I replied that I wasn't ready to choose anyone, that I was only sixteen, and he said sixteen's old enough for what he wanted to do.

I just kept struggling and pushing him away and he started to get angry. Our noise was growing louder and I was afraid others in the house would hear. He must have been afraid too, because suddenly he released me and backed away. I could tell he was very angry or maybe he was just hurt. Whatever it was, I took that opportunity to run to my room and shut the door behind me. All that night I lay alone in the darkness, thinking of what had happened and of what I would have to do now since it was clear I couldn't hope to stay there any longer, with Janek so anxious to enforce a relationship on me – a relationship I was sure I didn't want.

The following morning I went into the kitchen for breakfast with a certain amount of trepidation. Everyone was sitting there, quiet, as though nothing had happened. I thought that perhaps they just hadn't heard anything. Janek got up from the table when I walked in, excused himself and went outside. The rest of the family sat there without speaking. It was very uncomfortable as I couldn't tell what they knew about the goings on the night before.

We hadn't quite finished eating when there was a knock on the door. Banushka's father got up to answer it and I just sat there with my head down. When I looked up, he had come back and with him were Father Antonio. I put down my spoon in surprise.

Father Antonio was the first to speak. He said, "Wanda, can I talk with you?"

"Yes, Father, of course," I answered him.

"Wanda, we want you to come back with us. The boys are terribly unsettled without you and we've tried to hire other girls but the boys just won't take to them. We need you."

I was shocked. I guess my mouth had fallen open but nothing would come out.

"Maybe there were some misunderstandings," he continued. "I hope . . . I hope it was nothing that can't be fixed. But we want you to come back."

"I can't, Father," I said. "I'm earning much better money now. I can't work for such small wages anymore."

"What are you earning at the dairy?" he asked me pointedly.

The first week they had only paid me ten zlotys but I was about to start my second week there and they had promised me twenty now that I knew the rudiments of my job and I told this to Father Antonio.

"We'll pay you the same then, Wanda," he said.

"It's not . . . it's not just money, Father."

"Things will be better," Father Antonio smiled encouragingly at me. "I promise. The boys miss you terribly. And so does Lala."

I knew that Father Antonio was a very kind and sincere man and would not knowingly mislead me. But I thought he must surely be doing so now since Lala was not the sort who would miss someone like me. Still, he seemed so desperate to get me to come back.

"I . . . I don't know," I finally said. "I have to think about it." But I was already thinking about Janek and what had almost happened the night before and how difficult this had made my situation with Banushka and her family. It was one thing to be friends with someone and live in her house but quite another to reject her brother's advances – or even to accept them. I was sure my continuing there would now be a big problem for me, no matter what else occurred. Finally I decided.

"Yes, I suppose I can go back," I told Father Antonio at last. "But I can't do the kind of hard work I did before. I was hired to care for the children and that's all I can do if I come back. Otherwise it's better at the dairy." I was surprised at the newfound firmness I heard in my own voice.

"Of course," Father Antonio said. "It will be fine."

"You'll pay me what I can make at the dairy, too?" I asked.

"Agreed," said Father Antonio.

"Then I'll come back," I promised.

I packed my bags that same day and moved back to the Kosars' household. The boys were ecstatic at my return though Banushka had told me, as I was leaving, that she was genuinely sorry to see me go. She and I never spoke about Janek, either then or afterwards, and I never found out if she knew what he had done. But I was glad to be away from him from then on.

Life with the Kosars now changed dramatically. Not only did Lala treat me more fairly but I was no longer obliged to do all the heavy household work like a maidservant. I still did some of the cooking and cleaning but Lala was less demanding and I was able to spend more of my time caring for the boys. I also got paid a fair wage.

I never learned what had caused Lala to make such an about-face with regard to me but I like to think that Father Antonio had finally put his foot down. If not, then perhaps it was his love of his sons that at last overcame his deep devotion to such a woman, a woman who had so blatantly betrayed him and who daily made his household the sort of place even a priest must dread entering.

Chapter 21

The Eastern Front Collapses

THE WAR news was bad for the Germans but good for us. No one could deny that they had bogged down badly at Stalingrad and, more and more, they were sending their troops forward, to the front. We heard about the shifting lines of combat all around us. There were stories of Kolomyia being overrun by the Russians and then the Germans counterattacking and taking it back. I listened closely whenever I heard talk of Kolomyia because I couldn't help thinking of my family that was still there. Had they found a way to survive? Had any of them been able to escape the Germans and their ghetto?

We no longer saw as many German soldiers in our area as before but then perhaps they thought their work was done, having eradicated the Jews of Podhajce. By Christmas, Lala's parents were with us again. As before they moved in for a week and her mother settled down to busy herself with household affairs. Although I was now treated much better, nothing appeased the old woman who seemed convinced, more than ever, that I was a secret Jew. She used to follow me around and make comments about the things I did, perhaps hoping to unnerve me and cause me to give myself away. But I just pretended not to hear her, even when her comments were deliberately insulting to Jews, and she was never able to get me to make a slip.

I think she must have worked for Jews at one point because she knew a great deal about our household practices including how we prepared food. I had to be very careful about that because, more than once, she would look at me in the kitchen and ask if I was really sure I wasn't a Jew because, she would say, I handled food like they did.

I don't think Lala thought there was anything to her mother's concerns but if she did she was too pleased to have me back, caring for her two sons, to question who I really was. Whether Father Antonio ever suspected, I never knew but he and I continued to secretly put food out nightly on the porch for the people hiding in the fields and he always urged me to pray for them when we did this.

When Lala's parents left us, at the end of the Christmas holiday, I breathed a sigh of relief. It was very stressful to have such a suspicious woman hounding your every step, especially in light of the fact that she was on to something with me, though she could never find enough evidence to prove it.

After Christmas, the news got even worse for the Germans and by February we heard the most wonderful news of all. The German line had broken and their armies in the east had surrendered to the Russians. The Germans were in full retreat, withdrawing everywhere back to more defensible lines. Lala and Father Antonio were not pleased, however. I'm sure Lala's sympathies were with the Nazis though I don't think that was true of Father Antonio. Still, he was greatly troubled by the German defeat because, as a priest, he could only expect the worst at the hands of the Communists. It was well known that Stalin's forces treated priests and other members of the religious orders very badly. With the collapse of the Germans' eastern front everything changed in the Kosar household.

One day I awoke to find everything in an uproar. The Kosars were scrambling about, packing up their things. "What's happening?" I asked, coming out of my room, rubbing my eyes in surprise.

"The Germans are retreating," Father Antonio said, looking pointedly at me. "The rumor is that the Russians are only five hours away from here in Proskow. We have to go west, toward the German lines, because the Communists will soon be here."

"The Russians are coming back?" I asked incredulously.

"They'll be here soon enough. If what we've heard is true, we may have less than a day to get out. Hurry and pack your things and we'll take you with us. We're going to Styrj. The Germans have pulled back to there."

I was stunned. If the Russians were returning I knew I would soon be free of the ever present fear that I would be recognized as a Jew. I didn't know what to say to Father Antonio. He had always been good to me and, since I had returned to the household, Lala had ceased to tyrannize me as she used to. But I knew I couldn't go back with them, following the Germans.

"No," I finally said, shaking my head emphatically. "I want to stay. I've lived under the Russians before. It was better for me than the Germans."

Father Antonio looked at me intently. He seemed to be examining my face more closely than he had ever done before. His eyes were very, very sad. "If you prefer it then, Wanda," he said softly. "We wish you would come. The boys will be devastated if you don't. But you've got to do what's best for yourself. You won't reconsider?"

"No," I said, still shaking my head.

He nodded as though he understood. After that they said very little to me as they rushed to pack everything they could and load it onto a truck that was already waiting for them outside. One of the local Ukrainians had driven it to the church and sitting in it, waiting for them to come out. Lala mostly took their clothing and her jewelry, of course. There wasn't time or room enough in the truck to take much of anything else.

They were gone by the afternoon, the Ukrainian man driving them out onto the road, the truck's axle rumbling and creaking in protest. The boys, my two little boys, looked back at me from under the canvas covering of the vehicle, waving and crying, and Lala tried to comfort them. As cruel as she was to others, she loved her sons and didn't like to see them in tears.

Father Antonio gave me a slight, final wave, and a small smile, and then they were out of sight, leaving me standing there in the midst of the truck's exhaust – alone by the church. I was never to see them again though I have never forgotten what I endured in the time I spent in their home. I was there for more than two years I think, and there were times when it seemed even longer. Now that they had gone west, after the Germans, I was on my own again, with nowhere to turn.

Finally I pulled myself together and went to Banushka's house. I told her what had happened, that the priest and his family had run away, and she said she wasn't surprised because the Bolsheviks hated priests. I wondered what would now happen to the Catholic priest who tended to our spiritual needs and she just shrugged. "Where can he go?" she asked.

"West to the Germans," I offered, "like Father Antonio."

"I don't think the Germans will be able to help anyone now," Banushka said.

We Poles in the area were all glad the Germans had gone though the Ukrainians were more conflicted. They had sided with the Germans and done much of their dirty work for them and did not expect kindness from the returning Russians. When the Russians finally began pouring in, a day or so later, I was beside myself with happiness to see their long lines of grim-looking, battle hardened troops. They looked dirty and exhausted but unlike the first time I had seen Russian soldiers, these had the look of hard men and hard women, for there were women in their ranks now, too. They were the people who had beaten the great Nazi war machine. And they knew it.

I didn't want to remain with Banushka's family again because of what had happened before with her brother so I began asking around everywhere if anyone needed a girl in their household to help with family chores. Through Banushka and some of her friends I found two unmarried Polish sisters. They lived with their elderly mother, Helena, near our street.

Zoschia Dumbrowski was about fifty-five years of age and her sister, Juzia, about fifty-two. They earned their living as local teachers but their mother, who was about seventy-five, was sick with diabetes and needed a great deal of personal care. Since they were out of their house for most of each day, they needed someone to be her caregiver. When I heard about this, I went to their home and offered my services. After asking me a few questions they offered me the job. They already knew me from church, having seen me there on Sundays, and they knew, as well, that I had been working for the Ukrainian priest and his family until they had decided to leave. In those days these were very good recommendations if you wanted to hire someone so they took me on right away.

Zoschia taught me how to administer the insulin shots to her mother and I moved in with them and promptly took over responsibility for the old woman's care while Zoschia and Juzia were teaching during the days in the local school. Russians troops were now pouring steadily into our area, almost daily, going west, following the Germans who were at last in full retreat. The Communist authorities quickly established their control of Podhajce and we soon had a new set of officials to deal with, new rulers to replace Major Kleinecke and his kind. But for Jews, at least, things were a thousand times better since the Communists were not committed to our destruction as the Germans had been. In fact, they welcomed us back into society. I heard that Jews who had gone into hiding when the Nazis had begun the killings were starting to return. But I decided to continue to pretend I was a Catholic Pole, afraid of giving up an identity that had saved me for so long at that point.

It was around this time that I had to see a dentist and went to Dr. Kleiman's office. Like many Jews, he had returned to his home and, after a short time, begun practicing again. You had to make a living no matter what, after all, and a dentist is a dentist whether Jew or otherwise. I never said anything to him about being a Jew myself, of course, and continued to wear my cross and go by the name of Wanda Madeira, even after the Russians arrived. I knew anti-Semitism was not only found among the Ukrainians, since many Poles, too, harbored a resentment of Jews. The only people I had now were the Poles I had come to know in church and in the general area and I didn't think it would do to reveal that I was not really one of them after all.

Dr. Kleiman, for his part, never let on that he knew me from the priest's house or that he suspected me of having been there under false pretenses. He was very professional, as unsure of what the future might bring, I suppose, as I was, and so he preferred to keep silent about his suspicions about me when I was there in his office. He just examined my teeth and filled the cavities I had developed over the years when I had had no access to dentists and such. That was the entire extent of our contact at that time so you can imagine how surprised I was to have run into him years later in New York and to have him tell me about those days in Podhajce. Our world had been terribly disrupted during the war years and Dr. Kleiman had witnessed it with me.

The Dumbrowski sisters and their mother were not well off. They had no running water in their home so I had to pump it from the well outside and heat whatever I brought in on the wooden stove, if that was needed. I did all the household chores, washing their clothing in a tin basin with a scrubbing board. To soften the water I would add ashes from their oven. It was not easy in those years, especially in that part of Poland in the midst of the war. But I was determined to get on wherever I found myself.

Still I found time to write to Kolomyia, which I had heard was now completely free from the Germans. I wrote a number of letters to some of my old friends, one to Janka Bielinski who lived on my old street. I was hoping someone could tell me if any of my family had returned to the *korchma* because I had begun to think, more and more, about finally returning. First, though, I wanted to find out what was happening there, to learn if it was safe to go back.

But none of these letters were ever answered. Perhaps it was all the disruptions from the war, because the fighting was still going on, to our west, at that time. The postal system was now under the Russian authorities and they were more interested in beating the Germans than anything else. Without an answer I thought it was better to remain in Podhajce and continue to be Wanda Madeira and so I continued to live there with the Dumbrowski sisters, caring for their invalid mother and keeping house for them. But at night I was beginning to have dreams again of those I had left behind in Kolomyia.

One morning, before I had fully awakened, I heard a fierce knocking on our door. I pulled on my clothes and made my way to the front of the house. The old woman, Helena, was still asleep and no one else seemed to be about. Both Zoschia and Juzia had apparently gone out early so I went to the door and opened it. I was surprised to see the little man who was the principal of the local school there, Ivan. He was standing in the open doorway, looking at me.

"Wanda," he said, breathing fast. I could see he was trying to catch his breath. "Wanda," he repeated, "you have to run, get out of here now."

"What?" I asked. I was completely confused by his words.

"Run," he said again, as though he could think of nothing else. "They just shot Zoschia and Juzia for spies. They'll be coming here next to take you, too."

"Spies?" I said. "How can that be? What have I done?"

"It doesn't matter, Wanda," he said, trying desperately to make me understand. "Zoschia and Juzia had a radio in the basement and it was discovered. They were sending messages to the Polish underground and the Russians found out. They won't tolerate spies. They'll shoot everyone in the house."

"But I'm not . . . I don't know anything about a radio," I tried to explain to him.

"It doesn't matter," he said. "They won't believe you. You have to get out of here. Don't waste time. Run."

Ivan's face was so pale and his look of concern so sincere that I could no longer doubt his words. I ran for my jacket, the same one my brother Samuel had given me years before, and grabbed a few things and ran out of the house. Ivan was already gone when I left, afraid to be found there by the authorities I guessed.

I couldn't believe what had occurred. The two sisters shot? What would happen now to their mother? But I couldn't concern myself with such things. I just ran out onto the road, as Ivan had urged me, and started walking away as fast as I could, towards the nearby town of Brzezany. Some three years after running away from the Kolomyia ghetto, I was all alone and on the road again.

I was eighteen years old.

Chapter 22

The Road Home

I FOUND it surprisingly easy to be traveling again after all this time. I wasn't worried about discovery by the Germans any longer, of course, and was now just another Pole on the road. Naturally, there were the disruptions of war to contend with but the Russians were not the Germans and I felt many times safer, despite the brutality directed against the Dumbrowski sisters that I had learned about in Podhajce.

I walked and hitched my way toward Brzezany and found a Polish family there to take me in for the night. They let me sleep on their kitchen floor and I left the following morning. After that I was walking along the road until I came to a place where there was a young woman who was traveling on the road as I was, a Ukrainian nun. I stopped to speak with her and she told me her name was Anya. I was badly in need of a friend by this point and was glad of any company and so I said I'd like to travel with her if she were willing. She seemed glad of my presence, too, and so we took to the road together somewhere outside Brzezany.

We walked and hitched for a while and I learned a great deal about her as we waited, sometimes for hours, for rides from the military vehicles that were moving back and forth along the roads. Anya told me she had been forced to become a nun because she had become pregnant and given birth to an illegitimate child some three years before. I explained that I was from Podhajce where I had been working for a number of years for the Ukrainian priest in that town but was now trying to get back to my hometown of Kolomyia. It was all I could think of, once I had left Podhajce for good. Besides there wasn't anywhere else I could go.

I learned that Anya was headed to Lvov and I thought that as good a destination as any for the time being. She said I could get to Kolomyia from there though it was somewhat roundabout and so I decided to stick with her, at least until we reached Lvov. It was good to have someone else to share things with and I felt much safer in her presence, especially since she was a nun and both Ukrainians and Poles tended to be deferential to her.

Thanks to Anya, who came from a Ukrainian farm in Prohoslavna, we were able to find a welcome at many of the farms along the way. With her convent clothes and my tin cross, we were both accepted as fellow Christians and I even ceased thinking of myself as a Jew while on the road with her. It wasn't so hard because I had almost lost myself in my identity as Wanda over the preceding few years anyway. In fact, it seemed a lifetime ago, or more, that I had even been a Jew at all.

We went first to the city of Zloczow and from there made our way to Lvov. This latter town was quite a large city and reminded me a lot of Kolomyia. Anya invited me to stay at her convent and I slept the night we arrived in Lvov in one of the convent cells with her. We shared a small cot, because there were no better accommodations. That night I dreamed of my brother Samuel in his hole in the ground in Piadyki, and of my sister, Feiga, left behind in the Kolomyia ghetto. Perhaps it was the close quarters of the convent cell – or the austereness of the place, which lent everything a kind of strangeness, but I slept uneasily and couldn't drive the images of my brother or sister away.

The following day I told Anya that I had to go on to Kolomyia right away and she got me some breakfast and then walked with me along the road leading out of the city. There we said good-by to one another, having grown quite close during our brief time on the road together. We were both sorry to have to part so soon. I promised to stay in touch with her and we embraced and shed our tears together. The war years were hard for everyone and, though we had only been together a short time, we had become friends. But travelers on the road must often go their separate ways and I was determined to find my way home again.

I couldn't tell Anya why I was so set on returning to Kolomyia, of course. Perhaps she would have understood but you can never be sure. As a Polish Catholic girl I was her friend, but would she have felt the same toward me if she had known I was a fraud, that I was really a Jew who had been pretending all these years to be something else?

Anya showed me the best place on that road to find a hitch and stayed with me until a Russian army truck finally stopped to give me a lift. Then we kissed once in parting and I waved to her as the vehicle I was on drove off, watching her finally turn back and head toward her convent again.

I never saw her after that but I remember her many kindnesses and the joy of having found a friend like her on the road to this day.

The Russian soldiers who gave me that first hitch were going from Lvov to Lichakov. They weren't especially talkative but that was fine with me because I didn't want to do a lot of talking either. It was still early morning and I had a lot to sort out in my mind. I was also a little afraid to strike up conversations with any of these young men because a young girl on her own can't be too careful, especially in wartime. Still these Russian boys were generally very nice and understanding. For the most part most of those who transported me on the road back to Kolomyia were polite and left me to myself.

From Lichakov, I walked and hitched, by turns, to the town of Tshmenitze and then to Stanislavov. In one vehicle, a kind of jeep, one soldier sat in the back with me listening to his radio and passing information on to his comrades in the front seat. I listened, too, to the radio messages as they came in. I could see that they were communicating with other Russian units in the east, the area that I had just come from. I heard the reports that were coming in with some fear. Other Russian units were reporting Ukrainian partisan activity against the Russians in the area and said these Ukrainian units were killing all the Poles and Jews they could find. It was plain the Ukrainians weren't as pleased with the German retreat as some others were, nor were they happy at the return of the Russians. Worst of all, I realized, the ethnic hatred that had fueled and aided the Nazis' efforts against my own people had not abated in the least.

At Stanislavov, the Russians I was riding with let me off, saying they were no longer going in my direction so I thanked them and started walking again, maybe twenty kilometers this time, until I was finally able to wave down another military vehicle. I asked if they were going to Kolomyia but they said no, only as far as Verbizh. But that, I knew, was not far at all since Verbizh was within walking distance of my old hometown. I said Verbizh would be fine and took the ride they offered. My heart was jumping in my chest at the thought of being so close at last to Kolomyia.

They let me off outside Verbizh, as they had promised. It was morning by this time and they shared a little bread with me by way of breakfast. Besides this, I had barely eaten anything since leaving the convent at Lvov. I was so hungry but I didn't want to wait any longer and so I quickly started walking through Verbizh, toward Kolomyia. I was tired from all the traveling but so excited to be near my home again that I just kept walking despite my rebellious belly which was crying out for some kind of food.

I had to walk for several hours from Verbizh to Kolomyia but I didn't let that stop me either. I could almost feel how close I was now.

I knew I had to reach Sobieskego Street which ran out of Kolomyia toward Verbizh. After a while my feet began to hurt me terribly. The shoes were badly worn down as I hadn't been able to replace them in quite some time so I stopped and I took them off and continued along the road barefoot.

By early afternoon I came to the outskirts of Kolomyia and stopped the first Polish man I saw and asked him how to find Sobieskego Street.

He smiled and said you're on it girl. I just looked all around me in surprise. I told him I wanted to find the central marketplace, the Rinecke it was called.

"Go straight on Sobieskego and you can't miss it," he said.

I could barely contain my happiness. I hadn't recognized the street at first but was now almost floating as I ran along it. I walked straight into the city and tried to orient myself. Everything looked well cared for, clean and maintained, but I was unfamiliar with the part of the city in which I now found myself. Confused by the unfamiliar surroundings but excited to have made it back to Kolomyia, I pressed onward until I came to the municipal center where the government buildings were. There, finally, I began to recognize my surroundings. From the city center I knew how to find the central marketplace, the Rinecke, where my brother and other family members used to go to do their business.

It was to the Rinecke that the farmers and traders all used to go, and where they would be coming from in the days before the war when people used to stop by our little inn for food and drink or an overnight bed. I wanted to cry as I thought about those days and my family and friends and the life I had lived in our little *korchma*. I could barely hold myself back as I began to recognize the streets and buildings at last. Things hadn't changed so much, I thought, and there were tears in my eyes the further into the city I went.

Here and there I could still see traces of the barbed wire fencing the Nazis had put up but most of it had already been torn down. I couldn't believe that after almost three years I had come home again.

Life had returned to Kolomyia. When I finally saw the central market area ahead of me I just stopped in my tracks and stared. There were people everywhere, just like there used to be, though things did look a little grimier than I recalled. There were farmers and tradesmen hawking their goods and people moving among the stalls, testing and examining, and sometimes dickering for this or that. I made my way into the middle of the market, looking all around as I walked. The smells hit me first. The horse sweat and manure, the leather goods, the fresh produce from the nearby farms. It was all as I remembered. And there were Jews there, too. I was astonished to see Jewish faces again, it had been so long. One woman, rather stout and about sixtyish who was drably dressed saw me walking aimlessly around and came toward me. She introduced herself as Mrs. Marksheit, a Jewish woman she said, only recently returned from Russia where she had spent the war years. "If you need anything, a place to stay, anything," she said to me, "I can help you. My husband and I are working to help Jews who were displaced by the Germans."

I touched my neck and realized my little cross had fallen under my shirt. She had guessed I was another returning Jew. I left the cross where it had lodged and thanked her for her kindness. "Where . . . where can I find you again?" I stammered in answer.

"Here in the marketplace," she smiled. "I'm here every day. Just come and we'll see what we can do for you."

I thanked her again and hurried away, through the market area, breathing in the many and varied odors of the place, and heading for the central train station, the hub of old Kolomyia. Just beyond the train station Kozcaczwka Street began, I knew, and that was where I wanted to go. When I passed the rail tracks and saw my old street, I felt a great sense of relief, a feeling that I had indeed come home. That street looked so familiar to me as I finally turned onto it, all the memories of my childhood rushing back.

Kozcaczwka Street hadn't changed much from what I could see. As I walked along the road the old houses were all still there, just as I remembered them. Here and there a few looked abandoned and some had seemingly fallen into disrepair. But otherwise things were as I remembered. They were, that is, until I finally I came to a point where I could see our old house down the road. I hesitated, unsure of what would be waiting for me, but I had so many thoughts, so many dreams, such expectations. I couldn't stop myself from rushing toward the old inn. But the closer I drew to it the more concerned I became. The inn didn't look right to me. A wooden, clapboard structure, unpainted and set back from the road, it should have loomed larger as I got nearer but instead I thought I could see daylight coming from the middle of it. Its roof seemed to have been torn away. When I got close enough to it, I could see that it had been partly demolished and that part of the old driveway was covered in rubble. The well in front still seemed to be intact, but the front of the building had been removed and there was nothing between the two exterior walls which still stood on either side. There was no house left.

For the first time it really hit me that there was nothing there to come home to. Until that moment I had been thinking only about coming back. I hadn't given much thought as to what that would mean, to what, if anything, would still be left. I had believed I had a place to go back to and that, when I reached it, my journey would be over. But now I saw that there was no substance to my dream. Behind me I thought I heard a voice calling and I looked around. It was one of our old Polish neighbors, a woman I had known while growing up and she was coming toward me, staring. "Mutzka, is that you?" she was saying. "You're still alive?"

I just looked at her. I couldn't think of anything to say in response.

"What are you doing still alive?" she kept speaking as she drew closer to me. "How did you survive?" She didn't seem happy to see me there, in the flesh, but only perplexed that I was there at all.

I shrugged and said, "Yes, I'm back. I'm looking for my mother and sisters. Do you know if they're alive?" I wanted to say more to her but couldn't think of anything else.

She just kept standing there, looking at me, shaking her head. "I can't believe you're still alive," she was saying. Then she added, as if finally hearing my question, "No. No one else has come back."

I wanted to cry. I didn't know where to turn.

Suddenly I realized how hungry I was. I hadn't eaten anything since the morning when the driver who had let me off at Verbizh had shared a piece of stale bread with me for breakfast. And I was so thirsty. I just stood there, looking at this woman, aware of how forlorn I must appear in her eyes. I saw that she was already turning away from me and thought, why don't you speak, why don't you invite me in . . . a little food or something to drink, anything . . . I kept repeating these questions in my mind as she walked away. I dared not voice them because I didn't want her to think I was begging.

As I looked around, I saw others standing nearby, too, people I had known years before. They must have recognized me because they looked straight at me, as if in surprise, but no one waved to me over or tried to speak to me or offered to take me in. Not even a bit of food or something to drink. I was almost nineteen now, a grown woman, and I was still alone.

There was one place I knew I could still go. I touched the little tin cross that was still hidden behind my shirt and turned my steps toward the Madeira house by the river. Wanda, if she were still there, would take me in I knew. I was so tired and thirsty by this point that I thought for a moment I might run down to the river and throw myself down on its bank and drink from there but I decided first to go to my long time friend, the girl whose many kindnesses had saved my life before. As I walked along the dirt road that led up to the Madeira house from Kozcaczwka Street I couldn't help thinking about the many happy days we had all known as children playing along the river bank and how often I had run with Wanda along this very roadway up to her home or back again to our little inn. It all seemed so long ago and I had banished it from my mind for so long and suddenly I was here again. I was Mutzka, no longer a Polish girl named Wanda, a different person and yet the same, a girl who had lived in fear of the Germans but had done so in their shadow, shining their boots and keeping her silence, mutely witnessing the indiscretions of a priest's wife. I had been silent about so much for so long.

Wanda's house and the smokehouses, where they made the sausages and kielbasa, came into view. These looked no different than I remembered them, unlike my own home which was now nothing but a hollowed-out shell, empty of people and of the things the people I had loved had once filled it with. I quickened my steps because of the hunger and thirst I was feeling. It was late in the afternoon by this time and I had been on the road for a lifetime, or so it seemed to me.

As I approached the house I couldn't help thinking about the last time I had come there looking for help. I had been little Mutzka then, running from the Germans, desperately trying to save herself, her family lost, not knowing where to turn. How were things any different now I wondered? True, the Germans were gone and I had no reason to fear that anyone would grab and imprison me any longer, or try to kill me just because of who I was. The Russians were difficult to live under but they were difficult for everyone equally, not like the Germans who had seemed to have a special place reserved in their hearts for hating Jews. But here I was, still alone and without anyone to turn to. I was sure, though, that if anyone would help me, it would be Wanda.

But I was worried. What if Wanda were no longer living here? While Kolomyia had seemingly returned to some semblance of normalcy, it certainly wasn't the same as it had been. Many things were changed. I had seen that on the long walk back and especially now, in the faces of so many of my former neighbors. In only a few years they seemed to have forgotten us, forgotten the inn which Mama had operated for so many years on this very road, and forgotten my sisters and brothers who had grown up here. They, had, it seemed, forgotten all of us.

Suddenly I found myself standing in front of Wanda's old house, facing the front door. I knocked very loudly and waited. I could hear footsteps inside. How many times had I stood outside a door like this and knocked, hoping for the best? How many householders had I appealed to in this way in my years of exile? By now I knew I should have been a seasoned knocker-on-doors but knocking for the first time at any door like this always made me just a little queasy and it did so now, too. You never knew who would appear in the doorway – or what they would say to you.

The door opened slowly and I found myself face to face with Wanda's mother. "Panyi Madeira," I said, almost swallowing my words. "It's me . . ."

She just stared back at me. She was a lean, plain looking woman, her lank hair hanging loosely about her shoulders. Her face was long and almost leathery to look at, like the skins on those sausages she made for sale in her smokehouses. She seemed unsure what to say. I tried to smile but I was sure the dampness in the corners of my eyes gave me away. "I . . . I've come back," I blurted out to her.

"Where did you come from?" She seemed genuinely surprised to see me there now, on her doorstep.

"I was away," I answered. "I couldn't stay in Kolomyia, of course, so I went north. I've been living there."

I was hoping she would ask me to come in but she didn't.

I put one foot on the doorstep, thinking it might prompt her to remember the rules of hospitality but this, too, had no effect.

"Why did you come back?" she asked me suddenly. There seemed to be genuine curiosity and even surprise in her voice.

"My home," I said, "I came home. I . . . I'm looking for my family, for my mother and sisters . . . do you know what happened to them?"

She was shaking her head. "They're gone," she said. "They never came back."

"What about my brother . . . Samuel?" I asked hopefully.

"No one's come back," she said. "Only you . . ." She had her hand on the door and I saw that she was moving to close it in my face.

Desperately I said, "I don't have anyone to turn to . . . I don't know where else to go . . . my house is all broken up."

"People," she said, "have been taking it apart. It's been abandoned for so long. Wood's scarce and there's a lot to rebuild."

"Panyi Madeira," I begged her, "I need a place to stay. I've come so far . . . I haven't eaten . . ."

"I don't know what I can tell you. There's no room here."

"Where can I go, then?" I pleaded.

"There are people in town . . . Jews. Go there and find some of your own kind."

I was astonished at her words. Hadn't I been a Pole for almost three years by then? Didn't I carry a *kenncarte* from the Germans attesting to this. Of course, I couldn't say anything to her of this since my identity card bore her own daughter's name. But I suddenly felt as though I had been cut loose on the fast moving currents of the Prut, a piece of wood or a raft, adrift and captured by currents that were beyond my control. I was on the verge of tears as I saw her again moving to shut the door in my face. I wanted to put my hand out, to stop her, but how could I do that? I couldn't force her to take me in.

Mrs. Madeira's face seemed to soften as she looked at my confusion and distress. "All right, wait a moment," she finally said. Then she shut the door firmly and I heard her footsteps inside, moving away from me. I just stood there as she had directed. What could I say? I had come so far and had thought that, above all else, here in the Madeira household, where I had practically grown up with my friend Wanda, I would find a welcome. Instead I was shut out of the house.

I remembered the time I had spent there, when I had first escaped from the ghetto. Even then I had had to be careful, of course, because Wanda had insisted on hiding my presence from the rest of the family. Soon I heard footsteps returning and the door opened again. Mrs. Madeira had a mug of cool milk and a sandwich in her hand. "Here," she said, thrusting these at me. "This is all I can give you. But you can't stay . . ."

I took the milk and drank it down and bit into the sandwich. It was made with some strips of ham and a little cheese. It tasted delicious after all the hours I had gone since I had last had anything to eat or drink.

"You can't stay here," Mrs. Madeira warned me again as I finished the last of the milk, an air of finality in her voice.

"Where am I to go, then?" I asked her.

Her features were fixed, unmoving. She acted as though she hadn't heard my words. Behind the half-closed door I heard more footsteps. Another shadow and then the door was pulled open a little farther and I saw another face looking at me. It was Wanda. She was a young woman, taller than I remembered, hair bound back, her face more mature, but there was no mistaking her features. I realized then that I must look as different to her as she now did to me.

As she stared I quickly wiped my face to brush away the cheese and milk residue on my lips. I felt like a girl again, but wanted to be a woman in her eyes as she now was in mine. She was smiling. Her mother moved aside, a stern look still clouding her features, and Wanda stepped across the threshold to join me on the stoop. We looked at each other and suddenly we were both grinning and giggling like we used to. She said "Mutzka, it's you! You're back. I knew you'd be the one. I knew if anyone could come back it'd be you."

Suddenly we were clasping hands like schoolgirls again, her mother shutting the door behind us.

But Wanda was laughing. “Tell me everything Mutzka, everything,” she said.

Chapter 23

Beginning Anew

WE WALKED around outside, between the barn and the house, and Wanda plied me with questions. I told her everything I could in the short time we had and Wanda shook her head in amazement as she listened to my story. I couldn't tell her all of it, of course. The time was too brief. But I was able to recount quite a bit and finally, when I'd finished, she sighed and said, "Well at least you've come home, Mutzka."

I replied that I hoped this was so but added that my house was now gone. "And I have no idea what's become of my mother and sisters, or of my brother Samuel either," I said. "I know he was in hiding. He'll be looking for me, I know. And my sister in Horodenka. . . " I let these last words trail off as I found myself remembering Bertha's abandoned house which I'd passed in those first days after my escape from the ghetto. I knew I had to find out if Bertha were all right, too. But I didn't even know where to start.

Wanda said, "We haven't heard anything about any of them but maybe we can find someone who knows." Her words were gentle, even encouraging.

"But I no longer have a place to stay," I pointed out. "My old house . . ."

Wanda looked at me thoughtfully. "Wait here," she said firmly and left me to go back inside.

I waited by the front door of her house, as she had instructed, sitting on the stoop, sometimes getting up and pacing back and forth. I constantly touched the little cross under my shirt, rubbing it as though making a wish in some children's fairy story. I waited for quite a while in this way, alternately sitting and pacing. I couldn't hear any voices from inside. Still, I couldn't help hoping, remembering that Wanda had always been there for me when I had needed her. And didn't I need her more now than ever before?

Wanda took a much longer time to come out than I had expected and when she finally did almost two hours had passed. I was surprised as I carefully studied her face. She looked troubled. When she joined me on the grass she had an apple in her hand and handed it to me. I took a bite and, as I did, I saw that she was shaking her head.

"It's not possible," she said. "You won't be able to stay here."

"Why not?" I asked her. I was surprised at her words. "I don't know where else to go." It was already nearing sundown and I was worrying about finding a place to sleep.

"My mother says we can't risk taking you in. People wouldn't understand. I'm sorry." She looked genuinely unhappy at having to deliver these words.

"But the Germans are gone," I said.

"People will think we hid you during the occupation. Anyone who hid Jews against German orders put the whole community at risk and my mother's afraid people will think we hid you and will blame us for it . . . even though we didn't."

"You helped me," I blurted out.

"I've never told anyone . . . and you shouldn't either," she said, looking around quickly to be sure we hadn't been overheard.

"So what am I going to do?" I asked her.

"Don't worry," said Wanda, brightening, "we've talked it over. I told mother I'll go with you into the city again. There are Jews there. We'll find someone you can stay with."

I didn't know what to say. "Okay, if that's all you can do . . . maybe when I find my family . . ."

"I hope you do," Wanda said.

We started walking back to the road and Wanda was quiet for a while. Finally I couldn't endure the silence between us any longer and said, "What about you, Wanda? What have you been up to in all these years?" I was still very worried about finding my family but I really did want to know more about what had happened to my friend.

Wanda looked at me. "Do you still have my little cross I gave you?" she asked me.

I touched my shirt and quickly took my hand away.

"No," I said. "I lost it on the road." I was afraid she would want it back and, though it was only a little piece of tin, hardly worth anything at all, I had grown very attached to it. It had saved my life so many times.

"Well, it doesn't matter," Wanda said, smiling. "I have others."

I felt ashamed that I had lied to her and thought for a moment I would confess and give it back. But I just couldn't bring myself to do it. That cross had begun to feel as if it were a part of me. I was afraid that giving it back would sap me of the good luck it had brought me. We kept walking in silence. Finally Wanda said: "I got married, Mutzka."

I stopped on the road. "Married? To whom? Where is he now?"

Wanda laughed. "You remember Kazhik, the little boy who used to work for us?"

"He was a very hard worker," I said. "But not so smart."

"Well I married him."

"I'm sorry," I said.

"Don't be," she laughed. "You're right. He wasn't. But Mama liked him and thought he'd be good for me. She was afraid I had become too wild and she wanted me to settle down. Kazhik was here and very reliable and Mama liked him. She convinced me to agree to marry him so I did."

"What happened?" I asked her.

"He's gone," said Wanda.

"Gone?"

"Yes, the Russians drafted him when they took over. They put him in the army and sent him to fight. I haven't heard anything since."

"Sorry," I blurted out again.

"Well, maybe he'll come back," Wanda said.

But she didn't seem broken up by her loss to me.

"What of your sister Angela?" I asked.

"She's all right," said Wanda quickly.

"And her husband?" I pressed. Angela had married Jaschek Hudema, the younger brother of that same Rudeck Hudema who had courted my own sister, Regina, so many years ago.

"Jaschek's in hiding," said Wanda.

"Hiding?"

"He was working for the Germans and the Russians found out about it. Now they want to arrest him but he's staying out of sight. He's still around though."

"Oh," I said, remembering what the Russians had done to the Dumbrowski sisters in Podhajce.

"Everything's changed, hasn't it?" Wanda said, taking my hand.

I held tightly to hers as we walked.

"Yes," I said, "everything."

The walk back to the central market brought back many old memories and I struggled to push them aside. I had averted my eyes when we had walked past the old *korchma* and now I felt like I should be averting my eyes from everything. It was Kolomyia all right, the city I had lived my childhood in, but it wasn't the same. It no longer felt like my home and only Wanda beside me allowed me to feel that I had any friends left in the city at all. We hiked straight past the train station and headed for the market. It was getting late in the day and I was becoming very nervous. If Wanda's family wouldn't take me in, who would? Wanda, I think, could see how uneasy I was and she did whatever she could to encourage me. At one point she whispered not to worry, that she would stay by me as long as it took.

But, in fact, it was not to take very long at all. As soon as we entered the market area I saw a familiar face, an old friend from my days in the Jewish gymnasium. Her name was Hilda Spiegel and she was a year older than I was. A little taller with blonde braids, I recognized her as soon as I saw her looking at me and we started walking towards one another. Wanda followed beside me and Hilda came running over and said, "Hello, Mutzka. Where have you been?"

It was a strange question, as though I had been away on a short vacation. But everything was so strange in those days. I said that I had been in another city, Podhajce, and that I had only that day returned to Kolomyia. Then I introduced Wanda to her. They didn't know each other because Wanda, being Polish in background, had not gone to the same school with us after the Russians came. But they seemed to get on. I hurriedly told Hilda my predicament, that I had no place to stay the night and that Wanda had promised to help me find somewhere.

Hilda listened and finally said, “You'll stay with us. We have a little house in town, just my mother and father and two brothers.”

“You're all . . . you're all right?” I asked, incredulous.

“We hid from the Germans,” Hilda said. “We stayed out of the ghetto.”

“How?” I asked. I couldn't believe it.

Hilda looked at Wanda and said she would tell me all about it later on but that if I wanted to stay with them I had to come with her now because it was getting dark. I could see that she was uneasy talking about how they had survived in front of a non-Jew. I turned to Wanda and thanked her for coming with me to the market. “You had better go back,” I said to her. “It's getting dark and your mother will be worried.”

“All right,” she said. “I'm glad you found someone to take you in so quickly. She turned to Hilda and said, “Take care of our little Mutzka. She's seen a lot.”

Hilda said: “Haven't we all?”

Then Wanda turned to go back as she had come and I waved at her retreating form. When she looked around, she gave me an answering wave and then she disappeared in the crowd, heading back towards the train tracks.

After she was gone I asked Hilda again how they had survived.

“Many people survived,” Hilda said. “If you had some money you could find a place, people willing to take you in. My father found a family in Piadyki, Polish people, who hid us in their attic.”

“All these years?” I asked.

“From the time the Germans started rounding up the Jews. They had an attic and lived in an isolated part of Piadyki. We had to pay them an awful lot but they were taking a big chance, too. We didn't come out for almost three years.”

I thought about my brother Samuel.

“My brother was in hiding in Piadyki, too,” I said. “Did you ever hear anything about him?”

“What was his name?”

“Samuel . . . Samuel Feuer,” I said.

“I remember the name,” she said, looking at me intently. “He was in the wheat business like my father, right?” But it was more statement than question.

“Yes,” I answered, “that’s him. He did very well in wheat before the Russians came.”

“I do remember his name,” she said thoughtfully. Then: “We never heard anything about him though. Are you sure he was in Piadyki?”

“I visited him there when I ran away from the ghetto.”

“Well, you were lucky to have gotten away,” she said. “Those who didn’t . . .” But she couldn’t bring herself to finish her thought.

Chapter 24

Loose Ends

HILDA'S FAMILY took me in without any apparent qualms. Her mother, named Regina like my oldest sister, was an especially wonderful woman and went out of her way to make me feel part of the family. In exchange for my bed and board, I did household chores. I was used to that anyway from my years in Podhajce and they were a well-off family, always used to having servants. Their house was small but they gave me a place of my own in which to sleep. Hilda's father was named Salek and her two brothers were Benya and Herman. They all made me feel welcome, except for Hilda's father, Salek, who was concerned about having another mouth to feed. Still, Regina Spiegel would not turn me out and insisted that I stay with them, at least at the beginning.

The very next day when I woke I decided I had to start trying to put my life back together. The first thing I did after breakfast was go back to the market. I found Mrs. Marksheit and told her where I was staying. She said they wanted to register me as a returning Jew and I agreed so she brought me to a nearby table where a man was sitting, introducing him as her husband. Mr. Marksheit was very kind and took out a big ledger and asked me for details about myself and my family. I gave him my name and where I was then living and also the names of my missing family members. I told him everything and watched as he made notes. He and his wife were very encouraging and said they would do what they could to find my mother and sisters and my brother Samuel and I thanked them and left. But the more I thought about it the more I realized I couldn't just sit around waiting for someone to bring me news of what had happened. I was used to being on my own by then but I missed my family terribly, the more so as I had now returned to Kolomyia and everything I saw in the streets of that city reminded me of them.

I told my friend, Hilda, that I had decided that I was going to go back to Kozcaczwka Street to take care of a few things and to try to find out what I could about my family and she asked if I wanted her to come along.

"You can, if you like," I said and so, by late morning, we were heading away from the marketplace again, back to the street where I had grown up.

Returning to Kozcaczwka Street had become terribly hard for me but it was also a familiar road and so it caused me both pain and pleasure simultaneously. The hardest part was passing the old *korchma* again, seeing it partially demolished, knowing that I could never go back to it and fearing that, perhaps, there was no one left to go back to it with. Hilda, who had survived the German occupation in hiding with her entire family simply could not understand what I felt as we passed that old inn of ours. She could not imagine, I thought, what it was like to be without those you loved. But she tried to be encouraging and I appreciated her companionship, and her silence when we passed by the inn.

I went to the Bielinski home because they lived across the road from our house and knocked on the door. Panyi Bielinski answered and let us in. I asked if Janka was around because she was the person I had written to from Podhajce after the Kosars had fled and her mother called her out. We spoke briefly though Janka was kind of distant. She said she had gotten my letter and written back to tell me no one from my family had returned. But I had never received that letter. I figured it had arrived in Podhajce after I'd had to run away from the authorities that morning when I learned of the execution of the Dumbrowski sisters.

I said: "I still have to find out, Janka. I have to know where my family is. So many Jews survived," I said. "Maybe they did, too."

Janka shook her head and I could see that Panyi Bielinski also had a very downcast look in her eyes. I just stood there, not wanting to leave. "I have to know," I insisted. "It's my mother and sisters . . ."

Panyi Bielinski said that I should wait a moment so I did, with Hilda and Janka standing quietly beside me in the hallway. Neither seemed to have much to say and it was very awkward. Finally, Panyi Bielinski returned and said I could follow her. She led me into their living room and I saw Mr. Bielinski sitting in a big chair. He looked much older than I remembered him and very frail. He had always been a kind man. He said, "Hello, Mutzka. It's good you've come back."

"Thank you Pan Bielinski," I said. "I'm trying to find out about my family though . . . no one seems to have any information about them . . . and our house, it's gone . . ."

"People have been taking it apart, I'm afraid," he said. "No one thought anyone would ever come back to claim it . . ."

"My mother would," I said. "She and Gusta were taken away by the Germans but Feigie was still there when I left . . ."

"Mutzka," Mr. Bielinski said, "I saw your mother . . . and Gusta."

"Where?" I asked eagerly. "When?"

"On the train," Mr. Bielinski whispered. His voice was very hoarse and he started to cough, as though his throat had seized up and would not let him express the words he wanted to speak.

"How were they?" I asked him.

"Mutzka," he said, "they were put on the train . . . in a freight car. It was in the night. You know, I work on the trains. I was there when they were put on board . . . with all the others."

"I don't understand . . ," I said.

"They took them away, Mutzka. The train took them to Belzec." He began to cough again. His eyes were wet. "Your mother saw me and said Pan Bielinski, if you ever see any of my children, if someday you see some of them . . . tell them you saw us here, that we said good-bye."

Mr. Bielinski was crying as he recounted my mother's last words to me. "I could do nothing Mutzka, you understand?" he said. "There was nothing anyone could do. We worked on the trains but the Germans had guns and they were everywhere."

"They took Mama to Belzec?" I said still not fully comprehending.

"Yes . . . and Gusta too . . . and the boy. They packed the train with people from the ghetto and shipped them out in the middle of the night. No one's come back from there . . . from Belzec."

I fell silent. By then we had all heard of places like the camp at Belzec, places of death, places where people just disappeared. No one liked to talk about such things but the rumors were everywhere and the names of the places were known.

"What should I do?" I asked finally, not knowing what else to say.

"Mutzka," said Pan Bielinski, "you have to move on. You can't bring them back. . ."

I was crying now as I stood there in front of Mr. Bielinski. He was too. So, too, were Hilda and Janka and Panyi Bielinski. All of us. At last Mr. Bielinski turned his face away and I could hear him coughing quietly in the shadow of the chair in which he was sitting. "There wasn't anything any of us could do." He just kept repeating this over and over into the arm of his chair.

"What do I do now?" I asked finally, knowing no one could give me an answer.

Mr. Bielinski caught himself and looked up at me. "You still have that house," he said, "what's left of it. You'll need money. I'll tell people you're back and that it's yours. No one will do anymore damage to it. You can sell what's left. I'll see you get paid for any materials they take from it. You can't live there anymore and there's no sense trying to rebuild it but the wood is worth something."

"I don't know where to go . . . what to do," I whispered.

Hilda said, "You'll come back with me of course. You're not alone here, Mutzka."

"I need to find out what happened to the others," I finally blurted out. "My brother Samuel. He was hiding in Piadyki. And my sister Feigie. I left her in the ghetto. And Bertha . . . she was . . . she was in Horodenka."

Mr. Bielinski said, "The ghetto burned," Mutzka. "Everyone in it . . ."

"Maybe they got out," I said, "maybe Feigie found a way."

"If she did, she never came back here," Mrs. Bielinski put in gently.

I felt weak all over and put my hand out, leaning on a small table. I said, "I have to find out what I can, Pan Bielinski. Will you help me?"

"I don't know anymore than what I've already told you," he said. "I'm so sorry. Terrible things have happened . . ."

"But who can tell me about the others? My brother . . ."

"Mutzka," he said, "you have to make the best of this . . ."

"I can't Pan Bielinski," I said, "not until I know . . ."

He tried to rise but I could see he was so frail that he lacked the strength for it. He was no longer a well man.

"Look," he said finally, sitting back down, "do you remember Panyi Chanowska?"

I nodded. She was an old woman who lived on Kozcaczwka Street, not far from the Bielinskis. She was not well off and lived by herself.

"I think she saw something," Mr. Bielinski explained. "She may know something about what happened to your brother. You can go to her and ask. Perhaps she can give you more information."

Panyi Bielinski was nodding her head as her husband spoke. I think she was worried about his condition because he seemed so weak. I could see she wanted me to go so I thanked Mr. Bielinski and wiped my eyes. He was wiping his, too, as I walked toward the door. Janka walked with us to the front of the house and I could see her younger sister, Staszia, peering around one corner, staring. Outside in the bright daylight I couldn't stop blinking my eyes and Hilda said "What do you want to do now, Mutzka?"

I said, "We'll go to Panyi Chanowska and speak with her."

Her house was rundown and in really deplorable condition. When she answered the door in response to my insistent knocking she just stood there, glowering at us. I knew she recognized me but she didn't seem to want to speak with us. She was very stooped over because she suffered from an arthritic hip. She had always been a poor woman and she seemed in no better condition now. I told her who I was and reminded her that I had been a neighbor, that my mother had owned the *korchma* down the street, but it seemed to make no impression on her. Finally I just came to the point. I said I wanted to find out what had happened to my brother, Samuel Feuer, who had lived in Piadyki and that I was sure she remembered him. I said that Pan Bielinski had assured me she knew something about what had happened to him.

The old woman tried to shut the door in our faces but I pushed my hand out and held it open. She was not very strong and couldn't force it closed as long as I kept my hand there. "Please, Panyi Chanowski," I begged. "If you know anything, you must tell me. I have a right to know . . ."

"I don't know anything about it," the old woman told me firmly. "How would I?"

"Pan Bielinski said you saw something," I replied.

"Well, how would he know?" she hissed.

"Please, tell me what you know," I repeated, desperate.

The old woman seemed at a loss. She couldn't push the door closed with my hand on it and she couldn't get me to go away. I saw her eyes darting around, as though she were afraid to be even seen talking with us.

"Panyi Chanowski," I said to her suddenly, "you know, maybe I can pay you something if you can tell me what happened."

She just stared, but I thought her eyes widened.

"I don't have much, of course," I said hastily, "but I have my mother's house . . . what's left of it . . . and when I sell it I'll have a little money. I'll gladly pay you something if you can tell me about my brother, what happened to him . . ."

"I . . . I can't tell you much," the old woman said after a moment. But I could see that the promise of payment had had an effect.

"I'm very poor," she added, by way of explanation.

"I know," I answered her. "Look, I don't have anything now but I will, and then I'll pay you for what you can tell me. I promise."

I was counting on what Pan Bielinski had said to me about making sure no one else would take apart the *korchma* until they had paid me for it.

The old woman's shoulders seemed to slump as she released the door which, until that moment, she had been pushing against my hand. "It was early in the morning . . ." she finally said.

"What did you see?"

"I had come outside to sweep the steps clean. I was pushing the dirt off the stoop when I saw the wagon going by."

"Who was in it?" I pressed her.

"It was coming from Piadyki," she said, her voice very low, almost swallowing her words. "Your brother . . . I saw him and his wife and the two boys. Nikolai, the one-armed fellow who used to do odd jobs for people . . . he was driving the horses. There was a Ukrainian militiaman on the seat beside him. And an armed German soldier on a motorcycle behind them."

"How did you know it was my brother?" I asked her.

"He was lying in the wagon," she said, "but his face was turned toward me. The woman and the two children were sitting on his back. The wagon was moving very slowly. The boys . . . they were crying. I put my broom down and went inside. I didn't want them to see me . . . I didn't want any trouble . . ."

"That's all you saw?" I asked.

"Yes. They were coming from Piadyki. One-armed Nikolai was driving. That's all I know. You won't forget your promise . . . to pay me something?"

"No," I assured her. "I'll remember."

I thanked her and we left. She watched us walk off and called after us, reminding me once more of my promise to give her money for the information she had provided.

When we were out of earshot Hilda turned to me and said, "Where do we go now? Do you want to go back home?"

"No," I said. "I want to find Nikolai."

Nikolai was well known to everyone in our part of the city. He was half-Polish, half Ukrainian. I didn't know how he had come to lose his arm but he had been that way for as long as I knew him. Because of this disability he found it hard making a living and would often do little jobs for people, whatever they would pay him for. He was not a bad sort but it was hard making ends meet for people in those days and especially hard for someone like Nikolai. He lived alone in Piadyki so that's where I went, Hilda following along behind me as we crossed the bridge over the Kozcaczwka River.

We found Nikolai by his little shack. He was puttering around outside, doing what few chores needed doing with his single arm. I stood on the street and called his name and when he looked up I saw recognition in his badly shaven face. He walked over to us and stood on the other side of the little fence that separated his grounds from the road. I said, "Do you remember me?"

He nodded and rubbed his chin with his hand.

"I heard you know something about what happened to my brother," I said. "Samuel Feuer, the wheat trader."

"When did you come back?" he asked me slowly.

"Only yesterday," I said. "I've been trying all day to find out what happened to everyone. A woman on Kozcaczwka Street told me she saw you driving my brother and his family . . . in a wagon."

"Yes," he said. "I guess she saw me all right, it's true. I drove the wagon."

"What happened to them?" I said. "I have to find out . . ."

"Some things," he replied, glancing at the empty sky above our heads, "are better not to know."

"Please," I said. "I'm all alone . . . I have to find my brother."

"I'm sorry little girl," he said finally. "You won't find him anymore."

"What happened?" I was afraid of his answer but I had to know.

Nikolai looked very unhappy. He shook his head and said, "You know the old woman, Anna, who was keeping him in Piadyki, hiding him from the Germans?"

"Yes," I answered. "I know her."

"She had a son, not right in the head, Ivan his name was."

"I remember," I said.

"Well, the Germans had taken him away. They sent him off to Germany to work because their own men were all fighting in the army. They didn't bother people like me because . . ." He raised his arm as if showing me his situation for the first time. "But that Ivan," he went on, "well you couldn't see right away that there was anything wrong with him . . . no one knew the old lady was hiding anyone."

I remembered that Anna had refused to allow me to stay with them. She had been afraid that Ivan, her son, would see me and give everything away. "The Germans sent Ivan away then?" I asked.

"Yes, they came and took him and sent him to Germany. But he wasn't any good to them because of his condition. So they let him return home. No one knew that they had released him though. When the Ukrainian militia heard he was back, they thought he had run away from the Germans and went out there, to the old woman's place, to look for him and send him back to Germany."

"Because of that?" I asked, astonished. "They went to find him because they thought he had run away from the Germans?"

"Yes. But they found your brother and his family instead." Nikolai was shaking his head. "They were sitting in the kitchen with the old woman, your brother and the others, warming themselves by the stove. It was in the middle of the winter and very cold, you know. When the militiamen came up to the house and looked inside, through the window, looking for Ivan, they saw your brother Samuel and his family. They knew he didn't belong there and burst in and took them. Then they sent someone to get me, to bring a wagon to take them back into town . . . to Gestapo headquarters."

"Why did they do it?" I asked, not understanding. "They were looking for someone else, for Ivan . . ."

"But they found your brother, a Jew . . ."

"He wasn't hurting anyone. He . . ."

"I'm sorry," Nikolai said. "I shouldn't have told you."

"No, please," I said, "please tell me what you can." I was pleading with him. "What did they do to them?"

"Some things it's better not to know . . ."

"You drove the wagon . . ." I insisted.

"Yes. I didn't want to . . . not when I saw why they had pulled me out of bed. But what could I do?"

"Where did they take them?"

"First to the militia headquarters," Nikolai said slowly. "Then they decided . . . they took them to the Gestapo."

"What did the Germans do?"

"The ghetto was already gone," Nikolai said flatly. "There was no place left for Jews."

"What did they do . . ."

"They had me drive the wagon into the woods." Nikolai stopped. I could see that he didn't want to tell me more but I stood there, refusing to walk away. Finally he shrugged. "They put your brother on his stomach in the wagon and sat the woman and children on his back. The little ones . . . they were crying. They kept saying 'Mama, I'm tired, I want to sleep.'"

"To sleep?" I said.

"She told them 'hush, you'll have time to sleep soon enough'."

I could feel my cheeks wet with tears.

"I drove your brother and his family to a little clearing and then they took thcm out of thc wagon," Nikolai went on, mechanically now. "They made me stay on the wagon. They handed your brother a shovel and told him to start digging. He dug for an hour, maybe longer . . . a big hole. Then they told him to get out of the hole. He was all covered with dirt and sweat. The German who was with them went up to the woman and the two boys and made them stand at the edge of the hole . . . and then . . . he shot them. All three . . ." Nikolai went silent, looking away. Hilda grabbed my hand.

"My brother?" I said angrily. "What about my brother?"

Nikolai looked at me again and hugged himself with his single arm. "Him, too . . . after the woman and boys. Then the German soldier kicked the bodies into the hole and the militiamen took turns with the shovel, burying them all. I'm sorry. I didn't know what they were going to do when I agreed to drive the wagon. I'm ashamed."

I stood there in silence. I couldn't think of anything more to say.

Hilda said "Let's go back home, Mutzka. You can't do anything more here."

"My family. . ." I protested.

"They're gone," Hilda said. "You can't change that . . . or pretend the war never happened."

Chapter 25

Mutzka

MR. BIELINSKI sent a man to see me a day or so later about my house, what was left of it anyway. He said he wanted to buy whatever was still standing because he needed the wood. I was in a terrible state and couldn't think about such things and said yes, of course. I would have agreed to anything at that point. He said he wanted to talk about the price but I told him I couldn't, not then. I was still trying to get over the terrible news I had heard about my brother and the others. I could only imagine how horrible their deaths must have been.

Had my brother been able to persuade the old woman who was hiding him to let me stay as I had wanted him to, I would have been with them, too, when they were found, I knew. I would have been shot with them in the early morning hours beside a hole my brother had been forced to dig with his own hands. I would have been lying there like they were now, one on top of the other in the bottom of an unmarked grave. How strange, I thought, that I, who had had no place to run to, should have survived the war while my brother and sister-in-law and my two little nephews should have been discovered when the war was almost at an end and killed in such a fashion. Nikolai had told me that these events had happened just before the Germans were forced out and the Russians returned. The terrible injustice of it was overwhelming.

If only that foolish son of Anna's, the half-witted Ivan, hadn't come back. If only the militia hadn't gone out looking for him, thinking he was a fugitive, though he hadn't been. If only my brother and his family had stayed in the hole on that night and endured the cold instead of coming out to share the warmth of the old woman's kitchen. If only things had been different. I couldn't rip these thoughts from my mind. I couldn't make them go away. If only things had been different.

But they hadn't. And now Samuel, too, was gone – in the most horrible way.

I sat for days afterwards in the Spiegel house thinking about all these things. I didn't want to go outside or see anyone. Hilda and her mother came to me and tried to console me but I was inconsolable. I couldn't believe that everyone was gone like this: my mother, my sisters, my beloved eldest brother. Others had lived – but not my family. Only I had survived, the youngest, the least important of them all. The more I thought about these things the more I hated myself for having run away, thinking that if only I had stayed I might have saved them. Maybe I could have gotten Feigie to run away with me if I had tried harder or stayed with her a little longer, I thought. Maybe I could have helped Samuel in some way when I had run to him. All I had left of him now was the now worn and somewhat ragged jacket he had taken off his own back to give me – that and the memory of his face on the day when we had said good-bye in the old woman's barn when he urged me to run into the countryside and become a Pole. I wanted to curl up in a tight little ball and never see anyone again. I was ashamed of having been the one who lived.

But my self-pity did not sit well with Mr. Spiegel, Hilda's father, and after my first week with them he decided I could no longer remain. Perhaps it was my sadness that troubled him although he explained this by saying that there were just too many mouths to feed, that times were hard. He said I would need to make other arrangements. I was devastated and didn't know what I was going to do. Fortunately Hilda's mother promised that they wouldn't put me out on the street. She began making inquiries and soon found an elderly Jewish woman in town to take me in. The woman's name was Rosa and she had come to Kolomyia from the western Polish town of Jesczaw on the eve of the Nazi invasion in 1939. She made her living selling religious articles and had come to our city to buy *talises*, the prayer shawls worn by religious Jewish men in the synagogue and when performing their devotions. Kolomyia had been famous for the beauty of its *talises* and Rosa had made the business trip to buy these articles many times before. But this time, when she had come, the Germans and Russians attacked Poland and divided it between them and she had been unable to return to Jesczaw as planned. Instead she remained in Kolomyia and was still there when the Nazis came in 1941, after they attacked the Russians. She was a very cultured, Polish looking lady and did not appear to be Jewish in any obvious way. She had paid a Polish woman to take her in and tell people she was a distant relative. In this way she had lived out the occupation as a Pole, just as I had done. Having no ties in Kolomyia she was able to maintain the fiction of being a gentile and remained largely untouched by the war.

When Hilda's mother brought me to her and explained my circumstances, Rosa took me in at once. I didn't end up on the street as I had feared when Mr. Spiegel had first announced that I would have to leave. Hilda helped me carry my few things to Rosa's home and got me settled in. It was a very rundown place. The people in the area were Polish, not Jews, since Rosa had continued to live among the Poles even after the Germans had gone.

Next door to the house in which Rosa was living, there was a man who was crippled and couldn't walk. He used to drag himself around on his hands and knees to get wherever he needed to go. It was very depressing, watching him, but the worst part was that he had no scruples and was known by everyone to be a great thief. You had to watch your things all the time because of this man, whose name I can no longer recall. He would crawl into your home if he could find a way in and help himself to whatever he could reach. He thought that because of his condition he was justified in stealing from others who were more blessed than he was. And, in truth, it was hard to contest his behavior with him. Who wants to berate such an unfortunate soul?

Rosa proved to be very kind to me, as we were both Jewish women on our own without any family to turn to. I think Rosa had decided just to remain in Kolomyia by that time because all of her family, indeed her very community in the town of Jesczaw, had been obliterated by the Nazis. What did she have to return to?

She did everything she could to cheer me up and her kindness had an effect. Still, I couldn't get my mind off losing my family. Sometimes I would find myself thinking that perhaps Feigie, at least, had survived. Or Bertha. Or Meir. But I knew deep down that the chances were very small. If they had, they would have come back to Kolomyia, as I had done. But none of them had.

Hilda used to come by to look in on me and tell me what was happening in other parts of the city, with the Jews who had returned. Sometimes she would tell me about the doings on Kozcaczwka Street or mention that she had seen Wanda who had asked about me. I was always glad to hear from Wanda, of course, but I had no desire to return to her house after her mother had turned me out. In fact, I never went there again though I continued to see Wanda on occasion in the streets.

We moved in different circles now though, for I was mainly involved with other Jews who had come back while Wanda ran with her Polish friends. She had always been something of a wild girl and now that her husband Kazhik had disappeared, she acted like a single girl again, looking for all the young men and partying with them whenever she could. She liked to have a good time as did so many young people at that time, whether Jew or gentile. The war had been a terrible time for everyone and people needed to feel good again, to forget the destruction and losses we had all endured.

One day when Hilda came by she found me busy cleaning up Rosa's flat. I was in a very somber mood and didn't feel much like talking. I guess she could see how sour I was about things and wanted to cheer me up. She said, come on Mutzka, leave this for now and come with me to the park. There was a large public park nearby, Mieske Park it was called, the young people used to go there to meet one another and to be seen. Especially the girls who were always hoping some of the young men would notice them. I said no, I don't want to go anywhere but Hilda said yes you do and kept pulling my arm and cajoling me. I don't have anything nice to wear, I told her. It doesn't matter, she said. No one has any better. You have to get out and see people again. That's the only way to reclaim your life, to get back what they've taken from you.

"I can never get back what's gone," I said sadly.

"But you're so young, Mutzka. We all are. How will things go on, how will we Jews go on, if we curl up and die like they wanted us to do? Will you give them the final victory, Mutzka, even after they've been driven out and defeated?"

"I don't feel like going out and singing and dancing," I said. That was what the young people used to do in the park, dance to the music the band played until the sun went down and it was too dark to see what you were doing any longer.

"Then you don't have to dance," said Hilda. "Just stop moping around and come with me. Keep me company. I don't want to go alone. Besides there are some nice boys there I know. I'll introduce you."

"I don't care about that," I said.

"Then come for me," said Hilda and so, finally, I put down my mop and said I would. I found the cleanest dress I could, one that was not in too bad a condition and took out my shoes. They were the same ones I had walked in since Podhajce and were very badly worn but my socks were even worse. There was nothing left to them but the tops, the part that wraps around your ankles. Everything else had shredded away. I pulled them onto my ankles and stretched them to my shoes, tucking their edges into the shoes. At least that way it would look like I had socks to wear.

Hilda and I left for Mieske Park which was not far away and she wouldn't stop chattering. I found it very unnerving but I just listened to her talk. I didn't have to say much in answer because she was more interested in talking than listening. The park was crowded that day. It was late afternoon and you could hear the music and people's voices a long way off. When we got there I almost turned around. I told Hilda I had changed my mind but she just grabbed my arm and hurried me along. "I promised some people I'd meet them there," she said. "You can't go off, now."

"You don't need me to meet them," I said. "Besides, I didn't promise anyone."

"Oh come on," Hilda laughed, "you've come this far."

We entered the park and there were people everywhere. I really didn't want to go in but Hilda was relentless and kept pushing me forward. Finally I just stopped fighting her and let her guide me ahead of her, through the crowd.

I looked at all the bodies, all the faces there and saw a couple of boys up ahead of us, where Hilda seemed to be directing me. Well they were young men, really, not boys at all. In fact they were in military uniforms, Russian militia. I froze. I had seen so many uniforms in my day. Too many. Uniforms usually meant trouble I knew. I tried to turn around again but Hilda said no you don't, Mutzka, and gave me a shove. Before I realized it I was standing next to the two soldiers or militiamen or whatever they were. There was a tall one and a shorter one. The taller one had a long sad, looking face and his skin was pockmarked. He still had a bit of acne I could see. He was obviously younger than his height suggested. When he looked at me he gave me a warm, friendly smile and his long, sad face lit up. I couldn't help smiling back. His eyes twinkled and, looking at my friend, he said "Hello Hilda, who's this?"

"I brought along a friend," Hilda grinned, already swaying to the band music as she looked up at him. I could see that she wanted to dance. But the taller boy didn't ask her to. He just kept staring at me. Suddenly I realized he was looking at my neck and I grabbed the collar of my dress and felt the cross hanging there. I had forgotten to take it off. I fiddled with it, unsure whether to tuck it away or leave it where it was. They had already seen it after all. I could see from their faces that they were Jewish boys and I was a little embarrassed to be wearing it, as though I was ashamed to be what I was and had to pretend to be someone else. But that cross had been with me for so long by then that it had become a part of me. I owed my life to it, in fact – or at least that's how I felt.

The tall boy was looking at Hilda. "Why'd you bring a Polish girl?" he whispered to her. After the war everyone was very much aware of who they were. Though many Poles had saved their Jewish neighbors, others had turned away from them or even actively collaborated with the Germans in the killings. Many of these were anxious to avoid recriminations now or, like Wanda's mother, they just wanted to avoid the disapproval of neighbors who might take them for Jew lovers. And, of course, everyone was keenly aware of the Ukrainians' role in the Germans' actions. Mixing between the different groups was a cause for tension among people now so everyone voluntarily tried to stay with their own.

Hilda was laughing. "She's one of us, Milek," she said to the tall boy. "That's how she survived – as a Catholic. Now she never takes that cross off."

The one called Milek looked at me very seriously and said "Is that true?"

I nodded, embarrassed by the situation and not knowing how else to explain myself.

He looked very impressive to me in his baggy military trousers and soldier's tunic, both hanging so loosely on his lean frame as to make him look as though he were wearing someone else's clothing. Hilda smiled and said, "His real name's Samuel, Mutzie, but everyone calls him Milek. You can, too."

I thought to myself that it was nice his name was Samuel – like my brother's. I had been pining away for my brother for more than a week now, since I had learned how he had met his end. It was hard to get him out of my mind. But here was this boy, a man really, also Samuel, and suddenly I felt a wave of warmth rush through me for him, such a tall, awkward looking boy he seemed in his oversized uniform.

There was so much noise everywhere in the park with all the people dancing and shouting at one another above the music just to make themselves heard. But everything around us seemed to suddenly go very quiet. All I could see was this Milek the militiaman, standing there in front of me. All I could hear was the soft drone of his voice as he kept talking, mostly to me. Hilda, I knew, was trying to talk to him, too, saying something or other, but I couldn't hear her words. I don't think Milek heard her either because his eyes were only on me. "Do you like to dance?" he was saying, peering down at me, leaning a little closer. I had always been fond of tall men and he was no exception. Something about him made me feel very safe in his presence.

"I . . . I don't know how," I said in answer to his question. "I never had time to learn. So many things happened . . . I had to run away . . ."

"Then, someone will have to teach you," he was laughing. He reached out to touch me and I felt his large, strong fingers brush the back of my hand and then, suddenly, he wrapped my hand in his. "Come on," he whispered. "This music won't last forever. Let me show you how to do it."

Hilda was still trying to talk to him as he dragged me off toward the other dancing couples and, when I looked back, I saw her standing there, exactly where we had left her, beside the other militiaman. I hadn't even gotten the other boy's name.

"Hilda says they call you Mutzka," my new dance partner said to me gaily. "That's a sweet name." He was laughing self-consciously at his own little joke. My nickname, "Mutzka," of course was a play on the Yiddish word, *mutek*, for sweet.

"I'm Milek Sorger from Obertyn," he was saying as we moved between the other couples in the park. "I was here in Kolomyia, in the ghetto for a while," he said. "But I got away. I'm glad you did, too."

The band was playing a very lively polka and, though I had no idea how to move my feet in time with the music, my whole body was already beginning to tremble to the brassy rhythms that were flying about us like little butterflies on the cool breezes, reverberating from tree to tree. It was nearly dusk and the sun was dropping swiftly, the air starting to cool off. Milek had both hands on my waist, lifting me up and swinging me into the sky in time with the crisp, driving beat of the park orchestra. He was grinning unashamedly at me as he swung me round and I thought I had never seen such a silly look of plain, unselfconscious happiness on anyone's face like that before.

It made me happy, too.

Epilogue

IT SEEMS strange to say but I married Milek only a few weeks later. Ours was a whirlwind courtship in keeping with the tempo of that first day when we met in Mieske Park and in accordance with the pace of living after the war. Everything was rushed. Everyone was anxious to move on, to forget what had been and start living again. Milek's eagerness caught me up and never let me go again in all the years we were together. After that first day, Milek said he wanted to see me again and I agreed. He came round on a borrowed bicycle to call for me at the little flat where I was living with the elderly lady from Jesczaw.

He was working for the Russian militia, having signed on with them after the Nazis had gone and he was finally able to come out of hiding. He had been hiding, at the end, with his parents but before that he spent time in the ghetto and on the work details the Germans organized for able-bodied Jews. He told me stories, later on, about how he would come back from digging in the fields, his bare arms raw and inflamed from the weeds the Germans made them pull out by hand. It was some kind of poisonous plant which people couldn't touch but they made Milek and the other Jewish boys on the work details do it without any gloves or other protection for their skin.

Milek's older brother and sister had both been killed by the Germans in the early days of the occupation. Rachel, his sister, was caught up in one of the earliest street actions when she was coming out of a movie theater. They grabbed all the people with Jewish armbands as they came out and put them on trucks and took them away to the Szeparowce Forest preserve where they shot them. They buried them in unmarked mass graves.

Solomon, Milek's older brother, lost his life when he tried to escape from a train on which he had been loaded along with hundreds of others. They were being taken to one of those camps the Nazis periodically shipped Jews to when he jumped off and tried to run. The German guard on top of the train shot them all down with machine gun fire, killing Milek's brother and the others who had tried to leap to safety with him.

My husband's parents, who had been very wealthy before the Russians came in 1939, but had lost most of their fortune, managed to hang onto enough money to be able to purchase a hideout for themselves from a Polish family they knew, the Nadkovskis, on a farm near their old hometown of Obertyn. They had fled there from Kolomyia when the Germans began building the ghetto. Like my brother Samuel, they lived in a hole in the ground, underneath a horse trough during the day and only came out at night. But they were luckier than my brother because no one ever found them there. Still, the dampness of their underground hideaway took its toll and my husband's father, Duvid Sorger, became very ill with pleurisy in his lungs from the time he spent lying at the bottom of that muddy pit.

After the Germans fled our area and the Russians returned, my husband's parents went to Romania to seek medical care for his father. The old man was hospitalized and my mother-in-law, Sarah Sorger, saw to all of their business affairs after that. She was a very astute woman and soon began smuggling contraband yeast over the border because yeast was easy to get in Romania but hard to come by in Poland and people were willing to pay quite a bit for it. You needed it not only to make bread but for beer and people wanted their beer. My husband, his friends and a few relatives who had survived the war served as the couriers. Soon Milek was sending me across the border, too, to smuggle back the yeast. That's how I met my future mother-in-law for the first time. She seemed to like me at first – until she learned from a cousin of Milek's that he was interested in marrying me. Then she became very alarmed and told him I wasn't good enough, that I had no money and no family and that he could do much better if he would just leave his marriage arrangements to her.

Milek loved his mother very much and he allowed her to interfere for a while. At one point she even arranged for him to meet a Jewish girl from Romania. She came from a moneyed family and Milek's mother sent her to us in Kolomyia. Milek went to meet her, because his mother had insisted.

I saw this girl from a distance and she was very lovely, tall and attractive, but it turned out her vision was so bad that she was legally blind. Milek returned to me, to the consternation of my future mother-in-law. One day, a few weeks after we had met, I found out I had been robbed. My best clothes had been taken from my room in Rosa's flat. I went to Milek crying and told him what had happened. I was very upset. He was still in the militia and he came back with me at once, in his uniform, and quickly figured out what had happened. He went to my crippled neighbor and confronted him. In a short time Milek returned with all my things and I kissed him, I was so happy.

Milek looked at me thoughtfully and said it was foolish for me to remain there any longer. "Mutzka," he said, "a thief like that can make your life miserable. You'll always be afraid to leave anything around, never certain when this creature will come and steal something else from you. Come move in with me," he said. "I'll make room and you'll be safer." By this time we knew we wanted to be married and so I said good-bye to my landlady, Rosa, and took my things to Milek's flat and set up housekeeping with him. My mother-in-law was furious when she found out. But it was too late for her to do anything about it.

Before I could meet my husband's father, on the day in fact that I was scheduled to cross the border with Milek to Romania for this purpose, we learned his father had died. So Milek went by himself, instead, to attend the funeral. After that he brought his mother back across the border to Kolomyia and she moved in with us. Before that, though, Milek and I had gone to the civil authorities and had gotten married and my mother-in-law had to make the best of things, once she moved in, like it or not.

I let Milek handle my few business affairs from then on and he made the arrangements to sell off what was left of the old *korchma*. It didn't bring us much money because there wasn't much of it left by that time but whatever we got was a blessing. I bought myself a new pair of boots with the proceeds and another pair for Wanda. I wanted to repay her for everything she had done for me. We also arranged to buy two pigs with the money and Wanda brought them to her mother who had them slaughtered and turned into sausage and kielbasa. We had these stored in several pails packed with pig fat. We also got several jars of pig fat alone from these creatures. Wanda kept everything for us in her mother's ice house. We planned to use these things as currency since we knew we could sell such goods anywhere in Poland. People would always need to eat. And if we couldn't find buyers at least we would have food for ourselves. By this time we didn't worry a lot about what was kosher and what wasn't. You had to survive.

One day, I ran into Mr. Kazhnovski, our old mailman, and he said Mutzka, did you know I have a letter for you? I didn't and was surprised to hear this. He pulled it out and handed it to me saying it's from America. I grabbed it eagerly and tore it open. It was from my mother's younger sister, Regina Rosenblatt. I sat down to read it and my heart nearly stopped. My aunt wrote that she had seen my name on a list of survivors in Kolomyia. I had been listed as M. Feuer and she thought at first that I was Meir. When she learned that it was little Miriam who had survived, she was astonished. She wrote me that the family in America wanted me to come there as soon as I could and that they were prepared to sponsor me. I told Milek about this and he told his mother and there was plenty of excitement in our house that day.

I began a correspondence with my aunt and wrote that I was now married and that my new husband had a mother to look after as well. My family wrote back not to worry, that they would arrange to sponsor us all. Not long after this, Milek's cousin, Lornyi Guttman, returned from Russia. Since he didn't have a place to stay, he moved in with us, too. He was a sad, unhappy man, no doubt reflecting all that he had lived through during his exile in Russia but my mother-in-law quickly arranged to find him a wife because she said he needed to start thinking about his future and forget everything that had happened to him. She was always very forward thinking, very practical. She contacted people she knew in Romania and before you knew it we were two couples, plus my husband's mother, living in the one small flat.

I was pregnant by this time and we were convinced that we had to get out of Kolomyia. We all wanted to go to America and now that my mother's family was prepared to bring us over, we had a way. My mother-in-law didn't do so badly with her daughter-in-law after all, even if she couldn't brag that her son had found a well-off girl. Though my own family was all gone in Kolomyia, and I had no money to my name, except for those pails of sausage and pig fat, I was to be their ticket to America.

My husband made the arrangements. He resigned from the Russian militia and got us tickets to Klotzkow on the border of western Poland, just before you reach Germany. It had been a German city before the war but, with the German defeat, all the Germans had been uprooted and forced to move over the border into what was now Russian occupied Germany. The area had been turned over to the Poles. From Klotzkow we hoped to find our way into the American occupied section of Germany.

We left by train and it was the last time I saw Kolomyia. I had little left to hold me there and wasn't sorry to say good-bye to it. I don't even think I shed a tear as the train pulled out that last time. I had lost so much there. We left with only a few bags of things, the clothes on our backs and, of course, the pails of sausage and fat that Wanda's mother had made for us. This would be our currency as we traversed Poland. And, when we couldn't get food ourselves, we would eat it.

Once in Klotzkow we had to find a way to go west, to get to the American sector. Travel had become very difficult by then, especially through the different occupied areas of Germany. Each occupying army was very careful about who they let move about within their jurisdiction. So we settled down for a while in Klotzkow in western Poland while Milek worked the angles as best he could. We were there for a number of months and sooner than I'd hoped I found myself ready to give birth. Milek arranged to take me to a nearby Polish hospital and as he was escorting me into the admitting room I turned to him, realizing I still had the cross around my neck. I wanted to give it to him, for safekeeping, but he said no, wear it, you never know what might happen.

They put me in a room with peeling paint on the walls and a large crucifix staring down at me and I waited to go into labor. When my water broke and the labor started the nuns and the doctor came in. The way they arranged the bed, the crucifix was just above my head. I had a very difficult delivery. The pain and pressure were excruciating. They put me out using a mask across my face but I soon found myself regaining consciousness. I could hear them talking through the rasping sound of my own breathing. They seemed very far off. It's a bad delivery they were saying. The doctor, a tall, distinguished looking man with graying hair at the temples, was speaking in Polish, saying it was going to be a breach birth. I knew what that was and was frightened. Even though I was sliding in and out of awareness I had enough presence of mind to realize that things could go horribly wrong.

The sisters who were clustered around the table I was on seemed very concerned, too. I kept losing consciousness and, when I would come to, the pain would be worse than ever. I'd be writhing and moaning, the sweat pouring down my face and seeping under the edge of the mask. They would quickly put me under each time they saw me start to waken.

I knew giving birth wasn't supposed to be like this. You went under and when you came out you had yourself a nice little baby. But I kept waking up to more pain and to the sounds of worry in the attending voices. At one point I heard the doctor speaking to one of the nurses. He was saying things looked bad and that he didn't know what was going to happen.

"Is she a Jew?" he asked. I thought I was dreaming as I rolled my head around. I could see the crucifix hanging above me on the wall.

"No," one of the attending nuns answered him. "See what she's wearing around her neck?"

"All right then," the doctor sighed. "We're going to need forceps for this one though, and there aren't any here. We're short of everything so send the boy and I'll wait."

When I finally woke again it was to see my baby in the arms of the same nun who had pointed out the cross around my neck. She smiled warmly when she realized I was no longer under the anesthetic and gingerly handed my baby to me. I took him happily, though I was exhausted and very, very weak.

I was in that hospital for several days and when Milek came to take me home I told him what I had heard while I was delivering the baby.

"It's a good thing you wore your cross then," he answered. "They say that several Jewish babies have been stillborn in the past few days in this place."

"Stillborn?" I asked him.

He shrugged. "Who knows what they do? Maybe they just don't try as hard when it's Jews – or maybe it's something worse. This part of Poland used to be Germany," he reminded me.

We left Klotzkow as soon as Milek could arrange it. He found a man who said that for a certain sum of money he would prepare forged papers for us. "You'll have to pretend to be German Jews," he told Milek. "Polish Jews are not allowed out of Poland. They'll be turned back but they're letting Jews from Germany go home again – those who are left."

Milek and his cousin Lornyi raised the money. I don't know how they did it because we had so little of anything left by that point. But they found a way and bought the forged papers from their contact and soon, with a large contingent of other Polish Jews intent like us on finding their way to America, we were on a train, traveling mostly at night.

The train took us west, through Soviet occupied Germany into the British sector on the way to the area occupied by the Americans. All the women with children were piled into one car and that's where I had to travel with my little infant. Milek went with his mother, his cousin Lornyi and Lornyi's new wife in another part of the train.

One night the train ground to a halt and suddenly there was a lot of hushed running around outside our car. Milek slipped back to where I was and said I had to give him everything I had that showed I was anything but a displaced German Jew. I didn't want to give up my *kenncarte*, which I had kept with me since Podhajce, or that cross which had saved the life of my little son in the Polish hospital in Klotzkow, but he said we had no choice. We couldn't stay in Europe any longer. Our only hope, he whispered urgently, was to find our way to America, where the bulk of my mother's family had settled thirty years before. To do that, we had to get past the British. If they realized we weren't returning German Jews, he said, we'd be sent back; and not just those of us who had incriminating papers but everyone because the whole charade would be exposed. Everyone was now at risk.

Reluctantly I gave Milek the card and the cross. It was the last I ever saw of either. He took them away and burned them in a big firc thcy had made in the woods, leaving me with nothing but the forged papers I had been given, claiming I was a returning German Jew, a concentration camp survivor.

But the ruse didn't help us. That very day the British troops found us anyway and when they showed up with their guns and trucks people began running in all directions. My husband's mother and cousin Lornyi and his wife all fled under the train and disappeared into the woods but Milek refused to leave me and our new baby. We were all arrested right then and there and shipped back to Poland by the British, to a displaced persons camp. The camp they sent us to was Bergen-Belsen which had been the site of one of the Nazi death camps. The very thought of being sent there made us shudder.

We were housed in abandoned prison barracks where so many Jews had been condemned to die during the war. But we weren't treated badly despite the hideous accommodations. We were given food and had running water to drink and to bathe ourselves with. Because I had a child, Milek and I got a little room to ourselves. The lavatory and the showers were public though and we had to go there to take care of our bodily needs with everybody else.

While in Bergen-Belsen we met others like ourselves. I met Lolek Baumgarten there. His face had been half burned away and he looked awful. I almost didn't recognize him. But he knew me at once and we were soon talking about everyone we had known. Lolek had been in the ghetto with us and I urgently asked him about Feigie, who had been seeing Lonek, his older brother. It was because of that relationship, I remembered, that she had refused to come away with me when I'd run off from the ghetto that last time after the killing of Bubbeh Shprintzer and the removal of my mother and my sister Gusta.

Lolek just shook his head in answer. The Germans, he said, had been systematically stripping the ghetto of its occupants after I'd gone, collecting people and taking them away. That was what had happened to my mother and sister when they were taken to the Belzec death camp. Feigie and Lonek had managed to avoid this and hang on with him to the end, Lolek said, but that spring, after I had gone, the Germans decided to finish things. They locked the remaining people inside the ghetto, shutting down all the gates and putting guards on the outside so no one could get away. Then they threw fire bombs over the walls and fences, making a terrible fire and burning everything to the ground. People ran everywhere trying to get away, Lolek said. That was how he had been burned across half his face, fighting his way out through the flames.

He said that while he had managed to break out and run to safety in the fields, Feigie and Lonek hadn't been able to follow and had died in the fire. Lolek told us that he ran blindly into the woods in all the confusion and found his way to Piadyki where he went to the place my brother was hiding with his family. Lolek either guessed where they were or had known all along. He told us that he begged my brother to take him in and that my brother, seeing his situation, had finally agreed. Lolek was with them when the Ukrainian militia came looking for the feebleminded Ivan, only to find my brother and his family instead.

Lolek said he hadn't come out of the hole with them that night because he was still too weak from his ordeal during the last days of the ghetto. He had been too ill to climb out of the hole even to warm himself in the old woman's kitchen. Otherwise, he said, they'd have gotten him, too. I cried all that night because of the things he told me and Milek held me in his arms, trying to reassure me that it was all behind us now, that we had new lives to look forward to. But I couldn't think about anything but my sister and what had happened to Samuel.

While we were in Bergen-Belsen we made the best of things until one day cousin Lornyi returned to us. He had managed to make it to the western sector, with his wife and Milek's mother, despite the British units patrolling the roads and towns. They reached the American sector and had finally been able to contact my American relatives, telling them what had happened to me.

As good as their word, my mother's family arranged to sponsor all of us so that we could come to America and Lornyi had gotten the necessary papers and now he had come back for us. He showed the papers to the authorities at Bergen-Belsen and they agreed to release us. After some delay they finally put us on a train to the American sector and we ended up in an American DP camp in Benzheim outside Frankfurt in the western part of Germany.

We were there a long time, waiting to have our papers processed so we could be accepted into the United States as new immigrants. There was a lot of concern in those days about letting people in who were ill and my little Joseph had contracted bronchitis. The officials wouldn't agree to allow us to go to America until Joseph could be given a clean bill of health and so, between Joseph's health problems and the usual bureaucratic wrangling, it was some three years before we were finally allowed to immigrate to America, early in 1949. It had been a long terrible struggle to get out of Poland and, before that, just to stay alive. America promised us the chance of a new life.

While we were still in Benzheim, waiting for the immigration papers to be approved, I learned that a friend of mine from Kolomyia, a girl I had gone to school with, was in the nearby town of Ulm with her new husband. Eva and

Benny Muntzer were being housed in an old armory there and Milek said I should go visit Eva if I wanted to. "You need a break so go see your friend," he told me. "I'll look after the baby."

We were all together again, his mother and cousin Lornyi and his wife, so I didn't worry about leaving little Joseph. I was glad of the chance to get away because life in the DP camp was almost mind numbing with its relentless daily routine.

I took a bus into Ulm and found the old armory where Eva and Benny were being housed and went inside. It was a very big, dark building with high ceilings and poor lighting. In the middle was a large indoor parade area which the Germans had used for military drills. I climbed the stairs to the mezzanine area where the displaced people were being housed. Eva was there and when she saw me she ran over and we embraced. It was good to see another face from Kolomyia and we talked a while and then Eva introduced me around. I noticed a small man, very thin, staring at me as Eva made the rounds of her friends and acquaintances. He just kept staring at me in a very intense way and it made me feel uneasy. Finally he seemed to get up the nerve to actually come over. He pushed his way through the others, excusing himself, and when he reached me he stopped. "Miriam Feuer?" he asked me, his soft voice sounding almost as thin as he was.

"Yes?" I said.

"My brother's wife was a Feuer, too – from Kolomyia, like you," he said.

My heart jumped and suddenly I gave him my full attention.

"Eckhouse is my name," he explained slowly, "Zisie Eckhouse, from Horodenka."

"My sister married an Eckhouse in Horodenka," I answered. "His name was Yakuv. . ."

"Yes, my brother," the small man said, nodding. "Your sister . . ."

"Bertha . . ."

He took hold of both my hands. "We should sit and talk," he said.

I followed him to some chairs and we sat down opposite one another. I looked at him very carefully and could see the resemblance to Yakuv, Bertha's husband. Although he was a little shorter than his brother, they both had the same frail, scholarly look.

Zisie Eckhouse asked me if I wanted something to drink and I said no, I just wanted to find out what had happened to my sister.

"Don't you know?" he asked.

"No," I said.

He looked away for a moment and then turned to stare out the nearby window. "They were living in Horodenka . . ." he said quietly.

"Yes, I know that. My grandmother's house . . . I remember when they took it over."

"In the early days, before they put everyone in the ghetto," he went on, "the Germans sent all the Jewish men out to the fields . . . or to build roads. Yakuv went out with everyone else and Bertha stayed behind in the house to look after the baby. One day men came to the house, while Yakuv was away. They didn't say what they wanted, they just kept banging on the door and Bertha didn't know what to do. After ignoring them for as long as she could she finally opened it and they came rushing inside, shouting, tearing everything in the house apart. She tried to grab the baby and get away but there wasn't anything she could do. They dragged her outside with the baby . . . into the street."

"The street?"

"They took the baby from her and there was a lot of shouting. Everyone was shouting. Your sister tried to argue, to demand her baby back. People were watching on the street but there wasn't anything anyone could do. The baby was crying and one of the Germans turned her upside down, holding her by her feet, shaking her. The baby was terrified. This German . . . he swung the baby by the feet and your sister cried out. She tried to stop him, but the other German soldiers shoved her away and she fell. The one who had the child smashed her head against a street lamp . . . to stop the crying."

"Oh my God." I held my hands to my mouth.

"Your sister screamed and ran at them, trying to get her baby back, but one of them shot her and she fell."

I just stared at him as he was telling me all this. I had no words.

"They killed them both," Zisie said, his voice barely audible now, "in front of everyone on the street. No one could do anything . . ."

I felt my throat tighten but he was still speaking, his voice droning on in that same flat undertone: "My brother came home at the end of the day, like he always did, and people told him what had happened. He ran into the house and saw the shambles they had left and that Bertha and the baby were gone. He knew what they'd told him was true. He locked the door and wouldn't come out again. He loved your sister very much, Miriam."

I remembered how Bertha had resisted accepting marriage to Yakuv Eckhouse at first and how disappointed she had been, how angry, to see her life decided for her by others, all her dreams of a singing career brought to such an abrupt and irrevocable end. I was embarrassed to have such recollections now, in front of this man.

"They found my brother the next morning. He'd hanged himself."

"I'm sorry . . ." I reached out to take his hand.

"Well, that's what happened to them, Miriam," he said finally, shrugging, as if nothing in the world mattered any longer. But his eyes were already beginning to fill up with his tears. "That's what happened to us all."

PHOTOGRAPHS

In front of the *korchma* before the war. Miriam at far right, Feigie far left, followed by Regina, Bertha, mother Adela, Gusta and Meir. Samuel's two sons, Lazar and Israel, are pictured in the first row on the right, with cousins. Samuel and Breina are shown separately below.

Lazar and Israel Feuer were shot to death, together with their parents, shortly before the war ended, by the Gestapo.

האראדענקער וואס זענען נפטר געווארן אין אמעריקע

בני הורודנקה שנפטרו בארצות־הברית

עליה לקבר־אבות בבית־העלמין בהורודנקה

אויף קבר־אבות אויפן האראדענקער בית־עולם

NER' DOUGHTERS HUDEL - YENTY - RECHMAN

MEYER KIRSCHNER'S GRAVE IN HORODENKA, GAL

Adela Kirschner Feuer with two sisters from America, Yetta and Regina (kneeling), and Bubbeh Shprintzer at the grave of Adela's father, Meir Kirschner, before the war.

Milek Sorger and family before the war. From left to right: Milek, sister Rachel, father Duvid Yusher, and older brother Solomon. Milek's mother Sarah is seated. Only Milek and his mother survived.

Duvid Sorger and daughter Rachel in happier times. Rachel was taken off the streets by the Nazis in the early days of the occupation and never heard from again. Duvid contracted pleurisy while in hiding and died shortly after the war ended.

Milek Sorger in Russian militia uniform, as Miriam first met him, after the war.

Milek Sorger (center top) and friends after the war.

The Nadkovskis of Obertyn who hid Milek and his parents on their family farm during the war years.

Miriam (center) and Milek (top right) with three friends on the day of their marriage in Kolomyia.

Miriam with her new mother-in-law, Sarah Sorger, after the war.

Miriam and Milek in Benzheim during their stay at the Displaced Persons Camp.

Miriam, center, with fellow survivors in the Benzheim DP Camp. Miriam's mother-in-law, Sarah Sorger, is pictured to her right with baby Joseph.

Miriam with baby Joseph outside the DP camp.

Milek and oldest son Joseph in the streets of Benzheim.

Survivors in New York on New Year's Eve 1949. Miriam is seated in the second row, third from left, with Milek directly behind her.

Miriam Feuer Sorger shortly after the war ended in 1945.

Other Books from Paul Mould Publishing

Order from: Paul Mould Publishing
15 Standish Grove
Boston
Lincolnshire
PE21 9EA
United Kingdom
Tel. (01205) 363462

Hannes Klar (**ISBN-13**: 978-1904959410) *by Steven Porter* (257 pages) – A member of the Hitler Youth who became a Nazi soldier in the waning days of World War II, young Hannes Klar lived to regret his role in the Nazi war machine and to seek redemption in his later years, culminating in his support for the democratic revolution in Russia which brought Boris Yeltsin to power and saw the downfall of the old Soviet Union. A work of fiction, this novel is based on the memoirs of a real individual who was befriended by author Steven Porter. *Published May 2006.*

The Yellow Badge (**ISBN-13:** 978-1904959090) *by Stephen Clements* (361 pages) – Edward Cooper hated Jews. He had been brought up in a country where the people knew the right thing to do with infidels; kill them all. But he had also been raised to respect women and protect the weak. When he witnesses an assault on a Jewish couple by two wealthy young nobles, he is faced with an impossible dilemma. Against a background of rampant anti-Semitism, young Cooper finds himself drawn into a world he doesn't understand, a world of violence, prejudice, murder, and rape. Set in the England of 1320, ***The Yellow Badge*** mixes history with fiction to create a disturbing picture of English racism and hatred over six centuries before the world had ever heard of the Nazis. *Published November 2004.*

Conscript Heroes (**ISBN-13:** 978-0952870876) *by Peter Scott Janes; Edited by Keith Janes* (228 pages) – Thousands of British soldiers were captured at St Valery-en-Caux on 12 June 1940. Many managed to escape during the long march to Germany. Hundreds were hidden in the Pas de Calais for weeks or months, and scores were brought home by the Pat O'Leary escape line. Though a few of the survivors have written about their experiences in Nazi captivity and their desperate efforts to escape, the complete account survives in the diary of only one man. Private Peter Scott Janes had been in the army less than five months when he was sent to France to fight Hitler. Within weeks he was a prisoner at St Valery. Twelve days later he was rescued by two young French girls and spent the next sixteen months living clandestinely among the ordinary people of the Pas de Calais. In September 1941, he made his way south to Marseille to finally find his way back to England. Peter's son, Keith Janes, has combined his father's diaries with other supporting documentation to write ***Conscript Heroes***. *Published April 2004.*

Detachment W (**ISBN-13:** 978-1904959007) *by Derek Richardson* (232 pages) – In the chaos that followed the fall of France in 1940, hundreds of British soldiers managed to escape from their German captors, or evaded capture entirely. They were helped by French resisters to reach the unoccupied south of France but were rounded up there by Vichy French authorities. By 1941 and '42 they were joined by dozens of RAF airmen who had bailed out or force-landed in France. The French authorities called them 'Detachment W'. ***Detachment W*** recalls how the French military tried, with only limited success, to prevent escapes by many of these men. Author Derek Richardson spoke with surviving veterans and studied relevant War Office and Foreign Office files to write his account and uncovered hitherto unpublished information in the archives of Edinburgh, Washington DC, Bern, Switzerland, and Paris, France. *Published May 2004.*

Bitter Freedom: Memoirs of a Holocaust Survivor (**ISBN-13:** 978-1557791573) *by Jafa Wallach; Edited by Stuart W. Mirsky* (209 pages) – Trapped in Lesko, Poland with the coming of the Nazis, Jafa Wallach, her husband Natan, and her two brothers managed to escape the transfer camp to which they had been consigned pending transport to the Belzec death camp. Helped by a long time family friend, Polish mechanic Jozio Zwonarz who was secretly working with the Polish resistance, the desperate escapees dug a bunker for themselves under the dirt floor of Zwonarz' workshop, less than thirty feet from Gestapo headquarters. While Zwonarz oversaw the safekeeping of the Wallachs' four-year old daughter in a nearby forest, the fugitives struggled to survive in a living grave for twenty-two months as the war raged on overhead and their protector desperately foraged for enough food and water to keep them alive, despite a jealous wife, who imagined he was keeping another woman on the side, and frequent inspections of his workshop by the Gestapo and the Ukrainian militia. The true story of the Wallach family's survival under the most trying circumstances, ***Bitter Freedom*** traces the impact of the Nazi occupation on the Jewish community in southern Poland from 1939 until the liberation. *Published by Hermitage Publishers, April 2006; distributed by Paul Mould Publishing in the U.K.*